DOWNSTREAM TOWARD HOME

River Stories

Horton

Barren Grounds

Deschutes

St. John

Grande
Ronde

Deerfield

Charles

Green

Egypt's
Creek

Big Sur

Great Falls
Rock Creek
C&O Canal

Cache
la Poudre

Shenandoah

Verde

Blackwater

Gila

Greenbrier

Rio Grande

Juniper

Buffalo

Atchafalaya

Horn

Wolf
Red

Bayou Sorrel

Pearl
Old River

Shell Bank
Bayou Savauge

DOWNSTREAM TOWARD HOME

A BOOK OF RIVERS

Oliver A. Houck

LOUISIANA STATE UNIVERSITY PRESS

BATON ROUGE

Published by Louisiana State University Press
Copyright © 2014 by Louisiana State University Press
All rights reserved
Manufactured in the United States of America
First printing

DESIGNER: *Mandy McDonald Scallan*
TYPEFACE: *Whitman*
PRINTER AND BINDER: *Maple Press, Inc.*

Portions of this book appeared previously in the following publications:
Harvard Magazine, "Reflections on the Saint John" (November–December
1981); *Harvard Magazine,* "Running the Shuttle" (May–June 1994); and
International Wildlife magazine, "Strangers in the Barren Grounds," ©
1978 National Wildlife Association. Reprinted from the July/August 1978
issue of *International Wildlife*® magazine, with permission of the copyright
holder, National Wildlife Federation®.

Library of Congress Cataloging-in-Publication Data are available at the
Library of Congress.

978-0-8071-5745-9 (cloth: alk. paper) — 978-0-8071-5746-6 (pdf) — 978-
0-8071-5747-3 (epub) — 978-0-8071-5748-0 (mobi)

CONTENTS

PRELUDE

A Caliph in his shaded Alhambra was once asked about the most beautiful sound in the world, and he is said to have replied that there were three, the clink of gold coins, the laughter of a loved one, and the fall of water . . . in reverse order.

I've come down out of the firelight to wash the cooking pans at the side of the creek, scrubbing them with sand. Dark water brushes by and swirls away. I can hear a snag bobbing up and down out there, and I will go to sleep tonight with the sound in my ears. The snag has probably been there for months, before it there were others, there will be more in the future, and the river will keep on coming around the upstream bend as if from nowhere, pass by this very spot, and then disappear below. It is more than a physical phenomenon. It is close to magic.

I should admit that I am not objective about rivers, not even close, any more than I am about other parts of the natural world. In my world they have equal rights to exist. I have spent forty years of my life teaching, writing, and litigating about environmental things but, stepping back, most of them related to water. I poked around little creeks as soon as I knew they existed, and when others in college were in the library I was tying into an eight-oared shell and shoving off under an evening sky. Lisa and I spent many early weekends hauling an old canoe on top of our VW Beetle to one river or another, each with its own surprises, and it was yet another river, a very large one, that brought me to Louisiana and changed everything about us from then on.

There is a geographic track to these stories as well, the plates of my life shifting from the East to the North and West and finally, as if guided by an unseen hand, toward the South, where I remain taken by a landscape so filled with beauty and so casually abused. I am on a southern creek right now, with my pots and pans. Some friends up on the sand bank are talking in low voices but for the moment I feel closer to what must be thousands of people around the country, indeed the planet, who at this very moment are on or by the water, or looking down at it from tall buildings, mesmerized by the flow.

This is a book about rivers and a life spent enjoying and defending them, sometimes more successfully than others but always with the conviction that they were worth it. Here in New Orleans I still venture out on a weekend with family and friends or simply alone, except for my dog, Ms. Bear, up in the bow, as Lisa says "a tower of strength and inconvenience." Every piece of water has a tale to tell. These stories are an invitation to join us and, I hope, to remember your own.

Part I

EXPLORATIONS, 1954–1981

EGYPT'S CREEK
New Jersey, 1954

"Let it down *slowly*," I urge Peter, me safely behind him as he lowers the trap.

Peter, intent on his stick, gives a little grunt.

"On his *head*," I whisper, peeking around his back.

Slam, down goes the trap on top of the snake, missing the head by a good foot, but the trigger pan has hit the creature's back and there is an explosion in the water as it wriggles to get free.

"We *got* him!" I whisper triumphantly as Peter pulls the chain to him, drawing in the trap, drawing in the snake. It is a poisonous snake, we know that. We had looked at snakes in the book and this one had all the marks, a deadly black, a mean-looking face. Our problem is now what to do with it.

I offer to step on it while Peter opens the trap's jaws and snaps them back onto the head, which I figure will dispatch it. Peter looks at me skeptically, as this will put his hands within striking range before the jaws close. "We'll use a belt," he says, and looks at mine.

We manage to noose the belt and drop it over the snake's neck, if it had a neck, and start pulling it tight. All the snake does is wiggle harder. Peter gets a rock from the creek to bash its head but I am leaking enthusiasm freely at this point and I say, without much confidence, "There must be a better way."

We cannot think of one of course because there isn't one, while the snake, more slowly now, turns in the mud by the edge of the water, its home for a long time no doubt because it is several feet long. In the end, without saying more, I place my sneaker on the creature to still it, Peter leverages the trap jaws open, and we let it roll free. In shock, but alive. We are a little in shock too. When we get back to my house we check the book again and discover that it was a common water snake, "often persecuted by those thinking it harmful." Which defines us perfectly. I never harmed a snake again, but we haunted Egypt's Creek for years. My mother says it got me into college.

The creek on Egypt's Hill was tiny, perhaps five feet wide and dropping to half that when it rolled over a downed tree or through a tire. Way off to one side was State Route 22, a poster child for commerce on the cheap, and on the other lay a scrub of woods and field leading back to town. A companion creek came down past the golf course and a veterinary clinic, joining forces at Mindawaskan Pond on Broad Street, where a few listless ducks hung around looking for handouts. These little streams were our Hudson Rivers, our Mississippis, whatever we wanted them to be.

Peter and I waded up Egypt's Creek, turning our socks brown with mud, looking for things. We started an aquarium with pollywogs and insects but they died soon after. When we added plants they died too. If he and I had been commissioned to create the world in six days, nothing would have survived.

The summer I turned fourteen I discovered the creek behind the vet clinic where I tended the dog cages. A black man named George had the cats, which he maintained was the better job because there were only about ten of them, and besides a dog pooped ten times more. I said that my job won because the cat cages smelled like chemicals, which we knew well being downwind from the industries of Perth Amboy and the drolly named Jersey Meadows. The challenge of my job came when opening a dog cage to clean it, not knowing whether the animal would come bolting out like a lion with only me in the way. I held a noose of clothesline which gave me one shot to snare the animal's head, only one, and if I missed it was "Dog loose, George!" and he would come running to help me corral it. The German shepherds scared me to death.

There was one job worse. Dr. Shahalye would put a dog down from time to time and I would come hold it. The animal seemed so trusting, although it may have sensed that this was the end, and the holding part was easy. The needle slipped in a vein, a sudden sigh, the body went limp, and it was over. But not quite. I began having nightmares, always the same ones. I would be standing in darkness before a point of light, which kept receding and receding. Then it winked out. I would wake up banging my head on the wall.

My favorite job turned out to be water pollution. Looking back it is hard to believe I was so unaware, but then again everyone was. Every day I'd let the dogs out onto concrete runs behind the clinic where they went wild with joy, barking and leaping and releasing all that product that, by instinct, they would not soil their cages with unless in extremis. I would throw them tennis balls, chase them around, pick up the little ones to hold, and they returned inside happy campers. Then I took the hose and began to wash down the runs, right into the creek.

Any fool could wash a run, you'd just put the hose down and wait a while and enough water would finally do the job. But not always, because some of this product had been baking out there in the sun since noon and was stuck hard to the concrete, which called for strategy. I developed an aerial approach, lobbing down long arcs of water followed by direct hammer blows and accompanied by running commentary taken from war movies of the time, "They're coming toward us, General!" It never crossed my mind that I was flushing massive loads of fecal coliforms down to Mindawaskan Pond, which smelled like a sewer and whose few waterfowl didn't even try to fish. These days dog handlers use scoopers—if not, they are certainly violating clean water laws that I have invested considerable energy trying to enforce—but, lamentably, the romance of hosing those runs down into the creek, the tactical decisions to be made, the accompanying sound tracks, are lost forever.

That winter, Egypt's Hill grew a new dimension. Rummaging in the attic, Peter and I came across a trunk of my father's memorabilia, and in it a book with a tattered red cover called *The American Boy's Handybook*. Published in 1887, it proposed an assortment of exciting and near-impossible projects such as building your own crossbow. The materials called for, barrel staves and railroad spikes, so at-hand in the day, were by this time rare collector's items but one activity needed nothing but a hatchet, wire, and twine. Toward the end of the book was a dissertation on Traps, Snares and Deadfalls, each with its own illustrations. Back in a rush came the image of our badly abused water snake. This time we'd go back and do it the right way.

It took nearly two winters before we caught anything. The ground-level snares we placed along the creek banks were brushed aside as if little tanks had rolled through, and our bent-tree snares were so temperamental they would spring in a hard breeze. We placed nooses on logs crossing the water figuring that they would channel our prey, but they were no more successful. Deadfalls, a heavy stone crashing down, were slow to react and the animal would take the bait and be gone. We found many animal tracks and some afternoons after school, traipsing out to the hill, we'd be greeted by a strong odor of skunk saying that it knew all about us. Animals were certainly here and they ate about anything we put out for them, apples, hot dogs, whatever we found in the refrigerator. At last, the second February, we scored, by coincidence twice in the same day.

The first was a squirrel, plastered under a rock we'd pulled from the creek and whose trigger mechanism we had honed to a fine art. It sprang almost as quickly as a metal trap. I was stunned by how thoroughly the impact had transformed this lively creature into a dead rag. Still absorbing this, we walked out toward our snares and were greeted by a whimpering oddly similar to that of a dog, and from my stint with the vet I knew dog whimpers by heart. It had snowed lightly the night before and tracks were clear on the ground. Our bent tree snare was shaking like a fishing pole with a whopper on the line. As we approached I thought that we'd finally caught the skunk, only there was no smell, and besides, skunks did not look like hound dogs with big ears, white patches on their fur, and skinny tails. It was a beagle. Caught by the head, too heavy to be lifted up entirely, it had spent the night with its front quarters in the air and its hind paws dancing on the surface, leaving a semicircle of pain and bewilderment on the snow. I examined the dog closely: there were no visible injuries. We cut him loose and he went limping down the hill toward a line of new houses that were replacing the woods below. Stakes marked with bright yellow tape signaled yet more houses to come. We unset the traps, buried the squirrel, and walked home. We didn't need to say anything. Trapping on Egypt's Creek was over. But not quite. As my mother later said, there is a good chance it got me into college. That same winter, a senior in high school, I was called to Newark for an interview. The university I'd applied to had alumni scattered across the country and they were recruited to assess local candidates, perhaps those on the margins, I have no idea. Academically I had little to distinguish me from a class of students whose achievements were daunting. Still, the interview was arranged and my mother would drive me because the license age at the time was eighteen and I was not yet within range. I was to see a lawyer in a tall brown building. My mother would wait in the car outside. It would take twenty minutes.

The first ten minutes or so were a disaster. I even found myself feeling sorry for the man because he could find nothing to talk about with me. As I recall, it went something like this:

He: Do you like to play sports?
Me: One or two.
He: Do you play for the school?
Me: Well, swim and track but not in the meets. I'm not that fast.
Small silence.
He: What about music?
Me: Some, but I stopped taking lessons. I'm not in a group or anything.
Longer silence.
He: What do you like to do after school, then?
Me: Read books. Ride bikes. Play stickball.
More silence. He checks his watch. Still half the session to go.
Tell me, he says finally, as if dealing with a reluctant witness, what did you do yesterday afternoon?
Me: We checked the trapline.

A very brief silence. He stops looking at his watch.

He: The what?

Me: The trapline. We make our own.

He, quietly: Can you show me?

In what seemed like a couple of minutes I brought over his standing lamp to use the cord for a spring snare, which meant that he had to hold the lamp to keep the tension while I made a trigger out of a fountain pen with a rubber eraser for bait. His desk blotter was the creek. His ruler was the log. When I tripped the trigger he seemed delighted. We had caught a stapler. Without thinking I moved on to deadfalls, his big law books were as heavy as rocks and when they came crashing down on his pencil and eraser, as the rabbit nibbled in, he almost applauded. We got deeply into the triggers, including one involving a lock of three separate pieces called the Figure Four in *The American Boy's Handybook*. I drew it out for him, showing how the pressures go and how they fit together. We held three pencils to get the idea and I said that I could bring him a real one if he wanted. I was that naive. I do believe, though, reflecting, that he was tempted to say yes.

My mother had dropped me off at four in the afternoon. When I emerged from the building it was already dark. The clock in the car said five after five. My mother seemed happy about the wait. Sometime later a university envelope came in the mail with forms to fill out. My mother said she knew I'd be accepted the day of the interview just by looking at the clock. Then again, she was an intuitive person.

You could not find Egypt's Creek today. I went back years later and it was gone. Not even the hill. A Chicken a la King occupied the highway side, and beside it the storage area for Tire Man, whose large, tire-muscled arm swung out over the heads of motorists passing by. The hill had been leveled for tract housing with street names like Poplar and Elm, not exotic species but ones no longer found on this particular piece of earth any more. The creek was nowhere in sight. Probably down in a pipe somewhere. Memories these days can last longer than the places that produce them.

The reason I went back was to attend a high school reunion, an event I'd avoided up to then. I hoped to see Peter, but he wasn't there. I wound up talking with a woman named Carol who was one of those girls who was first in everything, but nice about it. I told her what I would never have dared tell her back in the day, that she was as lovely as always, at which she looked me straight in the eye and said, more curious than inviting, "Then why didn't you ever ask me out?" I was floored.

Groping for something to say, deflective, I said that I spent time up on the creek at Egypt's Hill. "Oh," she said, as if it were nothing, "I used to go up there with Peggy all the time." I was floored again, twice in the space of a minute. I asked her what they did up there and she said that they played in the creek, floated sticks, made mud men with funny faces. I told her the only thing that I could. That we did the same things, and that I like to do them still. A comet went by.

CHARLES RIVER
Massachusettes, 1957

The snow has given way during the afternoon to a fine sleet that hits the water with a hissing sound. My fingers are cold but I need them free to lace my shoes into the bottom of the shell, and then to grip the oar. They will be cold for the next two hours; I may not even feel them again until I am back in the shower room, small needles of sensation returning. It will be full night by the time we leave the boathouse and cross the bridge toward campus, and the sleet may have turned to rain. This could be a warm front. It is March and for several months the river has been ice.

Back in my room I make a tired pass at my course books and turn in. I am not an easy roommate to live with because come ten o'clock when others are really perking I am going to bed and asking would they keep it down. My morning classes are a blur, my mind is on the river and, more particularly, what the lineups for the boats will be that day. They are posted each morning just before noon on, of all places, the front window of Liggett's Tobacco Store, which also displays a large assortment of cigars and cigarettes from Egypt and France. That no one, even in a center of science and learning, saw anything anomalous about using a cigarette store as the university signboard for a sport like crew seems unreal, but that is another story. This one is about the river and the boats we rowed on it and what that did to us.

Grayer is standing in the middle of his room throwing a wadded ball of paper into the air, catching it, and then turning to me to insist, "Ollie, whatever it is, it is not a sport!"

Easy for him to say, of course, he is on the basketball team. "Hell yes it is," I say, as if a curse word proves my case. Grayer tosses me the paper ball.

"It's like doing pushups," he says. "That's exercise, but it's not a sport."

"This is eight guys doing exercises together, in rhythm," I say. I toss him back the ball.

"Maybe it's dancing, then," says Grayer, smiling evilly. Then he has an inspiration, "Were the guys rowing Cleopatra around playing a sport?"

I'm running out of arguments here and besides I am late to lab, in part because I dislike going. Grayer is toying with me now. Throwing the ball in the air and catching it, very deliberately, he says, "And besides, in crew there's no ball."

You do not row crew idly. It is more like a job and for me, perhaps because I had never rowed before and was way behind the curve, it was an obsession. I'd rush down to Liggett's during a class break to receive the life-determining news of which boat I was listed in, first, second, or third, and what time it would depart. First boat was an A. Third was just hanging on. Anyone beyond those twenty-four oarsmen, eight per shell, was flunking out. The fall season started with one hundred or so candidates for the heavyweights, and nearly the same for the lights. By the following March three out of four of us would be gone. That was just to make the team. On race weekends in spring, which were quite few in number, only the first eight would compete. We rowed five and sometimes six days a week for eight months (when the river froze over there were indoor tanks) before the first competition, capped at season's end by the one that really mattered, the Eastern Sprints, the grand rendezvous of the schools. You could win four or five matches against other squads, collecting their rowing shirts as prizes along the way, which was quite pleasant, and then lose the Sprints and never quite forget it.

It took several months before I was permitted even to step in a shell. They are called shells for a reason and are as unsteady as pirogues; you work your way up from rafts. I went out for crew because my brother had: that I would too was a given. Philip was one of those people always on scene when a camera showed up, and to this day he keeps a clip from the *Boston Globe* of a mid-Charles rescue: his shell had rammed something and sunk like a shot, but not before the coach's motorboat could ferry them ashore where an enterprising reporter snapped the photo. Philip was front and center, dripping wet and grinning. He soon went on to another life but I was skinnier and stayed with the sport longer. Assuming of course it was one.

We float out from the dock in the late day, streetlights reflecting off the river, streams of car lights like rivers of their own. We have tied in, only the cox at the far end from me is saying anything, telling numbers two and four to trim it up, calling out to another shell for position. Beyond that, just the rush of distant traffic and the patter of sleet on the river, and now on the shell and the top of my hoodie that I will not keep raised for long because my body will soon heat like a stove and the cold down my neck will feel friendly. None of the rest of us talk. We will not talk for the next hour, maybe more, it depends how many bridges we are going today, perhaps all the way to the turning basin which will be a long run indeed. I am clenching and opening my hands to keep them warm. I dread the start because it quickly turns to pain and it will be five minutes or so before that subsides and then the only thing to deal with is fatigue, until my wrists start to seize. These are only workouts. In a race the pain never goes away. Maybe Grayer was right. In the meantime, though, in the quiet time before blastoff, this is the most peaceful moment in my existence.

"NOW BOW!" Joe Brown, nearly invisible in the gloom, screams into his megaphone, "NOW BOW!" he repeats, as if I might have been elsewhere like the men's room instead, and then he lays it on me. "You are checking your slide on the catch!" he tells me, and now all the others know that I am slowing the boat down with my poor slide control. "And you are leaning out again," he continues, so now everyone knows I am destabilizing the boat as well. I just nod. Why he kept me in first boat I'll never know.

I could not help the lean out. The shell we were using was a newfangled rig from Germany, said to be very fast, but it was as tippy as a soap cake and the oar locks were set so low that the handle pulled right into my lap. For a bow man, because that was my post, this was fatal because the boat also had a tendency to nose down at the end of each stroke and I could not get my handle low enough to extract the blade, sticking out there seven feet or so in the darkness with a mind of its own. If I failed to get my blade out the handle would whip into my stomach like a hammer and either stop the shell or throw me into the water. The term was "catching a crab," which was like striking out with the bases loaded only the ball knocked you out as well. So I would dodge that handle like a dancer, bending to the side to wrist it down, twist it out, and then away, following it up the slide for the next catch.

We'd practice starts for twenty minutes or so, sometimes in a race with the second boat, sometimes on a stopwatch, sometimes just power-tens, everything you had into the oar. Then a rest, the boat gliding, all those automobiles passing by and the people behind the lights in the office buildings nearby completely oblivious to this ancient ceremony, or to what it meant, if it meant anything at all. "NOW BOW," Joe Brown yells, "YOU'RE STILL LEANING!"

I usually went out with the last boat of the day no matter where I was ranked because I had labs. I was intended to be a doctor and every afternoon found me in the biology room (which was entertaining, dissecting dead pigs), or the chemistry room (less entertaining, all the tubes did was change color), or physics lab (total boredom, rolling a ball down a chute and measuring how far it rolled). The protocols called for three conscientious hours of experimentation but I did not have time for that so I would massacre my pig in about thirty minutes, cadge some observations from a partner for my report, and be fleeing toward the river by four. The day was already dying. I was not really going to college. I was going to crew and taking some classes on the side.

Joe Brown is clearly frustrated with us this evening. The Eastern Sprints in Annapolis are less than a month away and the unbelievable has happened. In our practices the second boat is beating the first boat. Joe slams his megaphone against the side of his motor launch, which accompanies us every inch of every day for all these same months, and announces, "FIRST BOAT! I do not care WHICH boat is going to Annapolis, do you understand?" We are crestfallen. The unsung oarsmen in boat number two, ten yards off to the side, are trying to keep from grinning. Our shell has all the ringers. Six of our eight have rowed in prep school, prestigious squads. I am one of the few from a high school that, I can attest, had never even heard of the sport of rowing. If, as Grayer said, it was one.

April has come and the Charles turns green. There is grass on the banks and on that grass are coeds in light dresses chatting, reading books, dreaming. Sunshine has been rare around here. The girls are so pretty and so unaware of us floating by. We make no noise, we just appear from under bridges and, all of sudden, there they are, fifteen feet away, nuzzling their boyfriends or just exposing their legs to the world, to our world anyway, and nobody says a word. Nobody ever does. Then Joe Brown says, "We'll go up to the Slaughterhouse Bridge and race on down. Boats one and two."

The slaughterhouse no longer exists. The bridge crossing there even has another name now, which seems to me like changing the name of Chicago; whatever they call it, it is where they slaughtered the cows. On the Charles they did cows too, a huge business into the twentieth century, and it all went into the river along with just about everything else. Even in the 1950s we were catching strange things on our oars. The Charles was so filthy that we stopped dunking the cox after a winning race for health reasons. All of that has changed too—indeed the river has become a comeback story in the short history of pollution control—but this was then and the slaughterhouse was not all that far into the past. Its bridge would also be the start of the big face-off over which of our boats would go to the Eastern Sprints. As usual, rowing on up, we do not say a word.

Life is not fair, and the next few days are a roll of the dice that simply fall where they do. The trial for the right to Annapolis does not turn out well for us; the second boat, smelling its chance for glory, leads the first all the way. Joe Brown cannot believe the outcome and begins to play with the lineups. The power section of his first boat is clearly the cream, so the problem has to be toward my end in the bow. He starts switching us out, replacing first boaters with seconds to see what happens. I am the first one switched and I have the good fortune of riding the second boat's continuing bubble, and of being pumped with anger that people thought it was me. In the next face-off we pull hard beyond reason and beat the firsts again. So I am not the problem, concludes Joe Brown, and he next switches out number threes, replacing my friend Chris for another oar named Pete. We line up again at Slaughterhouse. Joe Brown says, "This is it, first boat. Whoever wins goes." He seems flat serious. He is not yelling, which is a sign. I am back in first boat at this point and somebody breaks the silence code. A voice ahead of me says, "Let's do it," which passes for high enthusiasm in this New England culture. Heads nod. We beat the second boat by three lengths, hands down. I am in. Pete is in. Poor Chris is out.

Annapolis is an experience. All the visiting crews are triple-bunked in a large gymnasium that echoes with the slightest sound and holds about ninety young men about nineteen years old, who of course make sounds. Some laugh and talk. Some snore. In the end I catch a little sleep, I think so anyway, because finally it is light. At breakfast we eat in the main dining hall, the midshipmen in spotless white served by black waiters in what appear to be tuxedos. At regular intervals during the meal young plebes march smartly up to our table, part of their hazing I suppose, puff out their chests, and say loud things like "[name of college, name of college] . . . bunch of fairies!" And then go back to their places. Then another plebe comes. I imagine these young men going off to the dangers of war and suddenly the thought doesn't bother me a bit. Then we go down to the boathouse.

The race is a disaster for us. The Schuylkill River is intimidating, wider here than anything I'd seen in my life and churning in a stiff crosswind. Our light German craft bounces on the waves like a cork, slapped to the side one moment and back the next; it is hard to keep her in position even for the start. We are favored to win this race, we've already beaten several of the crews here, but this is another river and another day. About halfway down the course we pass under a high bridge designed to pass oceangoing vessels but that also funnels the wind in a fashion I'd understand had I managed to stay with my class in physics, which was rapidly chasing me away from a career in medicine. We go under the bridge nose to nose with our closest competition when Pete, bless his heart, rowing number three, loses control of his oar and catches a crab. It does not launch him from the shell. Rather, his oar drags like a corpse and skews the boat to a crawl. The shell next to us blows past. By the time we have lined up again, taken a racing start and power-tenned our way back into the pack we can no longer take the lead. We come in third. There is a picture of me handing my shirt to the winning bow man. I no longer have it but I remember that I looked anorexic. I weighed 137 pounds.

I also remember this, like an unexplainable dream after an unexplainable accident, but it happened. I talked to another crewmate about it years later, the only time I saw him again, and this is what he remembers too. We are alone on the water now, after the race, making our way back to the boathouse. A straight channel leaves the Schuylkill River toward the dock and it is free of wind and current, more like the Charles on a calm day, and someone says, "Hit it." No one else says anything. The cox does not call for a power-ten. No one seconds the statement. We just come alive. The boat leaps out from under us, our dig into the water is so ferocious that each blade sends a large whirlpool spinning behind us, and then the magic happens. After the leap, after feathering the oars out with a single snap, the dull thunk of the oarlocks, each of us squeezing back up for the next catch, no check on our momentum, the water running fast below, we are flying over it, we enter another world, one that we tried to be in all year long and sometimes nibbled at but here, this one last time, perhaps in anger, perhaps in sorrow, we have reached it, and when we dock and lift the boat out we do not say a word, we never do, but some of us have tears and others have smiles and I think I have both at the same time.

GREENBRIER RIVER

West Virginia, 1970

Lisa is sitting in the canoe which is beached on a rock in the Greenbrier River. She is wearing a bathing suit, in full sun, absorbed in a book by Gore Vidal about a Roman emperor who was either very clever or a lunatic or both. Backlit by the shine of the water, she looks like a child bride. I am supposed to be reading too, a book of short stories, but I have not turned a page, so intent am I on not missing something that might be coming down to the bank for a drink or a redbird flashing by. I am sneaking peeks at Lisa as well. We have been wedded less than a year and this is our honeymoon. We are also in about as remote a spot as you can find on the Eastern seaboard, and a setup for a horror movie. The one where Basil Rathbone comes out of the woods, claps his hand over her mouth, and drags her away, a glimpse of his mouth showing fangs.

There is something uniquely raw about West Virginia, its mountains jammed together like tall ships with jagged tops, side ridges like sails, and valleys leading off every which way. There is also something Old Worldly about it as well, as in Transylvania. It lies in the dark of the hollows, the hanging fog, the sudden appearance of humans who, beyond the cities and towns, look surprising in this landscape, isolated houses in strange places, not all of them welcoming. The feeling that one is a foreigner is very present. This, too, plays into the movie.

Lisa and I are novices out here, and to each other as well. We had married in a whirl and set out on our wedding night to camp in the woods. Walking in, Lisa turned to me and said, brightly, "I've never camped out before"! I was very still. It had not occurred to me that someone from Vermont had never camped before. What else did people do up here? We got through it in a borrowed sleeping bag, on the coldest evening of the year. The baked beans congealed in the pan. The next day we hurried back to our lives in Washington, D.C.

I was prosecuting criminal cases at the time, one led to another, we kept postponing the honeymoon. One day, though, I was looking at a map of West Virginia and noticed a river snaking down the east side and very few towns. The small print read, Greenbrier. I said, I'll do the food.

Here we were then, in the isolation of this river bottom, pinched between two slopes of rocks and trees that began abruptly at the water's edge and shot up to the sky. The sun would not reach us until ten in the morning and be gone over the mountains by three. One side was scarred by a railroad track whose daily runs shook the valley with their roar. Seeing us on the water, the engineer would sound his whistle and the echo bounced back and forth in the valley. Then it was swallowed by silence.

Our campsites were memorable because they were no place you would think twice about if you had options. The first night a bull led his harem of cows right over our sleeping bags and down to the river, pulling our tarp on the way. Who knows where they came from, we'd seen no farm. We hadn't even seen a clearing. The poison ivy campsite that followed was toxic just to look at, and the ravine site filled quickly in the rain. They were otherwise untouched, pristine. If people actually paddled this river they were either models of outdoor etiquette, leaving no trash, or they were not really people at all. Everything about this trip had a spectral quality.

We brought along the usual backpacking fare, dried dinners in a package, tiny pots to heat them in, half a chocolate bar for dessert. We did not yet know that canoe camping lives on an entirely different planet with coolers, cold drinks, fresh vegetables, and fold-out chairs. Once we discovered these amenities we never looked back but for this maiden voyage we were on prefab noodles and powdered eggs. The eggs defeated us entirely, and defeated an animal one morning that pulled down our food bag, ate its way inside, sampled the egg powder, and then spit it back out on the ground. After we returned I wrote a letter to the company on the dried-eggs label, telling them this story, but it never replied.

The real challenge of the Greenbrier, however, was the water.

There wasn't any. You can work wonders in too much water, lining the boats, stuffing in flotation, portaging the gear, but you have few options with no water at all. The river at the put-in was perhaps two feet deep, backed up by a ledge downstream, but once past that obstacle it resembled a graveyard featuring different shapes of tombs. We started dragging within minutes, dragged much of that day, and many times in the days that followed. We found pools and little channels and learned to smell running water before we got to it because the dead-ends, warmed by the sun, had turned sour. Each morning we went forward on the hope that, today, springs and tributaries would kick in and give us an honest float. Our main chance was the entry of Stone Creek, described in a guidebook as a tipping point below which "the Greenbrier takes on the characteristics of a mighty river." That phrase has since become a family idiom for totally wrong predictions. Stone Creek was bone-dry, and the piddle of water that emerged beneath it would hardly fill a canteen.

We ran out of drinking water too, which led to our first Basil Rathbone moment. The plan was to take river water and boil it, but the quality was none too inviting and seemed high-risk. We also were confident that we would come across humans, houses where we could load up. For several days we saw nothing of the sort. Toward the end, running on empty, we floated under a rope bridge straight out of *Deliverance,* took a turn, and there was a town. To be sure it was very small, a single line of wooden houses on a dirt track that then simply vanished into the hills. But luck was with us. We'd get water.

We tied up at the landing and approached the houses, which were strangely quiet, not a footprint around them, not a trace on the road. We mounted the first porch and knocked. There was no reply. No barking dog, no noise at all. There was no noise outside either, not a child, not a chicken. We continued uphill, knocking as we went, no one home. The places seemed neatly kept, the roofs intact, curtains hung in the windows; only the people were missing. Perhaps this is where the UFOs had landed.

At the last house, around back, Lisa spotted a well. We lowered down our plastic jugs and let them slowly fill. We probably should have tested the water in some fashion but we were thirsty and drank our bellies full. Filling the jugs again we walked back down toward the river, house by house, a gauntlet of the missing. Passing the last one, the first we had attempted to raise, I do not know why but I turned and saw a white face in the window. There was only one front window, by the door, and the curtain was pulled back sharply. I looked at the face, it looked back, we both froze, and then the curtain dropped again to its place. Lisa saw the very end of it, the moving curtain. I said that I was going back to find out and she said find out what, and she was right, so we went to the canoes instead and pushed on.

I have thought of many stories that would explain that day, but I've no idea what the real one is. I cannot think of a happy one.

The other Basil Rathbone moment had come at the very start of the trip, and also remains in family lore. We had driven to a small town on the Greenbrier called Ronceverte, which is the same word in French. The famous Greenbrier Resort, pleasuring ground of the Roosevelts and the cream of the East, lay several miles above on a commanding hill. Ronceverte, tucked down by the river, was a world apart. We had left our canoe and gear upstream at a crossroads called Romney some one hundred miles upstream. We were now looking for a place in Ronceverte to store our Volkswagen for the takeout, find a ride back to Romney, and paddle on down. Patrolling the river we discovered a track through the woods that led to the bank. It might be a place to leave the car.

The track ended quickly in a turnaround and a litter of debris. We were close to the water at this point, though, so we started over to have a look at the landing and mark it with a bandana, a sign to recognize at the end of the journey. We did not get there. Between us and the bank was a man in dark suit pants, a white shirt, and suspenders and he was filling in a hole with dirt. His suit coat was neatly folded over a tree limb. His shoes were polished leather. He was standing at the edge of the pit and bent over his shovel to the task. A tangle of bushes screened us from view. He worked steadily. The pit was long and rectangular, the size of an adult human body. There was no earthly thing we could think that it was designed for but an adult human body.

The filling continued, shovel by shovel. We didn't say a word. We turned as silently as we could, went back to our car, and drove away. Once back in town we found that we were shaking.

I fear that this narrative has a dreamlike air, an embellishment on something quite natural, a play on the mind. Nothing bad ever happened, of course. What haunts us is that we have no idea what really did happen. Looking back, though, I would have it no other way. That there are still places where unexplained things can happen is an oddly comforting thought. Whether these places remain, whether they have the remotest chance of remaining, is not.

SHENANDOAH RIVER
Virginia, 1970

Lisa and I had both canoed when we were young, calling out "switch sides!" when we needed to steer the boat, and Lisa's paddle from Camp Wohelo is still out in the shed, gaily painted and slim as a girl's wrist. We learned again in Washington, D.C., up on the Potomac with a group called the Canoe Cruisers whose logo remains pasted to the side of our old Grumman, partially intact, a smiling, foolish-looking turtle. The Cruisers taught us to read water, make turns, ferry, tip over, get back in, and do it all again. We left without fear. Graduation would take place up on the Shenandoah River at a place called Bulls Falls. Which is where Lisa got her fear back.

The South Fork of the Shenandoah is one of the most scenic rivers in the East. It winds along a mountain range of the same name in large, lazy turns, sometimes facing straight into the hills and then out over the valley, low, farmed, and green. The sky is with you all day long, Montana-sized and full of character and change. You can feel comfortable out here at any skill level, put in at one bridge and take out at the next with a swim along the way. You also feel raw history here in the heart of Stonewall Jackson's Shenandoah Valley campaign, one of the most legendary fought on American soil. Jackson's battles helped keep the Civil War in doubt for four years and on the river below you are floating over spent lead bullets, rusty pieces of canteen, and the shadows of men dead for more than a century. Their blood, however, in these parts, after all this passage of time, has not entirely washed away.

The Shenandoah Valley ran like a beltway between Richmond and the still-new District of Columbia where the Capitol Building stood half-finished, its dome a scaffold in the air. As the Union army gathered for its first strike south a significant number of West Pointers resigned to cast their lot with the Confederacy, including Robert E.

Lee and a schoolteacher at the Virginia Military Academy named Thomas J. Jackson. Lee's job was to protect Richmond from the Union forces while Jackson's became to hold his flank on the Shenandoah, through which the Federals could otherwise descend like a scimitar, cutting off Lee's supplies and communications with the west. In a series of lightning strikes and forced marches, Jackson's men tied up Federal units more than ten times their number, week after week, removing them from the Richmond campaign. Most historians agree that, had these Union troops been freed for the march on the Confederate capital, it would have fallen.

The Shenandoah battle sites, Strasburg, Winchester, Front Royal, are the markers of the valley, high above the river and draining down. Jackson would tell a companion at the end of one bloody day, surveying the carnage, "He who does not see the hand of God in this is blind, sir, blind." His remark and its religious conviction, indeed the very face from which it came, strikingly resemble those of John Brown, who had brought this war to a head, in this same valley, along this same river, such a short time before.

Passing through this landscape on the way to a canoe run, crossing streams where men drowned simply while fording them under fire, I find myself torn. The southern cause was a catastrophe, but still. My father, raised in Upstate New York, had a friend who telephoned him every night on the anniversary of Pickett's doomed charge at Gettysburg to say, "Paul, Paul, the South has just lost the war!" as if it were terrible, breaking news. Neither man had the slightest use for the South. But they both felt the same thing.

Damping these tones into the background, Lisa and I drive toward the Shenandoah for our test at Bulls Falls. We review our moves, how to size up a rapid, scout it, exit a swamped canoe, we know all this. When the time comes we simply blow it.

Granted, Bulls Falls can be nasty. We drift toward it on still water blocked by a rock sill across the river with a single gap wide enough to pass a canoe, down which half the force of the Shenandoah is pouring, a five-foot drop. The scout to reconnoiter it is easy, a rise on the riverbank shows the falls as clearly as a battle from a balloon, or at least it seems to. The chute rolls over in a large tongue, splashes loudly below, and runs out to a flat boulder, around which we will have to maneuver, but we have practiced these moves many times. I feel no panic, but walking back from the railroad tracks I see to my embarrassment that I have a large dark triangle on the front of my shorts. I have, quite without feeling it, wet my pants. I do not tell Lisa, who is paddling bow.

We'd missed something important during the scout. Had we come down to the river's edge below the chute and looked up into it we would have spotted a pointy rock that divides it in two parts. The right side is wider, but carries the boat smack into the boulder. The left is tighter but requires less wiggle below. We do not make this choice because we do not realize that there is one to be made; our instructor is letting us skull this out on our own. He is standing out on the boulder below with a throw rope in his hand, waiting for the boats to come. It might as well be us. Our friends the Per-lees will follow. They know not to follow us too closely, but that is easier known than done.

We drop over the falls, slam into the pointy rock, tip sideways, swamp, and are swept into the boulder in a matter of seconds. I am overboard, floating, astonished. Lisa is out too, the proper way on the upstream side, and glides behind the canoe into the rock. Which would be perfect except that, behind us, the Per-lees have done exactly the same thing and their swamped canoe is now washing into Lisa with the force of the river behind it. Lisa is trapped between boats like a sandwich, she cannot move, and the pressure from the Per-lee canoe is shaking it at both ends. I am still treading water. Lisa is screaming. Our instructor leans down, grabs her life jacket, and pulls straight up, popping her out like a cork. We did go back and run the drop again, just to get beyond it, but it never got beyond for Lisa. We have run more difficult rapids since but she white-knuckles them all the way.

The end of the Shenandoah trip, however, is yet downstream at Harpers Ferry and if this river is a Civil War history tour, here is its epicenter. This is the confluence with the Potomac where John

Brown brought his tiny band to ignite a revolution, saw his own sons shot and dying around him, and was captured by forces under then U.S. Army Colonel Robert E. Lee. It was Lee's aide, Jackson, who came to the arsenal door where Brown was trapped to demand his surrender. The coincidences are stunning. An active press attended Brown's subsequent trial and transmitted his condemnation of slavery to a breathless country, prompting admiration, fear, hope, and loathing on both sides of the line. Not all of which has disappeared either.

Several years later, my back went out. We had moved into our first house, I insisted we'd do all but the piano ourselves and then found that I could not move. After months in traction, trying not to go crazy, not to drive Lisa crazy, neither successfully, the curtain began to lift. As soon as I felt up to it I turned to the Shenandoah.

I went in October when the leaves were in full turn. The water was low and clear, an easy float. After a few days I wound into the Potomac and met a nasty surprise, a flood of slime whose powerful smell hung on for miles. The stench was as bad off of the river as on it. There was no camping here. There was no escaping it. I walked a few miles to a store and called Per-lee to come get me.

It turned out that a pulp mill at Front Royal had experienced what is called in the trade an excursion, a malfunction spilling all of its waste directly into the Potomac and then on down. Pulp wastes endure. Even without excursions these mills top the nation's water pollution list, year after year. Federal laws have forced controls but the industry is still fighting a ban on dioxins, which government scientists have named the most powerful toxin known to man. The dioxins come from chlorine, which is used to bleach the paper, because what sells is paper said to be "whiter than white". . . which in its way brings us back to the Civil War. Whiter than white.

I still think fondly, though, about that last run on the Shenandoah. It was not spectacular, and I might not do it again if I had other choices, but I found peace out here and it invaded my body and I came home, hugged Lisa hard, and things got better from there. I should go back and say thanks.

JUNIPER SPRINGS
Florida, 1972

We should have taken my mother. There are certain phrases in English that mean exactly the opposite, and one of them is, "You go on along without me, I'll be fine here." That usually means, "I'd love to go." But we were in a hustle, bundling up my sister's children, packing a lunch, loading the car, running back in for a sweater, we simply swirled around her, she standing in the kitchen, staring at the frozen turkey on the counter that would take hours to cook. It was Thanksgiving; we'd be back in time for dinner. We were off to Juniper Springs in the Ocala Forest, where Marjorie Kinnan Rawlings set *The Yearling*, a jewel of water rising from a thirty-foot well and winding through hummocks of live oak and cypress, clear as glass. It would have been so easy to have asked my mother again, insisted on it, put an arm around her, told her that we'd do the turkey the next day, that we wanted her with us. I wind the movie back in my mind, hoping it will be different, but we did none of these things.

I only realized how fitting that would have been some years later, going over old photographs we discovered in the attic. One was taken from the side. She is about fifteen, her dark hair buried under a wide felt hat, wearing a wool shirt buttoned at the cuffs. She is lying on the bottom of a wood-and-canvas canoe, reading a book. When I showed her the picture and asked what she was doing in the canoe, she said, "Keeping away from the insects." That was her way.

My mother had been up in Labrador with her father and brother and a small crew of Canadian ex-lumbermen who, in other photos, are seen poling logs downstream, dancing on food barrels, and making camp beds from branches of hemlock and pine. Nobody else ran these woods in those years except the Cree, hunting and passing through. My mother was up there several summers in a row, it turned out. One thing of the few things she told me about the experience was how the Canadian guides took care of themselves in the out of doors, washing morning and evening, shaving in a little mirror they nailed to a tree. To this day when I camp, I shave. All of this was in her bones. We could have said to her down in Florida as she used to say to us when we were little, we can't leave you home, hop in the car.

Florida waters are largely secret because so much of them runs below the ground. They carve tunnels through the soft limestone, mass in great caves, pop up at unexpected places, then drop into sinkholes and disappear. The entire state is in flow. Scuba divers explore these subterranean passages with headlamps and air tanks, at some risk of getting lost. The springs where the water emerges are treasures and Juniper is one of them, but the largest of all is at Wakulla, 180 feet down with twelve miles of underground grottos and more yet to be explored. When the season turns cold, endangered manatees congregate here for the reliable temperature, their backs just bumping the surface and drawing cries from visitors, "There it is!"

Lisa and I went to Wakulla one February and, my mother's chromosomes kicking in, the spring water a constant sixty-nine degrees, I decided to go for a swim. As I floated slowly toward the source, the bottom receding below me as if I were leaving the earth, I felt a sudden nudge, the slightest brush, against my leg. Thinking it was an aquatic weed I shook it off, but then the nudge came back, nothing aggressive, just saying, "I'm no accident," and right beside me was a manatee, larger than I was, with a cub, floating at exactly my pace. I stopped to gape, and with absolutely no motion other than a brief undulation of those perfect aquatic bodies they shot away. I'd love to see manatees enter the Olympics some day, even an exhibition race, against our human phenoms. My money would be on them. And my heart.

Back on Juniper Springs, I am dawdling from the start. A perfectly round pool, ten yards across and translucent to the bottom, swells up and steams into the November air. I can look down and see the hole it is coming from. I don't need to go much farther that morning to have a full trip. When we begin to float out with the current I am the last. The paddle down is not long, perhaps six miles, which you could manage to do in a couple of hours, working steadily, and miss it all.

I keep slowing us down. Let's take a swim here, I propose, drawing blank looks. The air temperature has just hit fifty degrees. Let's pull out for a picnic, I say, although we'd eaten huge breakfasts and it is not yet noon. I have no intention of eating either. I just don't want to end things too soon.

My father is in heaven. He had been the classic Boy Scout, earned his Eagle badge, played bugle for the troop, and still played in a way that tugged at your heart, "To the Colors," "Taps," I could see soldiers in their barracks listening, some of them violent men, wiping moist eyes. He learned to paddle as he had to bugle in that same Germanic there-is-one-right-way of his, and it was all he could do to keep from coaching me as we made the Juniper run. One fall he had come to visit us in Washington and on a balmy day we went out and walked the old tow path from Georgetown. Several couples were in canoes paddling below, literally at our feet. I was half-dreaming, watching colors move on the water, when I heard my father bark out, "No, No! Not like that!" I turned to him, fearing an assailant, and instead found him gesticulating vigorously to a startled pair below us who had just bounced their bow off of the canal bank, quite happily for all that I could see. "Like this!" my father shouted at the young man in the stern, blading his arms gracefully through the air and then cocking his imaginary paddle to return the canoe to line. Behind his back, I raised my hands to the occupants of the boat in a sign of helplessness. My father was of course correct, about the blading, I mean. He was not trying to be superior, I don't believe his was even a conscious act, it was just an old reflex kicking in. But out here on the Juniper I know enough to end my steering strokes the way he liked. This is Thanksgiving and we are in it together.

If there is a yet prettier river in Florida than Juniper Springs a strong candidate would be the Wacissa, which rises from its own springs in a *Lord of the Rings* landscape choked with cypress knees and then opens into a wide river with long grasses underneath that trail downstream in braids. Large fish pilot the canoe, spooked out of one refuge and seeking another. One afternoon Lisa and I watched an osprey dive down to take one, a reckless, all-out plunge into the water, and no sooner rise with the fish in its claws than meet an eagle screaming down out of the sun and set to rob him.

The Wacissa is classic Florida because just when you think you are finishing the run you swirl into a dead-end lagoon, and the river disappears. It has gone underground. There is no way out. The nearest paved road is miles away and your car is somewhere on it. Lisa and I ended up here one afternoon near sundown, bewildered and thoroughly lost. We had missed a crucial turn, apparently. But luck often follows the lost and at the end of the lagoon we saw a couple with a large truck, just beginning to set up camp. He drove us out on a vehicle-busting track while his wife stayed with the children. He refused to take gas money. I forgot to take down his address. Driving back we did stop for a hitchhiker, though, keeping the karma going.

Back on Juniper Springs, I have managed to talk my father into stopping for lunch. No one mentions my mother. Shortly before her death, at the age of 101, my brother found a cache of old film reels in a box from her own father, who had bought an early 35mm film camera the way he bought a newfangled automobile, and then tried to learn how to make it work. Most of the reels were of clouds and trees swimming in and out of focus, spotted with light when he had shot into the sun, but then there was this one. It opens by panning a large pond, then down to the bow of a canoe, slicing through the water. My mother's back and wide-brim hat appear in the bow, and then a dark object is ahead in the water, the size of a trash can, moving away. As the canoe approaches the object becomes a very large head with wide antlers, a moose, rolling one huge eye wildly back at this strange thing that was chasing it, coming right along side of it, and then this body with a hat on jumps and lands on its back. At her father's urging, which means direction, my mother had mounted the moose and was holding onto its neck for dear life. The film shows them together like an old rodeo act, the moose swims madly for shore, my mother abandons ship, it stands a brief moment, shaking, and then bounds off into the brush.

Here is the odd thing. My mother never once mentioned that film. We had uncovered it by accident. When I asked her what she remembered about the incident she brushed it off as she had so many other questions. She said, "I remember the bugs," and pausing to correct herself, "the smell and the bugs." It was exactly what her father would have said too. My father, by contrast, would have waved his arms, exclaimed, made it a bazaar.

Florida's famed springs have run into trouble. The state is one big water system and it sets records for miles of water contaminated and the loads going into them. While there are several culprits here the dominant one is agriculture, which happens to dominate Florida politics as well. The Everglades Park has been in a knock-down with the sugar industry for more than thirty years. No state does well in regulating agribusiness for very similar reasons, but the equation in Florida is aggravated by its thin soils, which require huge inputs of fertilizers to keep the game going. Despite the abundance of polluted lakes and streams, state officials have spent decades resisting federal efforts to move them toward cleanup. Wakulla and other springs have gone cloudy for much of the year. Florida and its springs, Louisiana and its wetlands, West Virginia and its mountains, Oregon and its forests—it seems so hard for humans not to destroy the very things that define where they live, and what they swear they love.

We get off the Juniper run late. No surprise, we dawdled to the end, but this means that we pile into the cars as light is fading for the long drive home, quiet, savoring the day. We stagger into the house at eight o'clock, dirty and half-asleep. My mother is in the kitchen, her side dishes turned cold, the turkey still in the oven, stubbornly resisting the heat, a quarter inch of whiskey in a glass on the counter. We move like zombies, wash our hands and faces, throw packs into bedrooms, talk in low voices, my mother silent as stone. My father pours himself a whiskey. My mother refills her glass. My sister shushes her children as if there had been a funeral. Conversation at the table is minimal, "Can you please pass the potatoes," very polite. The one thing we could talk about, Juniper Creek, seems even to our dulled sensibilities the wrong thing at the wrong time.

I have not run Juniper again. One winter, though, my parents came to visit us in New Orleans and, by coincidence, we had a visiting professor at the law school who was alone and told me she liked the out of doors. I invited her to join us on a paddle up a small bayou called Coquille, just out of the city. Lisa stayed behind on boy duty. At the put-in my father went to the stern of one canoe and to my surprise my mother went to the stern of the other, taking ownership. I didn't say a word, the visitor and I got in the bow seats, and my parents paddled us through. I'd seen the same smile on my father's face back on Juniper Springs, but the one on my mother was new. She handled the boat like a pro. She swung the paddle with grace. She rested easily, as if she did this every day, only on this particular day, in this late light, she was radiant with joy. Driving home together, she didn't say a word. Unable to resist, I asked her how it felt and she said, "Rusty." But I caught the corner of a smile.

BIG SUR RIVER

California, 1973

The Big Sur seems barely a river at all, we'd call it a stream back East, but after a hard rain the kayaks come popping out like mushrooms and maneuver the tightest twists and drops imaginable, down to the sea. Most of the time the Big Sur is for hiking, and fishing, and back in the early 1970s, for smoking pot as well and going nude in the great outdoors. It is hard to say which was more widely enjoyed.

One of the pleasures of working for the National Wildlife Federation in the 1970s was an array of summer field programs that put families into the wild with a menu of courses like "Reflector Oven Cooking" and "Life in a Mountain Stream." A surprise favorite was the "Nature Creep," which consisted of sitting in a field and examining through a small hand lens everything within arm's reach, and no more, for an hour and a half. Which went by like quicksilver. I remember the dandelion, of all things, which outdid its competitors with gutter-shaped leaves that funneled rainwater down to its roots, a key to survival in dry climes. Who knew?

Following one of these sessions near Monterey, Lisa went off to visit her sister and I dropped down to the Los Padres National Forest and the Big Sur. Just under sixteen miles long, it runs swift and clear from the base of Mount Pico Blanco to the coast. Pico Blanco is the big dog of California's central range and it is named for a reason: extraordinary deposits of limestone that shine bright white in the sun, which in this region means just about every day. It had been Mount Ararat to the indigenous peoples here, the Ohlone, whose uncannily familiar creation myth had the world covered in a gigantic flood except for this single peak, which saved all three essential creatures: the Eagle, the Hummingbird, and the Coyote. Not the humans, who were not invented yet; they would descend later from the Coyote. Which, among other things, indicates that the Ohlone had a pretty good read on human nature.

The hike in was surprisingly steep, straight up through redwood trees and an understory so open it seemed a park. Once over the first lift it joins the Sur, bubbling along like a puppy, shadows of trout darting by. I met several groups hiking out who, in the custom of this particular time, in this particular place, were wearing sturdy boots, wool socks, and nothing else at all. Coming on them from below, my eyes on the trail before me, I would raise my head as they drew near, trying not to stare, their faces as casual and hello-there as they could be. Gearing up earlier at an outdoor store I had seen catalogues with nude campers advertising sleeping pads, tents, the full array, but I thought they were a come-on, Victoria's Secret ahead of their time. I turned to watch the hikers walk away, large backpacks over smaller pairs of buttocks, bouncing down the trail. Come day three I didn't even turn my head. It was normal.

I went rapidly, intending to get in deep, and ended the second day at a campsite described in my diary as, "If there is a heaven this has to be in it." The Sur at this point is in a sharp gorge with a narrow path alongside, winding upstream from pool to pool. It is overhung with downed timber and strewn with boulders that glisten with the spray, some flat as dinner trays and a perfect sit, feet soaking in the cool water, clothes washed and on a branch to dry in the dappled sun. The Ohlone had it right. You could take the famed California beaches, each as sterile as Muzak—the Sur was where life begins.

Actually, the Sur was about to be where life ended, at least here, below Pico Blanco. In the late 1950s a company called Granite Rock filed a mineral claim on the entire mountain. It planned to blow the top off with dynamite to reach the limestone below. It was a reasonable proposition for any miner, and indeed was supported by federal mining law that gave companies the unbridled right to enter public forests, take the minerals, pay nothing in royalties . . . and then, as a lagniappe, claim title to the land as well. This anarchism was enacted in 1872 to incentivize the development of the West and has resisted change ever since, despite the fact that every state from Colorado to California has become rather well developed, in some places wall-to-wall. The mining industry knows a bargain when it sees one. Granite Rock looked good to go.

Enter a new actor, the California Coastal Commission, created with the support of other federal laws attempting to bring a bit of balance to development on America's coastlines. The Commission took its task to heart, earning such a reputation for defending the coast that California real estate and other industries formed their own law firm to attack it. When it came to mining on Pico Blanco, the Commission was insisting that the Granite Rock project, although permitted by the U.S. Forest Service (which had little choice, given the mining law), would need a state coastal permit too. The effects that blowing up Pico Blanco were going to have on the Big Sur and the coast nearby seemed obvious to anyone who recognized that pollution ran downhill. To which Granite Rock replied, We're not on the coast and besides we have federal approval, and off they went into a legal fray that three years later landed in the United States Supreme Court. In a dog-eat-dog set of opinions, a majority of the justices upheld California's special interest in its coast, and its authority to require a permit. Which, to date, has not issued.

The legal battle won, Pico Blanco has not been mined and the Sur below runs clean and quick every day of the year. I caught a half-dozen trout the next morning, fishing upstream from pool to pool. In a kind of trance I leaped onto wet rocks, clawed through bushes, and stumbled like a drunkard in my eagerness to find the next hole where a big one might be hiding. I could have sprained an ankle in a heartbeat, which would have been a pretty fix. Two mornings from now I was to meet Lisa at the San Francisco airport for a ten o'clock flight, and I was a two-day's hike away from the nearest road . . . from which to hitch a ride. The Lord of Foolish Risks favored me this lovely morning, though, and I came back uninjured to fry the fish in shifts and lay them on a rock to cool.

At which point, pinch me!, I heard a splashing noise and around a boulder shielding my campsite, wading in the water, came an entirely naked young woman with her clothing in her hand. I was too stunned to do the obvious, offer her very politely some freshly cooked trout. Instead she asked whether this was the way to the hot springs, and I replied, no, they were the other way, pointing back in the direction from which she had come. She hesitated and then asked whether I had anything good to smoke and I, still a little stunned, gave her my second no in a row. To this day I ask myself about that scene, reliving the conversation, imagining different outcomes, but the Lord of Foolish Risks was with me here too because the young woman then turned, said of all things, "Sorry," and disappeared.

I sunbathed by the river until afternoon, naked as I was made, and then packed up to go. That evening I was down the trail at the first camp in, a dark hole under towering redwoods, empty of other people. I had to wake before dawn the next morning in order to be at the highway by dawn and begin thumbing a ride. And so, in the dark of early morning I was reading my watch by flashlight, 4:15, when the light winked out. No worries, but when I opened the shell to replace the batteries I heard an ominous springing sound, the switch had jumped away into the black. Without light to see, I stuffed everything helter-skelter into my pack including leaves and sticks and began to walk out, feeling my way.

The hitchhike was not without drama, it took several short lifts, but I arrived at the terminal just before takeoff, begged them to hold the flight (they did accommodating things back then) and came breathlessly into the cabin to find Lisa sitting alone, empty seat alongside, looking daggers. There were no cell phones those days. I had not had the time to find a pay phone, and even if I had, whom would I have called? I started to tell her about the beauty of the Big Sur but for the moment she did not seem to be interested.

SHUTTLES

West Virginia and Mississippi, 1970–1990

We are standing on the side of Route 49, a road that runs from Hattiesburg, Mississippi, to nowhere else in particular. I am in cutoff shorts and a baseball cap to hide my bald head, which for the business at hand would not be a plus. I'm carrying a canoe paddle. Lisa, standing uneasily beside me, is dubious about the paddle.

"They'll never pick us up if they see a weapon," she tells me.

"They'll see we are out-of-doors types," I say. "Canoers . . . friendly people."

I put on a friendly smile as a sixteen-wheeler roars by spitting gravel up to my knees. Lisa has retreated to the tree line.

It is near dusk on a Sunday, we are late off the river, and for all the traffic on this stretch of road, they could have closed it down several miles to the north and south. Our boys and two students are playing in the water below the bridge. There is a large sandbar and Red Creek ripples over it, shallow and clear. We can hear their voices, "No, look at me!" Jump. Splash. For maximum enjoyment of the outdoors through the most finely tuned sensory system of the human body—your children—there is nothing like a sandy creek in southern Mississippi. The only drawback is that, wherever you take out, you have to get back to your car.

That is what we're doing now. Rather, that is what we're standing around trying to do. Off to the west we can see a low moon ready to turn on in the failing light. From the distance I hear a deep motor noise. "Another truck," I say unhappily; trucks rarely pick up these days. Instead, over the rise comes a smaller vehicle rumbling loudly and trailing smoke. As it nears I see that it is also trailing sparks from its muffler, which has dropped to the road. I can not to this day remember the color of that car, although, in retrospect, I might have needed to.

About the latitude of the bridge, the vehicle begins to nose down as if the driver were placing invisible weights on the front hood. In a spray of burnt tire and roadside dirt, it struggles to a stop, heaving with the uneven drive of its pistons. Lisa and I sprint for the passenger door.

Like a gentleman I open the door and pass my wife into the backseat, only there is no backseat. You can see right into the trunk. There are some loose springs where a seat might have been, and a blue plastic milk crate. Lisa sits on the plastic crate and takes hold of my neck. I have sidled in front by lifting pieces of the car radio off of the seat and placing them on my lap. The dash is entirely open as if blown away by explosives, showing bundles of wire.

"Sumnabitch sold me this thing . . . ," mumbles the driver.

I look over and see a young man who has apparently not slept for a couple of days. His side of the vehicle, down by the brake and clutch pedals, is covered with discarded beer cans through which I can see the highway below.

"Paid two hundred dollars . . . oughta shoot the sumnabitch," he says, grinding the vehicle into gear.

Lisa's hand tightens on my neck. Pine trees and nothing else whisk by in the dusk. I turn to our host.

"Where you from?" I ask, very casual.

"Pensacola," he says.

He stares out the windshield. I stare out the windshield. "What've you been doing down there?" I ask.

"Time," he says.

"Time," I say, like it was the most natural thing in the world. Doing a little time.

I feel Lisa's fingers dig in.

"How much time?" I manage to ask. Maybe not much time, I am thinking.

"Five years," he says.

Five years, I think. That is more time than my younger boy has been on this earth.

We enjoy a little silence, which then begins to feel uncomfortable.

"What for?" I say, maintaining my casual.

"Cut my wife," he says. "Oh," I say. Silence.

"What'd she do?" I say.

"Come home too early," he says, leaving me to my imagination. He came home too early? She did? What was she doing? But I think I can guess that part. More silence.

"Where you going now?" I say.

"See my wife," he says.

I am figuring it has been five years in Pensacola, and he has been waiting all this time. What is he going to do when he sees her, I am on the verge of asking. But Lisa no doubt knows this, and is sending me signals by squeezing me so as to cut off circulation to my head: The signals that I should stop being so curious out loud.

Which, against my natural instincts, I do. Which might have saved our lives, who knows? Lisa is seeing a headline: Couple Found Brutally Slain in Mississippi Woods: Foul Play Suspected.

I tell our host that our car is down a spur off of highway 49, a couple of miles into the woods, where the two-laner crosses a bridge. We make the turn. It is about dark and the bridge seems a long way away down this lonely road. Through the roar of the car I think I can feel Lisa breathing. I can also smell incredible exhaust fumes coming up through the floor. The exhaust system has probably fallen off entirely by now and we are drinking carbon monoxide straight from the engine head. Couple Dies of Fumes is the headline I am seeing.

"There it is," I say, pointing to the outline of a bridge railing ahead. We roar down the hollow and across the bridge and on into the dark.

"Uh-oh," I start to think, "Where is he going?"

Lisa goes rigid. Her grip has become that of an eagle hooked into its last fish of life. I look at our driver. He seems more comatose than murderous. Perhaps, however, this is the way Jack the Ripper looked. "We passed it," I offer.

"Missed the sumnabitch," he says and, to my relief, begins to apply the great, shuddering pressure that seems to be this vehicle's braking process. I figure he's got about four more stops of this nature in the car and then it falls apart in the road.

He backs, fills, wheels a turn, and slows to drop us off. "Thanks very much," I say into the darkness of the car, slipping him some bills. Lisa tries to say something too, but she can't get it out of her throat, and then our host is off and away to live out whatever sad design he has in store. Lisa and I pad silently down to our own car.

"Where else," I say to her, "could you have a beautiful camping weekend like this with excitement at the very end?"

Lisa doesn't say a word. I see that I may have to run the shuttle on our next trip by myself or with one of the boys. Hitchhiking alone is difficult. Few people in their right mind will pick up a bald skinny man even if he is wearing a baseball cap and carrying a confidence-inspiring paddle.

We've hitched more shuttles since. Sometimes I take Gabriel, my youngest. He has straw blond hair, which is always a plus. We bring his schoolmates up on the Homochitto and the Bogue Chitto and other creeks as special and distinct as one boy from another. Wolf River has steep walls with moss, the Pushpatawpa has cypress knees, and the sandbars of the Big Biloxi lie in tiers like wedding cakes. I can't tell you what that sand feels like between your toes, but I know that it squeaks when you walk. At night, with the boys prowling around the tents, you can hear them, squeak, squeak, going by.

Unfortunately, these rivers can also be places people go to get rid of things like bedsprings and old Barca Loungers and to shoot their guns. Country road signs seem to be put here for target practice, and they are laced with holes. The danger of the out-of-doors these days is no longer nature, it is people. And yet, when you run the shuttle these are the people—not the ones in the latest SUV—who will stop and pick you up. Country can be raw, but it can also be very kind.

Country anywhere. Back when we were first married and ran the Greenbrier, we ended up stashing our car in the backyard of the Ronceverte chief of police, which seemed safe enough, except that while we were gone his son used it, ran out of gas, and killed the battery. Leaving the car there, we have to hitch north for the put-in and the following morning finds us standing on the edge of town holding a neat sign that says MARLITON. It might as well say PEOPLE FROM MARS or WE HAVE THE PLAGUE.

The early cars creep by us slowly so that all passengers can take a look at us. Later cars crammed with well-dressed families speed past on their way to church, returning two hours later to see the sinners still adrift at the side of the road . . . soundless, pale faces filled with curiosity pressed against the window glass. This is awesome stuff. A man and a woman just standing there on a Sunday morning.

Even the church traffic is better than no traffic at all, however, for by midday there is nothing moving north in West Virginia and we begin to suspect that Sunday afternoon driving is against the law. Lisa and I take turns holding the sign and going off to sit in the shade. I tell her that these are really warm people once you get to know them. She is thinking up a smart reply when up the hill from town chugs our big chance of the day, a VW bus.

Here is a Rule of Thumb: of all the vehicles likely to pick up a hitchhiker, the VW bus is tops. First of all, it has room. Second, it is not driven by families who go to church in West Virginia, or most of the time even by people who were married in a church; the chances are it is driven by guys with beards and women with very long hair who all eat with the same utensils and sleep in the back and believe in love and have no hang-ups about giving rides to strangers. This particular van, as it poots its way to where we are standing, fulfills our every expectation. Its sides are hand-painted with a rising sun and pictures of doves and its windows are draped with colored beads. The bus slows to a crawl just beyond us, and Lisa and I run to catch it, our duffels swinging from our arms, only to have the bus creep forward, stop, and, as we near it, creep forward again. A face appears in the beads at the back window, then several faces, laughing, and with a loud sputtering, they drive away.

"Those bastards!" I say. This is not part of the scenario. Lisa drops her duffel in the middle of the road and sits on it. "The next one is going to have to run me over," she says.

As if on cue, the next one comes right away. It is no VW bus. It is the largest truck out of Ronceverte in many a season, a full eighteen-wheel tractor trailer with its gears grinding up the hill like a box of tools spilling on a concrete floor. We stand there rooting for it while it thunders toward us, blasting exhaust from its stack and then, miraculously, stopping with a squeal of air brakes. The door is so high overhead I have to boost Lisa to the handle, and we pile in.

"HEY, HEY, HEY!" shouts the driver over the roar of his motor.

"Hey, hey," I say back, not even hearing the sound of my words, eyeing instead the dashboard of the cab that is rolling in bottles of Dexedrine, No Doz, and less familiar brands.

"Got to stay AWAKE!" the driver yells at us with a grin, catching my eyes on his pills.

He is wearing a sleeveless black T-shirt that shows arms the size of my thighs. The tattoos on his muscles shake with the vibration of the engine, a dancing woman and a dancing snake.

"Been driving since Miami," he shouts in explanation. "My FOURTH DAY!"

"His fourth day," I say to Lisa, who is holding onto the door like the strap on a merry-go-round. In case she hasn't heard.

"Isn't Ronceverte a little out of your WAY?" I shout back in what I hope is a friendly manner. "Got to go the BACK ROADS!" he explains, winding into his fourth or fifth gear change, his arms moving the two gear-levers like pistons. "I'm OVERWEIGHT!"

"He's overweight," I relay to Lisa, who is bouncing in and out of my vision to my right.

As we reach cruising speed, I say, "I'm glad you picked us UP!" and when he grins, I tell him, "A VAN right before SLOWED DOWN but then PULLED AWAY!"

"No SHIT!" he yells, still grinning.

"They LAUGHED!" I add.

"Let's GET 'EM!" he yells, and with a frenzy of pedals and shifting he grinds the big motor up another fifty rpms. With a rocking motion, the eighteen-wheeler accelerates into a left turn, a right turn, and then shoots down into a valley from which the road rises narrow and winding on the far side. Barely emerging from the valley is a small drop of turquoise, our target, the VW bus, oblivious to what is coming.

It may have taken us five minutes to catch the bus, I'm not sure. The trees fly by us, and with the height of the cab, they often seem below us; the very noise of our speed seems to arrest the idea of time. Pill bottles and tape decks dance on the dashboard, I hold onto my seat to keep from swinging into the gear shifts, and the only time I look at Lisa her eyes are closed.

Suddenly the VW bus is in front of us, one hundred feet, then forty feet, at which point it takes a curve, we take the curve, and we end up with the enormous grille of the truck perched over the van's rear window like the prow of a ship.

"Let's KISS 'EM!" yells the driver, and with the skill of a docking astronaut he proceeds to ease his bumper into the back of the bus, jolting it forward as you'd kick a tricycle with your foot. A white face appears at the VW's back window, several faces, mouths open, talking wildly, and then the curtains close.

The bus struggles forward. The truck eases forward, closer again. To my right I can see Lisa curling into a ball.

"Let's SAY HELLO!" yells the driver, and he pulls on his air horn.

A loud shriek splits the air and the bus seems propelled forward by the blast. It is shaking. Clearly, it can go no faster.

"HEY, HEY, HEY!" yells our driver.

"Hey, Hey," I say, adding, "that's probably ENOUGH!"

"ENOUGH?" he smiles, and for a moment I think he is going to kill them all.

"OH!" he shouts and slowly decreases our speed.

The bus struggles ahead to a side road, turns out in a cloud of dust, and lets us go by. I can see no faces at the windows this time. They are taking no chances. West Virginia has turned suddenly hostile to them, and it is probably not the first time these folks have seen hostility. They hunker down like a turtle and let us pass.

When we arrive at the Marlinton Esso station, hauling our canoe out of the back bay, our driver gets out, too, because he just has to "SEE THIS CANOE THING!" in which we are going to float the river. He disappears toward the snack machines as Lisa and I go down to the water, load our gear, and push off. We float under the highway bridge but as we emerge the surface of the water is plopping with what can't be rain, or hail, or fish . . . it is candies, handfuls of Milk Duds, Black Crows and Tootsie Rolls showering on the canoe. We look up and our driver is smiling down at us, tossing the last ones from a paper bag.

"HEY, HEY!!" he shouts.

"Hey, hey," I call back, and we raise our paddles good-bye.

These are the people who will give you rides.

Years later, boys in tow by now, we have moved to New Orleans and it is Mardi Gras weekend. We decide to do a river instead and try the Okatoma, but the water is so high and muddy it looks like the Mississippi, so we drop back to a thread of Black Creek, way up in the woods, running swift under a graying sky. We leave the cars and put in immediately—there is no time to do a shuttle—and paddle around the first bend into a tangle of trees that look like tank traps left by a retreating army. Dragging the boats over I can feel Lisa's unspoken question, was this really a good idea? We've never been up here before. It becomes a grand idea. The stars break clear around 8:00 p.m. and we cook by flashlight, closing in on the fire while the boys make jokes about their teachers and we pretend we aren't there.

The next afternoon we reach the takeout bridge and it is time hitch back to the car. It looks easy. We know people are at the bridge because we can hear them shooting their guns at something well before we come in sight. I make loud noises to alert them that the next thing they see coming around the bend wearing a welder's cap is not a deer wearing a welder's cap, and then there they are. They are two lanky men and a young woman so pretty and so faded it tears your heart, and a little girl, and a tricycle stuck in the mud, and two large dogs. And a cooler of beer. And a shotgun and a pistol.

I tell Lisa that if the parents of Gabe's schoolmate, who is with us out here, could see this scene they'd be calling their lawyer. But I put on a brave face and go up to the men and allow as to how it is a nice day.

They agree, and add that it is a good day for floating, although there wasn't anybody ever on Black Creek when it is not yet summertime. I say I didn't know that, and so we are able to discuss exactly where I am from and where I'd started out on the river, which finally allows me to ask about whether anyone might be able to give my wife and me a lift back upstream, seeing as we have these little boys with us and they need to get home—at which point the boys start to ram the canoes onto the beach like a landing party of Marines, whooping and cursing and generally destroying the impression I am trying to create.

For that or whatever reason, I get no takers on a ride, and so I walk back to the invasion of Iwo Jima to calm the boys down and select a hostage to accompany me on the hitchhike back. While I am pondering my choice, the taller of the young men I'd talked with approaches us, beer can in hand, loaded pistol safely protruding from the waist of his jeans. He says, "Y'all looking for a ride to Purvis?"

He is on solid ground here because I'd told him about two minutes earlier that I was looking for a ride to Purvis, where we'd left the car.

"We sure are," I say, adding that it'd really help the kids.

He looks uncomfortable and then says, "We'd like to help you, but we ain't got gas."

I offer at once to buy them a full tank of gas, reprimanding myself silently for not having put that part of the deal right up front, and Lisa and I accompany him to his pickup truck.

I don't know what it is about pickup trucks in rural Mississippi. They may have to be practically destroyed to get state registration. This one has no reverse gear. To turn it around, the driver has to steer it up an incline, throw it in neutral, and have the passenger hop out to give it a shove backward while the driver makes his cut. The operation is repeated as often as necessary. On the final pass here the other man picks up the dogs, each the size of a small calf, and throws them bodily into the flatbed like potato sacks. "Y'ole tick dawgs, y' ain't worth a damn," he says without rancor, more like a defining statement, and jumps in, slamming the door by reaching out through the window. There is no door handle. We head off, leaving the woman and the girl behind.

The driver is on my left, a beautiful boy gone to seed with a light sprout of beard and red eyeballs. Lisa and I are in the middle, she trying to press herself into my armpit, and the other passenger is at the side window, another tall one with so few teeth they looked like sunflowers in a cave. They are both opening fresh sixteen-ouncers of LITE beer.

"Good thing you're with us," the driver says. "Cops are mean around here. Bust you for anything."

I look at him, puzzled. Have these guys figured out I am a lawyer?

"We see a cop, you take the beer," he explains.

"Sure," I say, too quickly.

"This here's a dry county," he says. "You'd pull a lot smaller fine than we would," he said.

"Oh," I say.

"Yeah," says the passenger with some pride. "I'm already paying off $900."

"For what?" I asked.

Lisa gives me a blow to the ribs as a reminder about my curiosity.

"Driving on some guy's lawn," he says. It wasn't his particular fault, he explains. The driver of the car was drunk and had gotten stuck in a flower garden next to some girl's front porch whom they happened to know about the middle of the night, and our passenger was just trying to help back it out when he got arrested. He had to pay for the sidewalk, too. And a tree.

"The police sure sound mean," I say.

"You bet," he says, with emphasis. "My daddy used to go down to the main road and drink all night and nobody would touch him. Now they come looking for you." He trails off. "All I want to do is what my daddy done . . ."

Lisa tries to change the mood.

"I'd better finish my Coke if I'm going to hold your beer," she says, tossing back a final swallow.

"Here, let me help you," says the passenger, and gently and quickly, in all courtesy, he lifts the can from Lisa's fingers and sends it spinning out the window, clanking on the roadway behind.

Lisa stifles a small shriek.

"It ain't litterin'," he explains. "People come by and pick 'em up."

"Why don't you hold his beer?" I prompt Lisa. I am getting the hang of this.

And so we roll over the Mississippi countryside, past piney woods and small farms and fruit trees just coming into bloom, white dogwood and the shocking purple of red buds, a flower so wild and lonely I'll want it near my grave. Another shuttle done.

When we get to our car the driver swings up the road grade, leaving the truck's nose high, and throws it in neutral; the passenger, Lisa, and I jump out, run around front, and push; the truck swings back down in a graceful arc, the passenger leaps in, reaches out, and slams the door. As they pull away, he raises his beer to us in salute.

"A country boy will survive!" he yells.

We wave back.

GREAT FALLS OF THE POTOMAC
Maryland, 1974

I'd say that nobody runs Great Falls, but these days people actually do. They are wearing helmets and elbow guards and wedged into play boats that drop down from ledge to ledge, jabbing left and right, disappearing into holes and popping out again, shaking off spray and then on. There is no room to change your mind. This is a far more complex run than over-Niagara-in-a-barrel, a series of ten-foot chutes tumbling nearly eighty feet in half a mile, one of the steepest fall lines in the East. Red and yellow kayaks, tapered front and back, glint in the sun like minnows against an arc of roaring water which seems enraged by the hubris of it all.

Some of them drown. The Park Service used to post the numbers on the towpath nearby. To my knowledge, no one has tried Great Falls in an open boat canoe, but eventually somebody will. The water is too big and I-dare-you-to for someone not to try. Bungee jumping from high-span bridges may hold its charms for some, but there is a draw to these falls that is mesmerizing, that sucks me in. Out on the overlook I find myself having to step back from the rail. My knees shake. I do not stay long.

There are classic paddles along this reach of the Potomac, one starting at the very foot of the falls and sweeping down Mather Gorge, a granite canyon sheer as a box with a thin scattering of pine trees on top, way up in the air. The river has carved round holes, smooth caves, and swirling figures into the rock walls, feminine forms, softer than the more recent canyons of the West in geological time. The Potomac began on this one thirty-five thousand years ago. In a younger day, Per-lee and I, his red hair knotted behind his head in a bandana, would put in our canoes at the Old Angler's Inn at the foot of the gorge and struggle our way upstream like migrating shad, searching out the eddies behind rocks and ledges ahead where we could tuck in and catch our breath. A wrong angle of the bow and the current would whip us sideways and quickly downstream where we'd have to regroup and come back at it again. Once in the canyon itself, though, we could cruise up the eddy line close to the cliffs feeling as if we were inside an Ansel Adams photograph, a black-and-white poem to rocks and water.

On another day we'd float the gorge from the top, putting in at the base of Great Falls itself, deafened by its voice and wet from its mist in the air. We had to portage the boats down a steep trail to get here alongside the Fish Ladder, a narrow bypass on the Maryland side that was chiseled out for river traffic centuries ago. The ghosts of these rivermen accompanied us as we labored by, eighty pounds of unwieldy aluminum on our shoulders, plus a paddle and a spare. Once in the water, however, you could float for miles, past Angler's Inn, past the exclusive Madeira School high on its bluff, home of a high-tone scandal of a jilted lover, past a pond below where you could pull out and swim, down through White Horse rapids, a nonthreatening tumble of rocks curving left to right, you just followed the flume, and then out. A sweet day.

We did not talk much, Per-lee and I, but we felt the same things. At the pullout he'd turn to me, smiling, and ask if I'd heard the redtail or the winter wren, which has an excited, bubbling call. He ran a census track along this stretch of the Potomac every spring, counting the songs and the species. They were starting to drop in number. They have continued to drop since, small birds on diminishing floodplains, pushed out by forces they have no way to understand or adapt to. I have spent many years on their side.

My most memorable day at Great Falls, however, was not with Perlee and had nothing to do with canoes. It was not even daytime. It came with a cold winter and a foot-thick freeze. Between Christmas and New Year's Eve, the entire Potomac iced over at the latitude of the Key Bridge, from historic Georgetown to the recent clot of high-rises on the Virginia side implausibly called Rosslyn. Virginia commuters had favored this very spot to run an interstate from its suburbs across the Potomac, past Georgetown, and on to the Capitol.

The bridge, however, would cross several large boulders in the river called the Three Sisters and, of all things, they were part of the C&O Canal National Historical Park. Local environmentalists, my partner at the time in fact, brought a lawsuit against the bridge alleging harm to the park, which seemed a stretch, most particularly to the presiding judge, John Sirica, famous for his acerbic tongue and a tendency to intervene from the bench to ask his own questions. That tendency, disliked by both sides, led him toward the end of his career to intervene famously in the prosecution of the Watergate burglars, reject the government's limited evidence, and blow the case wide open, from which it did not close until the president had resigned. To some, this redeemed Sirica fully.

He would do the same for the new bridge over the Potomac, but it took a while. The lawsuit was limping along, the judge alternately checking his watch with impatience and dozing, until a government witness showed a map of how the bridge tied into the roadway running downtown from Georgetown. Little did he know, little did anyone know, that this was Sirica's commute to work. The judge sat straight up in his chair and barked, "What did you say?" The witness repeated his testimony. "How many cars did you say would be coming in from Virginia?" asked the judge. It would be several thousand an hour, the witness said, proudly, an achievement by his lights. Sirica, for his part, was looking at sudden, world-class, every-morning congestion. He remained highly attentive for the rest of the trial and then wrote an opinion favoring the environmentalists. The Three Sisters rocks remained unmolested, and on this particular winter day they became a rest spot for families out on ice for perhaps the first time in their lives, pulling sleds, wiping noses, and tying on skates. Lisa and I were among them. Which gave us the idea for New Year's Eve.

I have good memories of ice skating, but they were hard won. An early home movie shows me out on a frozen pond in northern New Jersey, perhaps age three, holding onto the kitchen stool and wearing three layers of wool socks instead of shoes, my rear end wet with many falls. I am not happy. That people could actually enjoy this was beyond me. Magic struck later in the form of a new neighbor named

Karen who, at the age of fifteen, was without question the most lovely girl in the world. One day she mentioned, casually, that she liked to skate. That is all it took. For the next year, away at college, I would go down to the hockey rink on Sunday mornings and circle the ice like a gerbil, learning to cut left because that was the traffic flow, learning even to wiggle my butt and go backwards, although not too fast. By late spring I felt ready for show but of course there was no ice around, so I bided my time. A few winters later, boyfriends later on Karen's part, we saw each other again. Both home on vacation, a cold front had come through New Jersey and I asked her, casually, if she'd like to go skating. We went up to a lake in the Watchung Mountains, I tied in quickly and glided out on the ice. It felt wonderful. I circled and turned for her to join me. She skated out hesitantly, quickly tired, and suggested we go home. The magic was gone. I was left with my skates.

Lisa comes from Vermont and her ice skates came with her into the marriage along with a coffee table that we call her trousseau. Neither of us was fond of New Year's Eve parties and she lit up at the idea of a midnight skate. I filled a thermos with rum and cider, grabbed a blanket and a box of matches, and we were ready to go. We'd no intention of trying the main Potomac River, out there in the dark. Rather, we would go up to the canal alongside the Great Falls Tavern, which had once served tourists to the falls, now a visitors' center. It was of course, at this hour, closed tight. We were the only car in the parking lot. One light by the center doorway illuminated the ice for about twenty yards. From there, it ran into dark.

The ice was smooth, it had been skated on only lightly during the day and only near the parking lot. I did a few turns and then, holding hands, Lisa and I glided out of the light and into the night which was starlit and lip-cracking cold. No one had been up here, a light dust of snow hugged the edges of the canal but the wind had swept the middle clear, a long, black mirror stretching ahead that groaned a little under the weight of our bodies but, at this temperature, posed no threat of breakthrough. We built a little fire on the bank up there, toasted the new year with hot cider, and then turned back toward the visitors' center, its pool of light like a beacon. That is when we saw the second couple. They had just pulled in to the parking lot. I am going to hypothesize here, because we did not know them, nor did we speak to them more than a few words, nor did they stay very long. I cannot swear what their situation was, or what they were thinking, or even who bought the skates. But this is what I'm willing to bet, just from the circumstances, which were these.

She was from Latin America, or at least she spoke Spanish, and was dressed in a light coat and stylish heels as if straight from a party. She was shivering even as she exited their automobile and would continue to shiver as she sat on a bench, smiling at him bravely, wanting him to be happy. He was Canadian, a flat accent like the Molson beer commercials, one tone short of Massachusetts. He wore a short jacket and no hat, which cinched the Canadian connection; people from D.C. begin donning wool hats at fifty degrees Fahrenheit. He was balding and I'd say in his early thirties, which I recognized because I was too. He leapt from the car and ran to the canal bank, opened a box and pulled out what was obviously his present for Christmas, a pair of black skates. The store tags may have still been on them. Doubtless, she had bought them. And doubtless she did not know much about skating because these were figure skates, jagged teeth in the front for quick stops and push-offs, and from what I saw he was all hockey. It was in his build, I'd bet on it. What happened next was tragic.

The last thing I remember him saying, looking back over his shoulder to his wife, stoic to the cold that was shaking her body, stoic to the idea of cold, was, "I haven't been skating for six years!" He took three strides out on the ice and his skill was apparent. Three more and he'd crossed the canal and turned back, beautifully, at a steep angle, in a sweeping hook, and his left blade broke. It snapped like a pistol shot in the cold. One second he was gliding, the next found him lifting his boot from the ice in wonder, metal stubs sticking out from the bottom, the runner God knows where. We were all stunned. I looked over at his wife and she seemed uncomprehending. Like a champion heart he went on pretending to skate out there, in front of her, having a fine time. But it could not last for long. He was hopping like a crippled chicken, flapping his arms for balance, it was not going to work. Head down, he retreated to the bank, his street shoes, his wife, the car, and then they drove away. My guess is that she bought them on sale, at a department store perhaps. Giving him, she was sure, just what he wanted.

The scene has stayed with me. I did not put the backstory together until later and even now Lisa reminds me that I don't know anything about them, which is perfectly true. What I try to do is isolate his happiness as he arrived at the Great Falls, caught a look at the ice, laced on his skates, and for thirty full seconds relived the exuberant feeling of his boyhood, so alive, so at one with the water that had been waiting for him, frozen to glass, ready to send him flying. I hope with every fiber that he got another pair. I hope his marriage lasted. I hope things went well.

DEERFIELD RIVER
Vermont, 1974

There are only the two of us and the river in the background, bouncing along, it seems to be playing. I am wearing a ski hat, it is cold out, and I have a brave smile on my face. The woman is not coming with me, that much seems clear. She is wearing a skirt and looks like anyone's mother, or perhaps the head nurse on the recovery ward, curly gray hair, glasses, kind face, no nonsense, and no topcoat. She is a Vermonter and since it is not below freezing she would not see the need. I have been married to her daughter for only a short while, which may explain why she would drive out to drop me off in the woods here and then come get me down below at the end of the day. There is nothing in the photo to suggest what she had been doing in this state, which seemed another country to me, or how much it affected the scene around us. Vermonters don't talk about themselves like that. As seems obvious from the picture, I couldn't wait to get on the water.

I first saw the Deerfield by accident, from the car window, driving across the mountains to Brattleboro. High on a slope, the slant of the road approaching thirty degrees, we crossed a rushing stream from one side that disappeared into a large pipe on the other, sequestered by a power plant downstream. I turned my head in time to see a dirt road cutting up along the stream and disappearing into the woods. On the drive back we went up to investigate. About a mile in the road swung next to the water with a narrow walking bridge to cross it. Looking upstream from the bridge, the Deerfield shot out from a wall of evergreens over smooth rocks of many colors, so transparent you knew it was water but you could only confirm it by the swirls and puffs of spray. It seemed to laugh. It was absolutely alive. The next day Lisa's mother brought me back to paddle it. With all the legends surrounding mothers-in-law, there are few that have them carting you around in glacial weather to float a river.

Vermont is not known for its rivers although it has some gems running east from the Green Mountains to the Connecticut, the heartland of the Atlantic salmon until we dammed them out of the region and whose remnants we are now raising in hatcheries and struggling to restore. These side streams in summer, the West, the White, become community centers, the gathering spots for locals at the end of the working day. One brings the inner tubes and the kids from home, the other joins them, changing clothes in the car, and they take a dip, pop a beer, toss a ball in the shallows and catch the late sun full as it pours in from the far end of the valley. Trying to figure out what is new about this scene, it suddenly strikes me: there are no roadside bottles or cans. There are no billboards either, and even the riverside development is stepped back a little, giving the water room to rise and fall, to breathe. Vermont did some radical things here in a few brief years, at a time before most of the country was even aware of these kinds of issues, much less inclined to do anything about them. Which is where the lady in the photograph came in.

At the end of the Deerfield run Marcia is at the bridge, waiting for me. I ask if she waited there all afternoon and she says heavens no. There was a restaurant up the road and it had a telephone. She had plenty to do. I didn't ask her what that could be, which I have come to regret; I now find myself triangulating her life from letters and fast-fading friends. It is frigid in the car and we turn up the heater. Marcia asks me about the paddle. I start to describe the rims of ice around the rocks, the feeling that they were crystal, the stones below in yellow and lime, but I could see she was more intrigued by what I was intrigued by than anything else. Her daughter had married a green one. She must have felt a bond.

Vermont first passed a bottle bill back in 1953 when America was just discovering the convenience of throwing things away, the years when General Motors led our industry in building things designed to fall quickly out of fashion, to say nothing of falling apart . . . so that we would continuously buy new ones. The strategy was called "planned obsolescence," and was widely hailed as genius. Vermont's bill didn't last long. The beer, bottling, and grocery chains saw an attack on a business model that was based on disposal at waste dumps miles away, at public expense, or better yet simply tossed from the windows of the car. They killed the program outright.

Fifteen years later an environmental wave rolled in along America's northern tier and, within a month of each other, Oregon and Vermont (again) had enacted bottle deposit legislation. The notion was hardly revolutionary. I had made my comic book money returning Coke bottles to Errol's Market up on Mountain Avenue at three cents apiece, and while the comics did little to advance my education, the deposits got the bottles off the street and back into commerce. Which would seem to be a win-win for all.

Instead, the bottle bills were wars. The industry formed the inno-cent-appearing Keep America Beautiful campaign featuring the face of an American Indian, crying: We should put our bottles in the trash, went the message, out of the kindness of our hearts. Deposits for returning them, however, were unnecessary, even un-American. It was the no-bottle-bill alternative and in many states it stopped the proposals cold. You can tell which states these are simply by looking at their roadsides, driving by.

How, then, did this bill and the bombshells that followed it man-age to pass? In the Green Mountain State, by several coincidences. One, quaint as it might appear today, was bipartisan leadership. Sens-ing the winds, both parties advanced these proposals as their own. Still, however, industry opposition was adamant and had large war chests on its side.

Enter Marcia, who had started out with the Plain Dirt Gardeners and was now president of the Federated Garden Clubs of Vermont. They were a formidable force, well-organized, used to staffing events, no stranger to lobbying, and no constituency to make angry. They were also mothers of children and tended to think about the planet in those terms. In Vermont they were often the wives of citizen-legisla-tors who led with professional lives in town and went to Montpelier only on state business. After which, importantly, they returned home.

The first time she went up to lobby, Marcia told me, she did not even get to see the legislative leadership. "Well now!" She said in as loud a voice as I ever heard her use, implying strong disapproval and that a fuller response was coming. It came quickly. The next week she showed up with two dozen Garden Club members and things began to change. They were not lobbying strangers in Washington. They were lobbying men who needed them for harmonious domestic lives. The new bill passed going away.

I knew none of this at the time. On my next visit north I went exploring up the Deerfield on foot with Lisa and her brother, and found it coming out of a reservoir built apparently for both power generation and recreation. As with all dams of this kind, the two do not mesh well; you can't have the water both ways. On this particular day there must have been a strong call from the utility downstream because the drawdown was huge, acres of mud flats separating boats and docks from the water's edge. I found myself in that era arguing against marginal dam proposals by pointing out that they were claiming economic benefits from two opposing scenarios, to deaf ears. Some of the largest dams in America now trap reservoirs of mud and sand.

In the meantime, Vermont was enacting two more laws that raised eyebrows across the country, the first to eliminate billboards and the second to create a new form of government for land use planning. Each met firestorms and, judging from a few clippings and what remains of Marcia's correspondence, the Garden Clubs were in the thick of them. She notes that three local members spoke at one public hearing "when the temperature stood at 29 degrees BELOW ZERO!" Her all-caps, not mine.

The absence of large advertisements along the roadside is the first thing one notices coming across the Vermont line from any direction. Like turning off a loud radio, there is a sudden sense of peace. To the billboard industry, however, surprisingly powerful everywhere it goes, the peace threatened basic American values: what is wrong with promoting your product? The fight was on and it too continued for several years. In one of the last conversations we had, I asked Marcia which of the environmental bills she felt best about and without hesitating she said, roadside advertising. It was a birthright thing. She was a multigeneration Vermonter, they were invasions. At the end of the day the billboard ban passed handily, none would be permitted in the future, those standing would be removed in five years. And they were.

When I went back up to the Deerfield the following spring this action was still off my radar. I remained a federal prosecutor in Washington at the time and Vermont was our escape from the contentious world. Our older boy, Cyprian, was barely six years old and I wanted him to see this magical river. A storm had brought heavy rains which seemed a plus, plenty of water. I would not need a shuttle this time; we'd drive up to the put-in, float down to the bridge, and then hitchhike back. With a small boy in tow, that part should be easy. My assurance had little foundation. The dirt road turned out to be lightly used, and on weekdays not at all. We ended up hiking it back at nightfall, Cyprian on my shoulders, sagging asleep. But at least we were okay.

The river caught me by surprise. Once out into the current it was like joining a freeway. Cyprian sat bewildered in the bow, his little paddle waving in the air, as I tried to hold us back, grab some eddies, slow us down. The day was as gorgeous as days after rain often are, everything washed clean, a pine smell you could package and the brilliant splash of the water, but I am not sure any of that got through to a six-year-old who was getting wet up front and who could hear me saying unsettling things to myself like "Holy cow!." I found a rock shelf near the far bank and rammed the canoe onto it from below. We ate lunch there, the water swirling past us like a hungry thing, me feeding Cyp peanut butter and pieces of our crushed Oreo cookies. His hands were cold.

In an instant, clouds took over the sky. Cyp began to shiver and after I jumped in the water to save our thermos that had slipped off of the rock I was shivering too. I am not sure whether there was a saint involved here or just a more prosaic shift of the wind, but the cloud layer then parted. The sky did not clear, it did not even open up, it just admitted a shaft of light that came creeping up the Deerfield River like a theater spot, landed smack on us, and then stayed there warm as butter. We floated on down and under the bridge, to land.

The land use bill was Vermont's most ambitious, Act 250, which put new development proposals before local citizen committees. The people would decide. The committees were designed to include all constituencies, but in this case it was the real estate industry's turn to go ballistic. It was far easier for developers to influence local officials than wild cards from the general public. The committees might be balanced, but they would stand in the way of getting the deal done. The Garden Clubs again countered with a barrage of debates, resolutions, and face-to-face lobbying. At one point Marcia went one better to form a larger coalition named Landowners for Act 250. "I'd like to see Vermonters decide their own future," she told the press, playing into a strongly felt state pride, "and not outside developers."

Even after the bill's passage the fight continued with lawsuits claiming the theft of private property and injury to the greater economy, an economy that, ironically, depended on green landscapes for its draw. The state successfully defended, which should have ended the matter, but no environmental protections are ever secure. Attempts to chip away at Act 250 continue to this day, as they do on billboards and bottles. The tensions between development and environmental values in America never sleep.

The day that Vermont's achievements finally dawned on me happened to be blustery and raining. We were driving up from the south and when we crossed into the state there was a long curve to the left and then a rainbow straight ahead, pink, yellow and purple, as big as the sky. There was no litter below it, and no fast-food chain. There was no roadside advertisement selling us something in the way. I told myself I would ask Marcia about it.

ROCK CREEK
District of Columbia, 1975

"Paddling this is impossible," I say convincingly, as to a child. For emphasis I add, "No way!"—only there is no one else around. I am standing alone on a small concrete bridge that crosses Rock Creek in its deepest trench, just below the Park Service headquarters on Beech Drive. This is a deeply wooded section and the water twists and plunges, making genuine whitewater sounds. Upstream from the bridge is a menacing fleet of boulders, worn smooth by spring floods that cover them briefly and then quickly subside. At normal levels the current splits three and four ways around these obstacles, forming small drops and eddies. Low water shows nothing but stones, more like a quarry than a body of water. Still, it is tempting.

I often stopped at the bridge while jogging the horse trail between the creek and the valley walls, examining the creek for Stuart Little, the canoe mouse in his tiny craft making his moves down toward me. Would he take the left fork and then veer back in a hurry, perhaps even back-paddle to line up for the next drop, or would he be able to make the double squeeze on the right? I played it several ways, like a game of chess, but it usually ended in mate. One way or another Stuart was going to dump, even lose his boat. Since the creek was narrow, he'd make it out to the side. But still . . . he just might get through.

I suppressed these thoughts for a long time, years in fact, until one spring we had unusually heavy rains and the stream came up out of its banks to cover the road, carrying debris and tree trunks along with it. The best part was that they had to close the road to clear it, which opened Rock Creek to hundreds of families living nearby. We'd walk down after work with our children, babies in jerry-packs and strollers, saying hello to each other, smiling at strangers, people from both sides feeding in. Briefly, it became a park again.

These occasional floods upset the established order. Although the pedigree of Rock Creek Park rivaled that of Yosemite—they were both established in 1890—starting in the 1920s its central feature, the creek itself, was turned into a highway corridor that, according to a Historic American Buildings Survey, was "one of the best-preserved examples of the earliest stage of motor parkway development." It was also one of the best-preserved examples of sacrificing urban amenities to commuters streaming in from the suburbs, some four thousand of them during a good morning rush, in larger vehicles each year, their roar heard for a mile in either direction and their exhaust lingering for hours. Nearing rush hour, twice a day, no sane mother would let her child go to the park to play.

The rare Rock Creek floods did not last long but they were glorious. On an evening following I'd walk up the parkway still choked by silt and branches to the little bridge, just poking its head above water. The creek would boil, the boulders were largely buried, this would be one whale of a run. Finding exactly the right level would be tricky. Too high and you'd slam into the bridge, slightly lower and you could be decapitated by it, lower still and you'd hang up like a truck on the rocks. By the weekend the water would have dropped and the chance to try was lost.

The rocks were only one deterrent to running Rock Creek. Another was sewage from a residential development that had nestled in upstream with a package plant to treat its wastes, which usually work a short time before breaking down. Even below the Maryland line steady doses of car oil, dog droppings, and other runoff also ended up in the creek, and that was before one reached the National Zoo whose exiting waters smelled like washout from the elephant yard. The only fish I saw in the creek were less than two inches long, when the water was clear enough to see them at all. On weekends we would watch small children wading in the shallows and floating small boats, mainly black families, and the choice was to warn them about the pollution or just let them have their Sunday afternoon in peace. I opted for peace, but uneasily. At some point or another our civilization or another will have to decide whether dumping wastes into water is really the best thing to do either with the wastes, or the water, but that day is not at hand.

Then there were the park rangers. I found nothing in the D.C. Code about paddling Rock Creek (unlike kite flying on Sundays, which was prohibited), but I was sure that if they saw me on it they would whistle me out. This was before the days of plastic boats that can navigate a flowing gutter. My canoe was seventeen feet long, solid aluminum, with a one-inch keel and about as maneuverable in close quarters as a tanker. Still, this is what we had. I called up Brent.

Brent would run anything. What I enjoyed about him is that although his boating skills would not win gold medals (nor would mine) his enthusiasm for the out of doors was triumphant. A walk with him through the park in spring might take an hour to cover two hundred yards, stopping every few feet for rising lady slippers or a lone trillium just peeking out from under its umbrella, I could never remember the names. Brent agreed that we would need a free day to run the creek, and a good rain. We'd take both boats solo, his was as banged up as mine, and take out at the zoo. I did not want to run through monkey poo.

That April, very near my birthday, we had a thunderstorm that hung around for a full day, and better yet, a Friday. We would go the next morning, putting in at the Maryland line. We didn't take a thermos or sandwiches. It looked like a couple of hours and out. We strapped on bricklayers' knee pads in those days to get a grip on the canoe bottom and pad the shock. We wore the kind of life jackets that you hand to tourists on ferries these days, the ones that tie with a bow in front and a pillow collar in the back. We were the very antithesis of *Outdoor Magazine*. They would have refused to photograph us at all. But this, again, is what we had.

The run started beautifully, the creek bank full but contained, the current right up to the bordering trees which were just then coming into leaf. New green was all around us. We zipped down the flats, fully half the trip, barely having to paddle forward, steering only to stay out of the woods, chatting back and forth. Then we entered the canyon. The volume came up ten decibels. The flow here was crammed between the road and the horse trail, less than thirty feet across, and the boulder garden began. Somewhere down below was the little concrete bridge. Maybe someone would be standing on it, dreaming about Stuart Little, but I doubted it. It was only ten o'clock on a Saturday morning and most somebodies were still drinking coffee.

When we sped past the Park Service station I knew we were in for it. We were losing control. I waved Brent back so that we'd not crash into each other, and took the lead. The big rocks were out ahead and then coming at me at what seemed like warp speed, no time to negotiate, no time to plan, just shoot for the gap and look for the next one, shoot for that one, and the next, and hope. I heard Brent behind me, banging off of the rocks like a tin can band, and he seemed too near to my stern for comfort but there was nothing I could do about it. I felt elated and scared. Then I saw the bridge. It was up out of the water— that was good. There was also a considerable gap under it, which was even better, but whether the gap was big enough to pass my boat, and Brent's, so close behind, was anyone's guess. We were going to have to guess in the affirmative because there was no pulling out of the creek now, there were too many rocks in the way.

We made it. We had no reason to expect to. We hadn't gone out that morning and measured the clearance. We hadn't pulled over above the bridge to walk down and check it out. We just trusted in luck and it held. My boat, with the higher bow and stern, scraped ominously under the bridge, me lying prone across the gunnels trying to make my rear end disappear, trying to will the boat down an inch more in the water, and then it popped free. There were more boulders ahead but they were more widely spaced, and then a twisty run around bends and under bridges where automobiles were passing, although whether anyone even saw us is doubtful. No one was ever on this water. To my knowledge, although I have no way of checking on this, no one has been since. I'd not recommend it. For one thing, you might become ill. The whiff of sewage hung in the air.

The Park Service has tried to balance the scales a little since that day. Rock Creek seems cleaner to the eye, if not to the nose, and there is even a small fish ladder at the Pierce Mill dam for migrating shad. Portions of Beach Drive, the one through the canyon, are closed to cars on weekends during daylight hours and they draw a diverse crowd of strollers, roller-bladers, and bicycles going too fast for the circumstances, but who am I to talk about a thing like that? For five days a week, though, Rock Creek remains consecrated to the motor vehicle and the rest, in the elegant language of wartime, is bugsplat. From time to time I dream of closing down this parkway and returning Rock Creek to its roots, but there would be a revolt of the suburbs were it even breathed out loud. As a former Speaker of the House once said, cheap gas is part of our pact with the American people. So, apparently, are highways through urban green.

Years later, on a return trip to D.C., I walked down into Rock Creek late on a Sunday afternoon before they reopened the road to a line of cars already gathering at the Maryland end. I had about an hour free, and jogged lightly up the horse trail, as in days of old. It was raining lightly, misting really, but enough to deter others and I saw only one biker out on the parkway, which explains what then happened. I turned at the bridge and decided to cross and go back by the road. It shone wet in the light of the street lamps just turning on, making the surroundings darker. I went slowly as if in a dream, remembering the turns from long ago as they came in view. Close to the end I rounded a bend and there was something ahead that resembled a dog, but it was not. It was more elegant than a dog ever could be. It was standing in a pool of light from a lamppost, the mist sparkling as it filtered down, a red fox, stock still, waiting. I slowed to a walk, hardly breathing, but it soon knew me for what I was and it turned, slowly, and trotted away into the gloom.

I've seen several wild foxes in my life, but this one was from the Garden of Eden. I'm not sure that its feet touched the ground. I had a vision of it crossing the creek and passing up into the hills. It was so lovely, so wild, and still with us.

BARREN GROUNDS
Northwest Territories, 1976

The last people on the face of North America to be reached by Western civilization lived up on the Barren Grounds, a wedge of rocks and tundra stretching across the top of Canada between tree line and the Arctic Circle. There was no wood for tools or shelter. There were no sea mammals for oil or furs, and nothing resembling a vegetable. They lived on caribou and they were careful to thank the animals. They saw no irony in that. It completed an environment of nine-month winters with winds that blew for weeks at a time, and brief, hot summers when black flies and mosquitoes hung like smoke and drove beasts insane. Within a lifetime after these people were discovered by whites they were gone.

We fly into the Barrens, three canoes on a pontoon plane. We are standing on the tundra, a flat jigsaw puzzle of green and blue pieces covered by a bowl of sky. It is thick with mosses and flowers that turn out on inspection to be two-inch rhododendrons and four-inch willow trees. That is about as high as things grow here, for that is about as high as the snows protect them. Anything that pokes above gets nipped off by the winds. For humans to live here—ideally—they should be about six inches tall and sleep most of the year.

The Barrens people lived here all year round. The eastern caribou herd migrated past them by the thousands from their shelter in the boreal forests to calving grounds along the Arctic Sea, and back again before the September snows. The hunters waited at points of land where the caribou had to swim for another shore and were vulnerable in the water. They ambushed them with arrows, drove sharp poles up the rectum and left them to struggle out of the water and across the landscape to die. They drank the blood and ate the flesh raw, which provided enough vitamins and minerals to survive. They made clothing from the hides and tools from the bone. They lived in this way for no one knows how many centuries, for as long as the caribou came north in the spring and south in the fall, past the places where the people lay for them in their caribou skin kayaks, using bows strung with caribou sinew and spears tipped with caribou horn. The Canadian writer Farley Mowat called them the People of the Deer.

By June, when we arrive, the herds are gone but the fish are there. The Little Lakes give rise to the Kognac River, which tumbles east over slippery rocks, sparkling under the sun and a grim gray in the rain. The water may never have seen a tied fly, a spinning lure, or even a metal hook. The lake trout bump each other to be first on the line, huge green fish with red sides. Sail-finned grayling bounce against the canoes as we drag through the shallows. The fisherman's art here is not to catch fish, one trout feeds six for dinner. The trick is to set them free again, softly, twenty-nine inches of green silver lying stunned in the water and then gone.

The people who lived here did not fish, the meat was too light and it had no useful skins. Years later, when they were starving, the Canadian government would try to put them on a diet of fish but they continued to die.

We travel for weeks in a world of sky and clouds, twenty hours of light each day. The sun is out full when we crawl off to bed and wakes us at four in the morning. Thunderstorms march across us in rows. We paddle in columns of rain, see bright sky one hundred yards ahead, and the next storm an hour away. It is a cold rain, almost sleet. It was seventy degrees a few minutes ago, and will be seventy degrees again in a few minutes. We stop occasionally to eat and to check the hillsides for stone scrapers, tent rings, traces the people left behind.

The first European through the Barrens didn't see them either. Samuel Hearne set out two centuries ago from Hudson Bay with a band of Chipewyans to look for a fabled mountain of copper on the shores of the Arctic Sea. He found no copper but during three years of hard travel he heard the stories of a people, not Indians at all, who were actually said to be making a living on the barren lands. The traders came later with metal traps and hard liquor, turning the people from subsistence hunters to peddlers of pelts in exchange for guns, blankets, and pneumonia.

Hearne's diary and others record another phenomenon that governed life on the Barrens, the flying insects, and they are still here, waiting. When the wind is up they swarm in the lee of anything that offers resistance—a clump of alder bush, a rock in the river. Mosquitoes hang upside down under my hat brim, just over my eyebrows, and I have learned not to disturb them lest they move to my skin. We face the wind whenever we can. Against all boyhood training, we pee into the wind as well.

The black flies are the worst. Small armies of them crawl over our hats and jackets. We have head nets and light-colored clothing, high collars, wristlets, bloused trousers, superstrength repellent, every precaution possible, yet they are in our drinks, cuffs, and buttonholes, even in our mouths. One week into the Barrens I have thirty-two bites on my right wrist, twenty-three on my left. They burn and have started to swell. My canoe partner injects me with adrenaline, stabbing three times before sinking the needle; he is no doctor but he is packing the medical kit. Besides, he says, he needs me to hold a paddle. It is a wonder the Barrens people endured it here, among the black flies and the mosquitoes on a windless day.

They lived on small rises around the Little Lakes where they could catch the breeze in summer and the caribou spring and fall. We also try living here, and we find ourselves grooming like creatures of the wild. We grease our lips, rub oil on split fingers, build pads around blisters, rest our eyes from the sun, dry our feet when we can, rub pulled muscles, clip toenails, and sleep ten hours at a stretch. We take flash baths in the evening, emerging from the water in a race with mosquitoes to our protective clothing. We knock on wood, keep our fingers crossed, and begin talking to the god of breezes. Stay here a year, we could be worshiping it.

Farley Mowat recorded the people in the 1940s, when they were beginning to crash. They were living in small camps, still trying for the caribou in the spring and fall, but they had gunned them down to a trickle with their new rifles and the trickles were passing them by. The people were starving, coughing blood and dying of pneumonia.

We find their graves along the rivers and lakes, cairns of rocks with sticks for markers. Peering between the rocks, we can see bones of some who stayed behind. On the sides of low hills we see kayak slips, shallow excavations in the rocky shore for landing skin boats. On the tops of ridges we find little stone men, a rock on a rock, more markers, this-is-the-way. The people themselves are gone. They were evacuated two decades earlier on a long trek to Hudson Bay.

We meet up with several of them during the last leg of our trip, where the Maguse River runs down to the bay. We do not expect to see them here. They have come out from Eskimo Point for a Sunday ride in twenty-foot power boats. They are camping nearby in nylon tents, cooking over Coleman stoves, and riding about on three-wheeled Hondas looking for caribou. They are open and generous and they offer to tow us through a gale to town. My boat driver made the evacuation out in his teens. His nephew is in the boat too and speaks good English. He works on machines at the airstrip. The first thing they ask me is, have I seen any caribou? I say, a few, but maybe a week inland. The boy has been to Seattle. He has not been that far inland, ever.

Two hundred years ago the last people on the face of North America to be reached by Western civilization lived up on the Barren Grounds. Now, no one does, except for newcomers laying pipe and searching for oil, copper, and gold. Helicopters fly overhead. With a big find, the price of gas might go down a nickel for half a year and more gold bricks will disappear into bank vaults as surrogates for money that few of us will ever see or understand. The people now live on the edge of Hudson Bay in cinder-block houses, surrounded by discarded cans and snowmobiles. They are heavily supported by the Canadian government. Their children speak good English, are on Facebook, and understand a world their parents never dreamed of. I cannot make up my mind about this story.

CACHE LA POUDRE
Colorado, 1977

I was rinsing out my oatmeal cup when I looked up and saw the bear. I could tell it was a grizzly from the hump on its neck hiding a muscle the size of my torso. It was watching me from the shadow of the trees across the creek and a small plain of grass. My hands were buried in the creek and burning with cold but I dared not move them. I dared not move a thing.

I was in shadow too, the sun was just rising over the ridge behind me and walking its light slowly down the far side, toward the bear. I figured perhaps twenty minutes or so for the sun to reach it, at which point I hoped the glare might induce the bear move on. I let my eyes wander to the left and right, trying to get a better read on the grizzly but it gave me no clues. It remained motionless, which is exactly what the book I'd brought with me said it would do. The grizzly was an intensely curious animal and had no compunction about tracking human beings that happened into its territory; it would loop around trappers and hunters all day long, following their moves just as they tried to follow his. And it had the patience of Job. It could wait all day. Well, I thought, I've just eaten, I can relieve myself if need be right here where I am kneeling, I can no longer feel my hands so that's taken care of, maybe I can wait all day too.

The odd thing was its total tranquility. I would have thought an insect would bother it, a bird would catch its attention, but none did. Then again not much was moving about that early, it was near freezing and a spray of hail lay half melted on the ground. At some point I allowed myself to twist my neck and get a better look. As the sunlight drew nearer the bear was getting increasingly thin, the dark bulk of its body looked more and more like a fallen tree, the point of its snout could even be a root, its hump the curve of a branch behind. And so it was. This was a stump bear. I felt a wave of relief, and then regret.

This was a bear's place. I was just visiting but the Colorado high country was where it belonged.

As beautiful as rivers can be, the places where they rise are small havens with water bubbling up from the ground or down from dripping ice, cheered on by early flowers or tracing black loops through the snow. You can cup your hand to drink. You can dangle a fly on a thin leader over a bend for five-inch trout, slip the hook gently, and let them slide back in. At the moment I was in headwaters of the Cache la Poudre, just below snow line, and the rivulets were less than a stride wide but already mimicking the rivers they would join, indeed that they would form, sharp angles, pools, and occasional sticks and snags. The one I was camped by bustled along like a youngster, uncaring about me and anything else around it and as innocent of its consequences as, come to think of it, a grizzly bear. They are both wild, magical forces for so long as we allow them to be. One of the blessings of growing old I have found, thinking back on scenes like this, is that they were still around. Even if that stump wasn't a real-life griz . . . and this makes all the difference . . . it could have been.

When I first heard about the Cache la Poudre I liked the sound of its name, and the fact that there was nothing else around it for miles. The story goes that in 1836 a trading convoy, trapped by a blizzard, cached its load of gunpowder in a large pit and then hightailed it to safety, hence the name, "hide the powder." There is no actual record of a trading expedition through this region in that year but no matter, names take on lives of their own. The reason I had spooked so easily up here, spotting the bear, was that at the last minute I'd packed in one of the most intimate histories of the grizzly ever written. In the late 1800s a naturalist named Enoch Mills lived in close proximity to *ursus horribilis*, whose very name speaks of the fear that it inspires. Mills traveled into grizzly country on foot, alone and unarmed, sitting for days near den sites, tracking bear movements, taking copious notes, and then promoting vast refuges to harbor it, resulting in today's Rocky Mountain and Glacier National Parks.

Mills begins his book, "It would make exciting reading if a forty-year-old grizzly bear were to write his autobiography," and proceeds to explain just how exciting. They rode logs for the hell of it, fooled each other with tricks, showed shame when caught out, let their cubs climb up their backs to reach the honey hole, dug out bunkers, built stone walls, sledded down snowfields on their backs, made plans, executed them, and sat on hillsides mesmerized by a blazing sunset. To Native Americans a grizzly was as close to human as animals came: it ate similar food, thought thoughts, stood on its hind legs, and even walked upright, its paws hanging like hands. And when crossed, it was a killing machine.

White men picked up on the killing part. In 1814, Governor Clinton of New York became one of the first to exhibit a captive grizzly, calling it, P. T. Barnum style, "the ferocious tyrant of the American woods—it exists, the terror of the savages, tyrant of all other animals, devouring alike man and beast defying the attacks of a whole tribe of Indians." Like shooting wolves and Native Americans back in the time, bragging rights went to the man with the most slain per day. Mills recalls one man killing "five bears with five shots, in rapid succession"; another killed nine "inside a minute, two of which were cubs." Lewis and Clark's Corps of Discovery shot at nearly every bear it saw and at one point Captain Lewis, with an empty rifle, found himself standing in the middle of a river fending off a grizzly with his "espontoon" (bayonet). American legends, every one. The last track of the great bear in the Bitterroot Mountains of Idaho, its home turf, was seen in 1946. Not until then did Idaho begin to restrict grizzly hunting.

By day, up on the Cache la Poudre, reading Mills in spurts, I even came to feel like a bear. I had little to do except to groom myself, tape a blister, salve a cut, examine the creek, spot fish, untangle a spool, wander the tree line, listen for birds, search for tracks, say things to myself like, "Well, will you look at that!," read a little more, grab a bite, and then settle back with a cup of steaming tea to watch the sun go down. In another day's time I would walk up and over the far ridge to a road indicated on the map, catch a ride out of the mountains, and then a bus to the airport. What could be easier?

The watershed moment for the grizzly in America came in, of all places, Yellowstone National Park, where they had retreated to escape the roads and the guns. Their natural range stretching from the Pacific to the Mississippi had been decimated. By the 1950s the iconic wild beast of the nation was down to perhaps four hundred individuals, perhaps fewer, no one really knew. Its refuge in Yellowstone turned precarious with a boom in tourists and dumps for their garbage that both maintained the bears and changed their behavior from wild and evasive to begging and volatile. The Park Service faced a lose-lose decision: close the dumps and starve the bears, or try to maintain both with unnatural and unpredictable consequences. After much controversy the Yellowstone dumps were shut down, and bear numbers plummeted even more, but then stabilized and slowly began to recover.

Meanwhile, *homo sapiens* was also hunting hard for high mountain water sources like the Cache la Poudre in the Rocky Mountain West. We had not simply discovered Yellowstone, we had discovered the entire Front Range of Colorado and were occupying it as rapidly as gated communities could eat up the farmland and spread onto the plains, all in need of the one commodity in shortest supply: water. Rivers from Montana to New Mexico were already oversubscribed. The closest available sources were up at tree line and ripe for the picking, unused and wasted it could be said, and was said at every opportunity. Since the early 1900s a string of water-supply dams began to tap the upstream tributaries to serve Denver and towns up the chain. By the 1970s a second land boom had put the search into overdrive and a showdown was inevitable. It came with a classic fight between old-style boomers and new-style environmentalists over a reservoir at the junction of two Platte River tributaries, the Two Forks Dam.

I first learned of Two Forks when a colleague of mine running a law clinic in Boulder called to say that he'd just been charged with contempt by a judge in Denver. We had filed a lawsuit against the dam, and when I asked how the judge's order might play with the university where we were piloting the clinic, Bob said not to worry, "everyone knows he's a nutcase." It was the tip of the iceberg. Feelings about water in Colorado were close to biblical and the Denver Water Board was the reigning prelate. To be sure, the board had a challenge on its hands; Denver had added half a million people in a decade and, counting the build-out on the eastern range, was anticipating another million more. The solution was a new billion-dollar dam impounding thirty-one miles of some of the most scenic water in Colorado, including a prize trout stream and a spectacular canyon. Its effects would be felt downstream as far as Nebraska, where Platte River flows were needed to maintain the badly endangered whooping crane. There were large stacks of chips on both sides of the table, not the least of which were the power of the state's water machine.

The politics were also intense. One Colorado governor called the dam a bad idea, and his successor had to agree, but said he wanted the construction jobs. For their part, environmentalists came up with an alternative plan at a fraction of Two Forks' construction cost based on measures rather obvious to the naked eye: water conservation and recycling. The federal government was even offering grants to use treated wastewater for lawns and agriculture. For its part, however, Denver still operated on promotional water rates, the more one used the cheaper the unit price, and was serving nearly ninety thousand homes with no water meters at all. Neither conservation nor recycling was welcome news to the water board. It was about selling water, not saving it. It was going forward with the dam.

The legal proceedings meanwhile turned ludicrous. Facing an environmental lawsuit, the board sued back claiming tortious for interference with its business, the environmentalists countersued claiming deprivation of their constitutional rights . . . more delay, more controversy, more mess. In the end, however, Two Forks managed to clear the only federal hurdle necessary, a Corps of Engineers permit, and was off to the races. But for a single hitch, a little-known provision in the permit law allowing the Environmental Protection Agency to veto it if the effects were too severe. The hitch seemed minor; such vetoes were scarce as hen's teeth and none yet had dared to challenge a western water project.

The never-happened-before then happened. In early 1989 the EPA administrator, new on the job, over objections from his top staff who feared the political repercussions, vetoed Two Forks Dam, straight

up. The environmental costs were too severe, he said; there were better alternatives. Shock waves spread across the plains, the veto itself
was challenged in court by home builders, water utilities, even the
national Cattleman's Association, to no avail. They would have to live
with the decision and, to the surprise of all, Denver itself led the way.
Within a short time a new water board director, declaring that his
agency had shed its "earlier adolescent personality," adopted both
conservation and recycling strategies and saved most of the water it
would have gained from Two Forks at far less expense. Out on the
ever-booming fringes, however, where dry land was cheap and bought
with unquenchable faith that water deliveries, from somewhere, anywhere, were theirs by right, the hunt remained on and it would lead
back to the Cache la Poudre.

In recent years the odds against both the grizzly and high mountain water have gone up another notch, maybe two. The fracking
method of producing natural gas has come into vogue, and, among
other things, its operations consume more fresh water than most
small cities. Meanwhile, though some of the West remains in denial,
fresh water is dwindling with climate change. The new response here
again is the old one, more new dams, and the North Colorado Water
District has proposed one, the Glade Reservoir which, granted, is a
lovely name. It will dam the Cache la Poudre River and bury its valley
for all time. Including my stump grizzly, which may still be up there.

There is a more insidious effect of climate change, well known to
biologists but seen by few of the rest of us. It has upset the biological
clock for millions of creatures who depend on its rhythms and cycles.
The grizzly is one. *Ursus horribilis*—despite its strength, intelligence,
and eclectic appetite—depends on the timing of seasons to fill its
larder. Gaps in the food supply are bridged by spring berries, new
litters of pica, and other sources as they come online. Scientists a
few years ago found families of bears gorging themselves at tree line
on a harvest of moths. These days, however, wild food is not arriving
on schedule. A recent attempt to remove the grizzly from the endangered species list failed when a court noted that climate changes were
jeopardizing a key supply at a key season, seeds of the whitebark pine.

Connections formed through eons of history are breaking down and those species—that cannot adapt rapidly, however long they preceded us, whatever their role in the landscape—are in big trouble.

There are those of us who accept these changes, in fact all changes caused by humans, as natural. For some of faith they are simply part of God's grand design, and for others who consider themselves scientific they illustrate survival of the fittest in an ever-changing world. In this light, writes one, the head of a large conservation organization in fact, the polar bear is not necessarily threatened by the melt of sea ice; it may do fine on the mainland, hanging around town. The morality of these propositions stuns me, but there they are.

I left the Cache la Poudre on a warm day, walking up the ridge toward the road that led back toward the land of *homo sapiens*. There was no path up and in this piece of wilderness the understory dissolved into a tangle of boulders, deadfalls, and trees. My backpack catching every limb, I decided to leave it on a rock and go up to verify the road. The climb was endless, and once out of the woods entered a field of barren scree. Scaling that and peering over, I saw a dirt road below me, pristine, without no sign of a tire. There had not been a vehicle on it for weeks, perhaps months. I checked the map. This was the road alright but it was many miles long, both ways, coming from nowhere in particular and going nowhere in particular the other way. Perhaps it was closed up higher by late snow, it had never occurred to me to ask. I ate my remaining food, drank some water, and started back for my pack. At once, though, the landscape looked all the same, the scree, the rim of the treetops below, my route could have been anywhere. Everything I had carried in save the map, a compass, and my water bottle was who-knew-where down in the trees.

God seems to smile on me at times like these, and often in exactly the same way. I heard the sound of a jeep, a chugging, puttering noise that I recognized from servicing my vehicle in the Army. It appeared below me, open to the air, oblivious. One of the few things I learned as a boy that remained useful in later life was a shrill, four-finger whistle and I blew for all I was worth, stumbling down to the road. The jeep stopped. It was a backcountry ranger, just checking things out. He knew I was out here, I'd signed in some days before. We went back and located my pack. He offered to carry it back up for me but, red with embarrassment, I wouldn't let him.

On the drive out I told him about my stump grizzly. He said quietly, as if he knew something, you might see a real one up here some day, you never know. We were both smiling.

CHESAPEAKE & OHIO CANAL
Maryland, 1978

The girl is kneeling on an island of grass and rocks in the Potomac River, wearing a short jacket and blue jeans, black hair in the wind, she is eight years old. Kneeling next to her is a smaller boy, younger, she is helping him with a zipper. Our canoe is beached at their feet, huge charcoal clouds are blowing in from the west, whitecaps dot the river, it looks like a front, we are hunkering down.

A few seconds after snapping the photo I bend over to cover them and say that this could be the seldom-seen marshmallow storm, they are going to fall from the sky already toasted, the best kind. A few seconds later a line of hail comes through pelting us lightly and then it is gone, the sun returns, we are not even wet, and the kids are smiling. I dig out the cookies. We are in the middle of one of the most unusual canoe trips in America. We have come down an old canal, one of the first attempted in this country, and ahead of us is another canal, one of the longest ever built, and in between is the Potomac, wide and shallow here and dotted with small islands. Above us a pair of fish hawks is circling, looking for prey.

The two canals bear witness to the vision and engineering of our earliest days. That the Chesapeake and Ohio Canal ahead of us is still intact, awaiting our return run to the car, is witness to yet another vision, that of William O. Douglas, America's greatest conservationist since the days of Teddy Roosevelt, Gifford Pinchot, and John Muir. It did not hurt that he was also a justice of the United States Supreme Court. Without Douglas, the canal would be gone. It would be a highway instead. That was the plan. What better use could there be for the bank of a river?

Canaling began here nearly two centuries earlier with young George Washington, who as a land surveyor had been probing west from Virginia as far as Fort Duquesne (now Pittsburgh) and returning with the dream of a waterway reaching the Ohio. The Potomac was the obvious choice but it was wide and shallow and, even discounting the barrier at Great Falls, had numerous rapids in the way. No sooner than the Revolutionary War ended, Washington organized the Patowmack Company to build a series of small canals to bypass them. One of these, of the few actually constructed, skirted the Seneca breaks about fifteen miles above Great Falls on the Virginia side, colloquially called the George Washington Canal. What remains of it is an almost secret piece of the river, beginning with a hard-to-find gap in the trees and bending like a stream past pieces of old masonry with several drops, none too big, easily done. But not without its surprises.

In another photo the children were the size of peanuts, holding their small wooden paddles with the face of an Indian on the blade, ready to go. Kimberly, who had zipped up my boy's jacket, was sitting at bow when at the first drop, past an old canal stone, a wild-looking man with a full beard not seen since the nineteenth century jumped out onto the block, his hands inches from Kim's hair, although she did not see him, so intent she was on the wave trail ahead. I cannot remember whether he had any clothes on. I shot past him in seconds, still steering, and we looked at each other with astonishment, as if I were the first white man in his world. Safely through, I turned, but he had disappeared. I never saw him again.

Years later, however, a friend sent me an article from a reporter in Washington entitled "Naked Ned Hunts for the Infinite along the Potomac." The man was real; his chosen name was Chaosmi the Infinite, after his belief that knowledge is based on "an infinite number of answers to every question, and an infinite number of possibilities." He apparently lived in a shelter of rocks topped by an old beach umbrella and spent his time building tiny dams in the river, some just a few feet long, strategically placed to create "calm pools and tranquil falls where plants and fish abound." His reasons were well ahead of the time: He wanted to see if his alterations "would slow down the flow of nutrients and the plants could absorb them before they got to the [Chesapeake] Bay." Judging from the look of things, the piece concluded, he had succeeded. It was a "beautiful spot," home to bait fish, plants, and ducks and geese that "frequently spend time resting here." One hopes that Chaosmi the Infinite is still alive, and that no one has sought to arrest him for wearing insufficient clothing. The fact is we have more than a little in common, his thinking and mine. This said, seeing him in the flesh out on the GW canal, and knowing no more, was a happening.

The C&O Canal, orders of magnitude more ambitious, began fifty years later on the Maryland side with the Chesapeake and Ohio Company, whose very name speaks its bold ambition. Company engineers built high canal walls that reached into the river itself, crossed tributaries with aqueducts so strong that attempts to blow them up in the Civil War failed their purpose, and blasted tunnels through mountains, the one at Paw Paw extending for two-thirds of a mile and so dark inside that the mules wore oil lamps to light the way. Where high floods erased their handiwork they repaired it, when the money ran out they raised more, and when the railroads were coming they raced them to the west but, here, they lost. After only a decade or so of profit the C&O went into steep decline and was sold in bankruptcy to, of all ironies, a railroad company seeking to deny the right of way to a railway competitor. Dozens of similar canals around the country were failing as well, including the mighty Erie with its famous ladder of locks leading right into the city. It was a brief and colorful life. Photos show passengers sitting on the roofs of canal boats in rocking chairs, reading newspaper and smoking cigars, the lockkeepers in suits and high, white collars. The brawls of the boatmen, the abuse of the mule boys called hoggees and paid pennies at trip's end, all these and more are history, which without tangible physical reminders will disappear as well.

Canal history would be no more remarkable than the subsequent passing of the railroads to trucks and interstates, but for the elaborate and ingenious works of engineering they left behind. In the 1950s, in the heady rush of federal road construction, the secretary of the interior proposed to demolish the C&O entirely for a superhighway. Congress backed the idea, believing that it would "provide better access to the beauty and recreational opportunities of the Potomac River Valley." The *Washington Post*, catching the fever, followed suit. Highways had become nature's best companion.

Enter a third force of man and nature, Justice Douglas, whose writings and passion for the out of doors had struck an old synapse in the American mind, not yet extinguished by the new. Appointed to the high court, his opinions on water resources in particular carried a feel for nature ("A river is more than an amenity, it is a treasure," one observed) notably absent from his modern successors. Following the *Post* editorial, Douglas published a famous open letter and issued a challenge. He would walk the entire length of the C&O Canal, 185 miles, and he invited "the man who wrote the editorial" to join him. If that writer did, the justice said, "he would return a new man and use the power of [the *Post's*] great editorial page to help keep this sanctuary untouched."

> He would get to know muskrats, badgers and fox; He would hear the roar of wind in the thickets; He would see strange islands and promontories through the fantasy of fog; He would discover the glory there is in the first flower of spring, the glory there is even in a blade of grass, the whistling wings of ducks would make silence have new values for him. Certain it is that he could never acquire that understanding going 60, or even 25, miles an hour.

The challenge took its toll. Of the sixty-plus participants, only nine made it all the way, in a remarkable eight days, the fifty-five-year-old Douglas setting the pace. Photos show his weary companions soaking their feet in buckets of water. One of the finishers, though, was the newspaper writer and he was converted. Shortly thereafter, the *Post* switched sides, editorializing this time in favor of a C&O national park. The fight was on. Unwilling to abandon their dream, highway boosters stalled the park proposal for the next fifteen years until, finally, in 1971, with the arrival of Earth Day and a new consciousness, Congress acted. It is that hard to preserve things. It is so easy to destroy them.

The canoe paddle back up the C&O is also a remarkable one. We cross the river to it, weaving through the small islands, the canal levee ahead topped by a high line of sycamore trees, their trunks and branches white and smooth as swans. One afternoon we started a wild turkey here. It shot out of a tree like a helicopter with a great beating of wings and lumbered away, a round bag of a bird with its neck sticking out like something it should have kept inside. How Benjamin Franklin could have proposed this species as our national symbol is hard to fathom. Except that it is quite tricky, which he apparently admired.

Up on the canal, paddling back to the car now, the water is table-smooth, rock cliffs on the right, and to the left the towpath, perhaps a foot above the canoe. Peering over the towpath, about twenty feet below, the Potomac rushes by. By late afternoon the sun polishes its surface a silver color, turning slowly to orange. Here is where I tell the children, "paddle me, I'm lazy," and they stab their little Indian paddles wildly into the water, me furtively sculling us forward in the rear. Soon, almost too soon, I no longer have to do it and they are paddling this run on their own.

Back at the parking lot we load the canoe on the VW, the three of us, Kimberly on her tiptoes, Cyp waving his hands in the air below. Our homemade canoe rack is a feat of engineering in itself, cars stopping alongside to ask, "What is that thing?" We had purchased a Beetle convertible that we enjoyed for perhaps two months before falling into canoeing and needing to transport the boat. I fashioned a contraption of metal pipes that were double-bolted to both bumpers and rose in a rectangle above the roof. With angle braces at every junction and strong tie-downs, it could carry the Grumman. I'd not foreseen the difficulty in removing this rack, though, whenever we wanted the top down. Over time the bolts corroded and fused together and the rack became permanent. We now had a non-convertible that leaked wind and hauled boats. And drew remarks.

I did regret the loss. But on a weekend morning as I drove out to the C&O run with the boat high on that ungainly rig, and then back home with the sun still coloring the sky, two or three happy kids spilling out of the car to run and tell someone how it was, the regrets disappeared. You don't need big water to have a big time.

VERDE RIVER
Arizona, 1978

The last time I saw the eagle it was ten miles from Phoenix, sitting up on the Verde River in a cottonwood tree. It was huge, black, and silent as a gunslinger waiting for the men from town to come.

The men from Phoenix had been itching to come for decades. They were just waiting for federal money—several hundred million or so—and they'd come take him twentieth-century style. No guns or rough stuff, we didn't treat the nation's symbol that way anymore, most of us anyway. Instead they would dam the Verde and funnel the water to the booming suburbs of Phoenix downstream. The project was called Orme Dam.

The Central Arizona Project was said to supply water for agriculture, but for the most part it would feed new subdivisions sprawling out into the desert with swimming pools and Bermuda grass, at bargain rates because the federal government picked up so much of the tab. As an official of one Southwest water district explained, "We don't want to change the lifestyle of people in Southern Nevada. That's why we are exploring all these sources of water." Sources like the Verde.

Orme Dam would put thirty miles of river, a rare flash of green in an arid landscape, under water for all time. It would take two-thirds of the Fort McDowell Indian Reservation, part of yet another, and half the nesting eagle trees in the state. The project had been authorized for more than twenty years and was grinding slowly toward Phoenix and the site of Orme Dam. Everything in the way was on borrowed time.

I rode through the Fort McDowell reservation in a four-wheel van. A medical doctor from Phoenix was driving, a biologist named Anne at shotgun. She knew where the eagles were. The point for us was to avoid them; it was early March, their season on the nest. We bounced along in silence through sage and sand. Ragged mountains stood like silhouettes in the distance and, off to the left, the tops of cottonwood trees, fruit of the Verde.

"This has always been a friendly group of Indians," said Bob, squinting in the glare and looking for a side road down to the river.

"I wonder how we ever gave them something this valuable," I mused out loud.

"Nobody thought it was worth much at the time." This was Anne.

"But they do now."

"They want the water," she agreed.

"But so do the Indians," said Bob, finding his turnoff. "They love this place. They think it's more beautiful than Phoenix, which is beginning to piss them off." He pointed to what appeared to be a geyser rising on the horizon, about as at home in this landscape as the London Bridge.

"That is the World's Largest Artificial Fountain," he said in a voice that trembled with false pride.

"What does it do?" I asked.

"It is the World's Largest Artificial Fountain," he explained.

Water in rivers is anathema to the western mind. The story goes that a family went for a picnic by a western river one Sunday, the current sweeping by. As the lunch was spread, the husband walked over to the riverbank and stared at the water. He said, finally, to no one in particular, "What a waste!" Which happens to reflect the law. The only way to obtain rights to water is to take it from the river, even for large fountains, the more the better. The government builds reservoirs and canals to bring the water to you, charging pennies on the dollar. Orme Dam comes to mind. Needless to say they are wildly popular. Except, in one rare moment, with the president of the United States.

In 1976 President Carter, who had come up against several marginal dams in Georgia, moved to cancel many of them pending with federal construction agencies. He drew up a target list of sixty from a backlog of several hundred, the least meritorious of the lot. Washington, D.C., where each of these projects was political treasure, was shaken to the core. Congress fired back and the horse trading began. By the end of year, with blood all over the Capitol, the president's hit list had been reduced to eighteen projects that by any measure were economic disasters, environmental disasters, and in some cases safety risks on a grand scale. The Central Arizona project was one of them.

Out of the West, screaming like a wounded eagle, came Representative Mo Udall, otherwise the strongest environmentalist in the House, arguing with no apparent discomfort that the federal money should keep on flowing into that bulwark of opposition to federal spending, Arizona. Certainly these projects were boondoggles, he admitted, everyone knew that—so long as they were located in somebody else's state. In the end, the final end, the president's list was halved again and nine more bottom feeders escaped. One, by a whisker, was Central Arizona. The fate of its Orme Dam component, however, facing angry Native Americans and endangered eagles, remained up in the air.

We walked past a shanty on a path to the Verde River. It could have been a tractor shed. Swinging wide to avoid the dogs, I realized it was a home. Laundry hung from the line.

"That's a pretty sad-looking place," I said.

"Yavapai Indian," said Bob. "They've been applying for federal housing money for years."

A silence.

"The feds turn 'em down," he continued. "They say that the Indians are living in the floodplain." Another pause. "Of course, the flood they are talking about is when they build Orme Dam."

"But the Indians won't sell, right?"

"Not now. But the feds aren't giving up." They kept raising the ante, and denying the housing money.

"How high is the ante now?" I asked.

"Seventy-three thousand dollars for every soul on the rez."

I wondered out loud what I would do under the circumstances.

"The last time they voted three to one to turn it down," he added.

We walked out on a bluff. A covey of quail jumped from the mesquite. A hawk patrolled the far side. Below us the Verde ran swiftly toward Phoenix though light-green trees. I focused my binoculars downstream and could see a brown smog of pollution against the mountains, the footprint of a city in the air. Between here and there, sitting high in a cottonwood, as visible as a marked man and just as alone, sat the bald eagle, waiting.

On the way back I asked Anne about the eagles.

"They won't live around reservoirs in Arizona," she said. "We don't really know why, although we can make some pretty good guesses."

"Make some pretty good guesses?" I asked.

"They like tall trees around their feeding grounds," she said. "It's where they relax. Tall trees won't grow around a reservoir because the levels fluctuate so much." We walk on.

"The dam people have an answer," she continued. "They are going to build concrete platforms for the eagles to rest on and truck dead fish in for them to eat."

The doctor dropped me off in downtown Phoenix. We had taken an easy float on the river later that day. Paddling through desert terrain is novel every time, the contrast so sharp, dry and wet, a secret, a privilege. Bob told me that the following weekend he and some friends were going out to plant cottonwoods seedlings along the Verde near the Orme Dam site. In twenty years or so they would be new roosts for eagles, he said. Considering the concentric rings of new development around us. I said this sounded like a pretty optimistic plan. There seemed to be a lot of money saying that those eagles would not be around.

My last night in Phoenix I sat in a hotel room one hundred feet higher than the cottonwood tree on the Verde in which the eagle sat that afternoon. I did the only American thing to do under the circumstances, I ordered up a sandwich and turned on the television. Within an hour I had seen twelve ads. Four had eagles in them. In two, the eagles were selling cars, buy this model and you would be free as an eagle, they implied. The third was for a bank in Phoenix, and the fourth an insurance company, each of which had an eagle on the door. You could trust these institutions; they would never let you down.

Following this visit the Wildlife Federation intervened on Orme

Dam, raising endangered species issues. They were not stoppers, but they helped slow things down. Behind every one of these water fights, however—or any environmental fight for that matter—are a handful of people who just will not quit, and every once in a while they save something as large as the Everglades. In this case, they were Bob's Maricopa Audubon Society and the Yavapai Indians living on the Verde River, all 452 of them. They pulled off a miracle.

In November 2011, the Fort McDowell Reservation celebrated the thirtieth anniversary of its victory over Orme Dam. Three decades before, the Department of Interior had surrendered. The victory was costly; the Yavapai people rejected some $30 million in return. Selling "fry bread and an occasional steer" for transportation, they had trekked to the nation's capital to make their opposition heard. In the end they were granted other water from the Central Arizona Project instead and they husband it to this day. They irrigate through underground pipes to reduce evaporation, and largely at night. They have enough for their homes and fields. Conservation is not all that hard. It is getting from here to there that at times seems insurmountable.

BLACKWATER RIVER
West Virginia, 1979

Rivers have attitudes. Some are simply greedy, daring you to come on down, while others are bordered by meadows and wildflowers that invite you to linger. If you like white water you look above the fall line for twisters named Whirlpool and Squeeze'm Dog. The ones on the Blackwater, however, had no names. They were almost continuous, for one, and besides we had never met anyone who had run them.

We are gathering at my house in D.C. for the ride to West Virginia. It is still dark out, the coffee is on the stove, and bluegrass music on the radio even today reminds me of those trip mornings, before we had children and our weekends went in other directions. Lisa is not coming with us; there are ice slicks in the gutters and patches of snow. We have wet suits, new to us at the time, and an assortment of canoes that we paddle solo, turning them backwards to kneel against a thwart, the better to keep control. Still, they are seventeen feet long and stubborn to turn, which in this case turns out to matter.

Perrin shows up first, then Jeff. We'll meet up with Shack and his dog coming from Charlottesville once we get over the Virginia line. Shack's hound is trained to sit up front on calm water, weight against a contrary wind, and then leap on signal to the rear when nearing a drop, lifting the bow. The three of them have boats made of Royalex that glance off of rocks like a ball. I still have my aluminum Grumman with a one-inch keel that sticks to anything it comes upon. Which will matter as well.

The Potomac River rises from several forks in West Virginia, three of them so dramatic they are called the three jewels of the crown. The largest fork is Smoke Hole Canyon near the Canaan Valley, fourteen miles long and three miles wide through a landscape famous for the density of its timber and the speed by which it all disappeared. Good forests in New England yielded fifteen thousand board feet an acre, and the finest stands in Minnesota and Michigan up to forty thousand; in the late 1800s lumbermen hauled one hundred thousand per acre from the Canaan Valley in prime red spruce. No such stands remain today anywhere on the continent. A historian writes: "It took such men a little more than a generation to reduce Canaan Valley to stumps. Shorn of the tall trees that had kept it dark for centuries, the dense valley floor lay open to sunlight. It dried and fires followed, enormous raging fires that burned to the bottom of the humus layer and smoldered for months." A timber company official was more prosaic: "We didn't leave a stick standing." Paddling down Smoke Hole feels like entering an old war zone, all of those bodies, unremembered.

We come out to West Virginia when the waters rise toward spring, reading the rocks and drops ahead, broken field running past ledges of ice and snow. The last time we were caught in a storm so strong it seemed to blow sideways. We found a motel, a godsend, but with only one room available so we slept as in the days of Lincoln, two on the mattress, two on the box spring, one on a rug on the floor. The next morning we walked out to find icicles dripping down from our flotation blocks that remained in place when we flipped over the boats to launch them, the ice sticking up now like the teeth of dragons and glinting in the sun.

This time we are going to run the Blackwater, which Perrin had discovered. The map shows a waterfall but there are no trip descriptions, which could have been a sign. There is also no road to it, only a railroad track up high on a bed cut from sheer rock. Perrin's eyes shine with excitement. In the warmth of the kitchen pouring coffee into the thermos and kissing Lisa good-bye, it all sounds good. I do not tell her that I won't be back this night, because I fully expect to be.

Blackwater Falls is a daunting sight. Water pours over a ledge forty feet in the air to a pool below that slops and boils in a circle before exiting downstream. We are looking at it from the railroad tracks across the ravine, feeling the power. The river below is almost invisible through a tangle of trees that cling to the slope like survivors. The tangle goes straight down. I have that bowel-loosening sensation

I always feel in moments like this, before taking the plunge. Perrin shoves his canoe forward with his foot until it begins to careen downhill like pinball, bouncing from tree to tree, then over a bank and into the water where it is caught by the current, swept downstream, and hangs on a boulder. Which could also have been a sign. In retrospect, everything was waving us away.

Jeff, Shack, and I lower ours by the stern lines, slipping over pine needles and old snow. By the time I reach bottom the others have ferried Perrin out to his boat and begun working their way on down. It is difficult to see them. Anyone who has run a river knows that there is trouble ahead when it goes out of sight. The gradient of the Blackwater is so steep that it is rarely in sight more than ten yards ahead, and then only through boulders protruding from the sides and midstream, the current swirling around them toward who knows what below. There is no way to get out and scout them. There are few places even to bank the boats. We go forward by pointing the bow at whatever looks best and away from whatever has jolted the boat ahead. Which is where mine begins to fail.

I am following the others in a chain, like an acolyte. Whatever route they find, that's good enough for me. This is no river to improvise on. If someone gets snagged we all brake hard lest we pile into him. I find myself grabbed by ledges that hold the Grumman with unseen hands, and even when I jerk free I am off-line for the next chute ahead. The Royalex boats are slipping freely but mine is scraping aluminum all the way. Withal, I am managing well enough, my companions still in sight, when the inevitable happens, a rock buried in pure foam tackles me and I flip. I climb out downstream and give a yell ahead, and by the time I get back to my boat it has wrapped around a boulder like a sandwich with both ends pointing downstream, both gunnels snapped and a thwart pointing straight toward the sky. Very little of the carcass is above water. Perrin tells me later that when they came up looking for me I was staring at it in wonder.

Useless as it seems, the consensus is to pull the boat out. We are past noon by now and have been making slow progress downstream but, like leaving no soldier behind, Perrin insists we make the rescue. Engineering on the fly, we hook a carabiner to a tree limb, thread a rope through it for a pulley, and tie it off on the bow. Three of us pulling hard, the front of the boat struggles up out of the water, the aluminum bending further with the force. Yelling "hey, hey!" in encouragement, Perrin jumps in the water and jams a beached log under the bow, levering it up further, and the canoe begins to deliver itself like an obstetrical nightmare, torn badly but out into open air. We drag the remains ashore. It takes almost an hour. The sun has slipped over the lip of the ravine.

We take stock. We are not two miles down from our drop car, and at least seven more remain to the shuttle car below. If they spend any more time with me the others have no chance to get out. We have no camping gear with us, I give them my dry matches just in case. I will walk back out to the trailhead. They will drive up to get me this evening. Nobody says anything about the aluminum body at our feet, badly wounded but, if I squint my eyes, still a canoe. As they leave, I grab what is left of my bow and begin hauling it uphill. We labored it out of the river. I can't just leave it behind.

I don't know how long it takes me to reach the railroad track, but by the time I arrive it is near dusk. I have pulled, pushed, crawled, cursed, and done everything but romance that carcass up the slope, hanging onto rocks with one hand and dragging it with the other, bumping it against trees, the jagged edges snagging, as stubborn a thing as ever existed. I have accepted not being able to finish the run. This, instead, has become my quest. Reaching the rails I feel light-headed but elated. All that remains is to drag the canoe down the ties to the road end, the way we had dragged them in, and wait for the others. Night is falling, they have to be off the water by now.

I remember little today from that final march, other than that the canoe kept on reaching out for anything it could grab onto, as if I were manhandling the wounded to a grave. At one point I heard a roar ahead of me and thought immediately of a train, which could have crumpled the boat like a can, but it was a chute of water instead, pouring out of a cut in the mountainside. Suddenly thirsty, I buried my face in it, mouth open, and met a foul surprise, acid and bitter. I spit it out and only then remembered that this was coal country and that it was my fortieth birthday. I am due home anytime now.

When I reach the road the moon is up but there is only the drop car belonging to Jeff. Wherever he is, he has the keys. In turn, I have a large hunk of metal and my wet bag. It is too cold to remain here. I leave the boat by the car and begin walking down the road. There must be a town out here although I cannot remember how far it is. We had been in a hurry, coming in.

I do not do well staying up all night. The last time I'd done it was pulling charge-of-quarters duty at an army post in Korea, which consisted of sitting at a desk by a telephone waiting for word of World War III until I fell asleep on the blotter. This time I would not get to bed until the following afternoon. No one had told me how hard it would be to hitchhike home from West Virginia, at night, on country roads. In retrospect, why would anyone need to tell me? For openers, there are no cars at that hour. I do find a gas station, call Lisa, and sit with my back against the Coke machine. The fellow closes at eleven, but he'd let me stay inside.

I got a call from Perrin a day later. They had spent the night in Blackwater Canyon, unable to get out before dark. He was worried, he said, but knew I'd get out. He added that he had a present for me. That weekend he showed up at my house with the hulk of my canoe. He had brought it back on top of his own. He had called around and found a fellow who fixed crashed airplanes and was told, sure, bring it by. So we did, the repair guy wasn't home so we left it on his driveway with a note. A month later he called and said it was ready. He would not take more than a modest amount of money so I snuck in some extra and said thanks and did not see him again. Until one day Perrin sent me a copy of *Canoe Magazine* and there was our man on the cover dressed in a white frock and holding a stethoscope over the wreck of my boat in his driveway. The headline read, "Dr. Robby Brown Fixes the Unfixable Canoe." I felt happy for him. I have a copy that will go to my boys.

The Grumman is still in my backyard. With four large patches

welded over the rips, riveted strips of metal supporting both gunnels, and a new thwart, it is about ten pounds heavier and steady as
a rock. My dog prefers it, there is more room to run around in than
my others. We use it exclusively for trips with tents, coolers, and lawn
chairs, well below the fall line.

SAINT JOHN RIVER
Maine, 1981

The Saint John was not my fight. When they called and invited me to float it I was in the midst of vacating my office in Washington, storing ten years of files, renting the house, and moving our family a thousand miles to New Orleans. I don't remember blinking, however, before I said, sure, that sounded like a fine idea.

We fly in on a day full of squalls. The sign on the door of Folsom's Air Service reads, "Getting things done around here is like making elephants: (1) It is done at a high altitude (2) It is accompanied by a great deal of roaring and screaming (3) It takes two years to produce results."

The sign gives the wrong impression. Folsom flies today. The radio crackles with reports from pilots who've landed on lakes to the north to sit out the storms for a while. Our pilot is old man Folsom himself and the storm-bound pilots are his sons; he tells them to stay put. He climbs into the small cabin, slams the door, and peers over the instrument panel at the thunderheads above Moosehead Lake. Then he says, "Christ, am I tired of this shit!" We don't know whether he means the storms or the flying and we don't ask. Soon we are up and over the north Maine woods, our bags in the rear and the canoes lashed to the pontoons.

By all rights there shouldn't be a river below us. We would be over an eighty-mile lake backed up by two walls of concrete at the towns of Dickey and Lincoln, the Dickey-Lincoln dams. The dams had a well-placed booster in Senator Edmund Muskie, who had been Maine's governor in the 1950s and watched the rise of hydroelectric power in the South, led by the Tennessee Valley Authority, which in the name of economic development wound up impounding nearly everything that moved in the lower Appalachians. Cheap hydro was also booming business in the Pacific Northwest, particularly since American taxpayers footed the bills. This was an attractive game plan, and Muskie struck an alliance with the public power industry to promote it back home. The industry's dream site was on Maine's longest river, the Saint John. The Dickey-Lincoln project was born.

Jon bends over his Oldtown canoe with a roll of duct tape, carefully pinching a guard down the center of the gunwale. He stops his improvement to pick up a pair of old sneaker laces I have discarded. He examines them a moment, tests their strength, and then ties them onto his newly purchased knee pads. "If the pads come unbuckled in the water," he explains, "the laces will hold them until I get to shore." It sounds just plausible enough to make me want to reclaim them. There is a northern mind-set that may come from spending long winters indoors, a passion for fixing and tinkering that produced the first steamboat and the nation's mercantile industry. It does not seem anomalous that a Yankee like Jon, back in the 1840s, on vacation in the Carolinas, would have come up with the cotton gin.

Our companion Bill is an exuberant man who moves through his day like a clothes washer on the heavy cycle. He has simian arms that draw oversize canoe paddles through water, leaving long wakes behind. No matter who is in the bow, his boat moves steadily ahead of the rest. At this moment he has been gathering firewood across the river, accompanied by crashes and the sound of breaking limbs. He brings back a boatload and then walks over to his duffel shouting, "Who'd like some coffee?" He is ready to make it for everyone. In the process he tells me that he teaches math at the state university in Orono. I tell him I'd been all right in mathematics until they started talking about integers. Then I'd switched to English. I can sense that this bothers him: it is like stopping paddling in a headwind.

The Dickey-Lincoln project rose on the momentum of public water projects dating back to the 1930s, part of the New Deal's approach to federal investment. Flood control power, irrigation, and navigation projects boomed forward as did the budget of the U.S. Army Corps of Engineers which constructed them. Hydro dams were seen as progressive and supported by labor and business together, over the objections of conservatives who grumped about their doubtful benefits and lowballed costs. When Muskie went to the Senate he made the construction of Dickey-Lincoln a priority and in 1965 he succeeded in having the Corps authorized to build it, tucked into an I-get-mine-you-get-yours omnibus bill whose lucrative components, doled out to many states, no member had the incentive to question closely. Faced with late but budding opposition from Maine sportsmen's groups over the impacts of the dams, Muskie retorted that if the Dickey-Lincoln site was blocked then he would authorize the project on the Allagash instead, an even more pristine river nearby. Their voices were temporarily stilled. Muskie took it for an understanding. He would throw his weight behind protecting the Allagash; the Corps would turn the Saint John into a power plant.

Tom, a Boston attorney who joined the late charge against the Saint John dams, is in charge of dinner. Jon, a former attorney general of the State of Maine, is maintaining the fire with economical, one-stick additions. The fire suddenly jumps into the frying pan and the wine is ablaze. "I think we're getting a little warm here, Tom," he says. Last night we had fresh beef bourguignon with a cheese and fruit salad, followed by port and Amaretto. This morning it was eggs Benedict on melted cheese and toasted English muffins, buttered. At the start of the trip I'd stood on the dock at Folsom's Air Service and watched them pack the food chests. There were cuts of meat in dry ice, more wines than I keep in my house, fresh artichokes, red cabbage, and a dozen or so cans of smoked oysters. The last item in the wanagan was a bottle of champagne. It would be opened at the site of the dam.

By the late 1960s, the Dickey-Lincoln project was ready to go and queued up for its first appropriations but the line for start money was a long one. The Corps at that time had hundreds of projects under way or authorized and waiting, all screaming like cowbirds for pieces of the worm. Then came another obstacle, largely unseen at the time, the National Environmental Policy Act. Enacted without fanfare in late 1969 and signed by President Nixon on New Year's Day, the law's simple requirement that federal agencies reveal the impacts of their projects before launching them proved to be hidden dynamite, because agencies did not want to reveal the damaging side of their proposals and twisted every which way to avoid doing it. Which left them vulnerable to challenges in court. The Corps took the unique position that since its dams were authorized by Congress the new law did not apply at all. Early litigation said otherwise, and the Corps lost a series of cases on river projects up and down the east coast.

As a result, up in Maine the Dickey-Lincoln project was now susceptible to litigation from the environmental community, which still held out hope against the dams. The opposition included my Saint John canoe partner Rob, who led the largest hunting and fishing group in the state. He had not been part of the earlier Allagash-for-Saint John compromise, and felt no need to honor it. To Maine sportsmen the dam was a disaster and that ended the inquiry. They would be up against the combined might of the public power industry, the Army Corps, and the senior senator from Maine who was a major player in Washington and at the same time, ironically, their environmental champion on Capitol Hill.

Dessert tonight is Bill's lemon cake. He has poured his mix into an aluminum mold, set it in a cast-iron pot, grated in orange peel, swept apart the fire with an ungloved hand, thrust the pot in the coals, shoveled more coals onto the lid, and created an oven in about forty-five seconds. "What's the baking time on this one, Tom?" he asks.

Tom squints to read the box by the light of the coals. "Forty minutes."

"We'll give it twenty," says Bill with finality.

Twenty minutes later he sweeps the coals from the lid and produces an impeccably golden cake, thick as a tire and light as leaves. It is his gift.

We build up the fire—over Jon's mild objections that so much wood is really unnecessary—and discuss Maine's moose season, its first in many years. Seven hundred permits were sold in the lottery and 635 carcasses were brought in, a remarkably high percentage. The moose were apparently quite tame. Jon defends the season. "It's not a question of sport. It's several hundred pounds of very tasty meat." He tells of a guide whom he met on the Allagash and asked if he had bid into state permit lottery. "Yep," said the guide, "but I wasn't gonna wait to see if I won."

Maine's moose season was crowded out of the headlines by Dickey-Lincoln. In the circle of the fire we pass around Tom's folio on the subject, a worn collection of letters and clippings dating back to the 1960s. There are hundreds of people like him around the country who have risen up against a dam, a highway, or a waste dump, burned out and disappeared. The unusual thing about Tom is that he lasted. Reversing the momentum behind one of these projects is like pushing bombs back up into a plane. Either you're Superman or you need a great many friends. Tom's letterhead is The Friends of the Saint John.

Rocks in the fire burst among the coals. "Comes from the moisture in the rock," says Jon. "That's the way the Indians used to split their rocks. Put 'em in the fire." The flame burns down. In the woods behind us, a ruffed grouse booms on a log. Rob says it sounds like a manhole cover dropping a mile away. Jon says it sounds like a heartbeat.

On the margin of the alder bushes a woodcock begins calling to set up its courtship display. We lean back and watch it rise, twittering, chortling, this dumpy bird with its outlandishly long bill spiraling up in flight until it is lost from sight. Then, on signal from a female below who has apparently approved of his performance, he dives to the ground to meet her and the alders go quiet. Meanwhile, across the river a snipe is up. Extraordinary luck. The woodcock is a rocket, up from the ground and down; the snipe is a long-distance acrobat, darting through the sky, with a moaning sound a hundred feet in the air.

We turn in to our tents but the night sounds continue, as they will for hours, for days, for years, for as long as there are places on earth for these creatures to live, whether or not we are here to see them, in a cycle that doesn't care whether we two-legged strangers are well fed in our tents or starving to death at the roots of the trees. A cycle in which we don't matter at all.

Chortle, twitter. Chip chip chip.

Boom . . . boom . . . boom, boom.

Senator Muskie's evolution toward environmental protection rose from the same roots as his support for the Dickey-Lincoln project: economic development. Early in his governorship he had succeeded in wooing an industry to Maine's Saco River, only to find that the water was already so polluted it had no capacity left to assimilate wastes from the venture. A light went on. The nation's waters needed to be restored not because pristine was nice but because it was profitable. From this first awareness it was a shorter step to Muskie's later advocacy of new laws that curtailed industrial pollution with little regard for costs. "Can we afford clean water?" he thundered at his Senate colleagues, "Can we afford rivers and lakes and streams and oceans which continue to make possible life on this planet? Can we afford life itself? Those questions were never asked as we destroyed the waters of our Nation, and they deserve no answers as we finally move to restore and renew them."

Muskie's clean water bill prevailed, and has remained rock-strong against a tide of complaints ("inflexible," "treatment for treatment's sake") that continue to this day. Meanwhile, however, he also stuck to his guns on Dickey-Lincoln and it would take a yet more dramatic turn of events to turn that tide.

We have one major rapid ahead, rather straightforward. It is also easy, however, to dump a gear-loaded canoe. The safe route hugs the west bank but I am in the bow, paddling with Rob, and I say what the hell and make several moves to the middle that put us over rocks and into holes. We run the waves at their worst angles, ship gallons of water, and pull out below half-swamped. Rob is delighted. The others can't believe we are still afloat. I am instantly credited with white-water prowess. I think about correcting them, decide it is too complicated, and enjoy the moment.

On Memorial Day, Saturday, there is a commotion on the far bank. Two trucks appear on what must have been an old logging road carrying a load of canoes. Out of the trucks, yelling like infantry, come young men and a frenzy of "Goddamns!" and "Let's get these bastards in the water!" We stand on our side in shock.

More surprises. They have brought motors for each canoe, six of them sputtering to life on the flat calm of the water. Growling like mastiffs they nose across the river toward us (heart failure), and finally chase each other with yips, cries, and flourishes of beer cans a few hundred yards downstream, putting in at an obvious bog. One by one the motors expire. Then the snarl of a chain saw erupts. Mother of God.

Bill says all motors are all relative. For someone who had hiked a hundred miles in to the headwaters of the Saint John, he points out, our arrival by an airplane was just as much an intrusion. I think there's something qualitatively different here, though. Not too long ago President Reagan's incoming secretary of the interior, James Watt, told his park rangers about a trip down the Grand Canyon on a large motorized raft. The first day was "spectacular," the second day was "a little tedious," and by the fourth day "we were praying for helicopters and they came." This may be the only point on which I ever agreed with him. For me, four days in front of a motor is three and one-half too many. Of course, we'd differ over the remedy. Watt would double the horsepower. I'd let it sink to the bottom.

Dickey-Lincoln came back before Congress in 1976 with President Carter's water project hit-list, which included the Saint John dams. Then came Ronald Reagan who had campaigned for reduced federal expenditures, and appropriations for new starts were squeezed. Meanwhile, Senator Muskie had accepted Carter's invitation to serve as secretary of state and, with the Reagan victory, he was out of public office entirely. The project now found itself in hostile territory and facing a growing campaign to kill it in its own home state. Muskie's Senate replacement, George Mitchell, had strong ties to his mentor but none to the public power industry. In 1984, sensing the political winds, he backed a bill deauthorizing the Dickey-Lincoln. It is said that Muskie, who was largely responsible for Mitchell's political success, never forgave him.

The Saint John sweeps into a broad valley running flat over sandbars and through the low-sloping hills of French Canadian–American farm country. We float this section in a daze. Rob is draped over the bow of the canoe with a sudden fever, face to the sky, shivering under his long johns, wool shirt, and rain jacket, helpless as a deer on a fender. He sits up when the nausea passes to point out of the several locations where hydropower dams have been proposed. We'd measured much of our trip down river by how far underwater the Dickey-

Lincoln site would have put us today—twenty feet, fifty feet—until the numbers lost their meaning and we were simply buried under acres of snags, mud, cold, and the silence of the dark.

The river rises through forests owned by seven timber companies. The companies cut trees and manage access for hunters and fishers and for others who have simply read Thoreau and are going back to look for his sign. To the south are Maine towns, largely coastal and swelled by weekenders from Boston. I fly out on a Sunday in a plane with men in khaki pants, tweed jackets, and ruddy complexions. They are going back to the city and comparing their weekends.

"Been upstate, Elliott?"

"Spent all weekend clearing clam shells off the tennis court."

"Damn shame."

We all have different dreams.

INTERLUDE

River stories run like movies, they start here and end somewhere else, sometimes just another place in the mind. Then there are the memories that do not move. Like photographs they bring back a single place, a single thing recalled as vividly as the first time we heard a song.

One such snapshot comes from a trip to the far North. Rocking on the metal canoe seat all day long had left me lame and unable to move. That evening I crawled into the tent and listened to the others planning a walk up a rock formation behind camp. I must have dozed off because the next thing I heard was Joe unzipping the tent, jumping in quickly to keep out the flies, and saying "you'll never guess what we saw, pardner . . . a Gyrfalcon!" The hunting bird of Saudi kings, the royal falcon of the world. Sensing my despair, he said, "Go on up in the morning, I'll pack for us." I was awake at first light and found in my excitement that I could stand. I hobbled up slowly, looking for a bird to fly, for a ledge that might hide a perch, perhaps even a nest, but there was nothing. At the top, with no place left to examine, I started back down when I noticed a crevasse in the side of the hill so ragged it appeared to have ripped open last evening. I sidled over and, seeing nothing, all disappointment and anger, I picked up a rock and exploded it against the far wall. Immediately, rocketing out of a shadow on the rock face came a large hawk sporting a wicked black mask over its eyes and sleek as an artillery shell and as I turned to follow it came another, trailing, browner in color, the female. They swung out together and then, as if delivering a get-well card, wheeled back over me and again away until they were specks in the sky. I did not see them further, nor have I any others in my life. I fairly bounded down to the camp, rigged a life jacket under my rear end to ease the pain, put on my paddling gloves, and as we got into the boat Joe handed me a piece of breakfast. Some things have no words.

Another time capsule comes from the Glover River in Oklahoma which was slated for a marginal Corps of Engineers dam said to support the aquaculture industry, which turned out to be the McCurtain County catfish farm, which turned out to be three mud ponds the size of a football field. The term pork-barrel could have originated here. Local opponents invited me out for a look. They had invited every media outlet in the state as well. The headline was to be something like Washington Expert Joins Fight Against Lukfata Dam. We would launch a canoe trip down the Glover, a premature celebration of victory. It had been raining and the river came pounding through a culvert in the road. I was given a large companion who had never been in a canoe before but came armed with a large box of ginger snaps. We had no sooner pushed off into the river than my bow man, in all innocence, swung his large torso around to offer me some cookies and we flipped right over. I still see him surfacing with a lock grip on his ginger snap box, which was now pouring out cookie goo. The following day's paper had the headline we expected and a photo of me and my companion with his dripping ginger snaps, looking as if his dog had died. Years later the dam was stopped, but this is the photo that remains.

Yet another comes from Louisiana on a weekend when the Pearl swamp was draining and I should have known to choose a different route. I was with several students and all went well until we got quite deep in and ran out of water, a horizon of cypress knees sticking up like hairs on a dog brush, downed logs and mud. We didn't have time to go back so, pulling out the compass, we began to drag the boats to the west, knowing that at some point, like Columbus, we would run into something. As we struggled forward, the boats banging over roots and ridges, a man appeared suddenly before us as if dropped from the sky. More startling, he was dressed entirely in camouflage and his face was painted like an Indian, assuming Indians liked black and green. More startling yet, he was holding an automatic rifle topped by a telescope nearly the length of the barrel. If this was an invasion of America, they had surely missed their drop zone out here. The apparition addressed us accusingly, "Where's your orange?" Our orange? The question seemed strange, but the apparition went on, "I had you in my scope and you'd be cold dead if I hadn't seen writing on your T-shirts." It turned out that this was opening day of deer season. He had spared our lives and we had ruined his. With all the ruckus we'd been making there wouldn't be a four-legged creature left within miles. Here he had been, all year long, dreaming of opening day, living the shot in his mind, and instead he almost shot three goofballs from the city playing Lewis and Clark. He did us the courtesy of turning and walking away.

More fragments come flooding in now but this last is particularly distinct for what will become obvious reasons. Back in the 1980s one of my first wave of students produced a crew so adventurous that on spring break we drove from New Orleans halfway to El Paso to float the Rio Grande. At trip's end, tired and none too clean, we noticed a hot springs indicated on the map perhaps thirty miles away. What the heck. There was only one car parked at the springs, and locating the trail we hiked in. I expected what I had seen elsewhere, a tub the size of a desktop bubbling like a chem lab with dead vegetation and lumps of whitish sulfur along the sides. Instead, rounding a bend, all eight of us looking like dropouts from the school of life, we came onto a transparent pond the size of a living room, surrounded by a flat shelf of rock, and beyond, perhaps twenty feet down, the river running by. Lying in the middle of pool, eyeing us curiously but without panic, was a young woman pretty enough to grace the cover of a magazine and entirely without clothing. We reacted in eight different ways, none of them graceful, but none aggressive either. With studious inattention to her we slid into the water and began to talk as if just meeting on seats in the plane. Nothing more happened. After a while she got up como si nada, toweled off, slipped on shorts and a blouse and walked away, wishing us well. I think that if she had offered to marry one of us instead she would have had takers. I look at her now as another Gyrfalcon, a gift so natural and beautiful I could do nothing but thank it and store it away.

It is time to return to fuller stories, but we all know that the photos in our memories are far more numerous than the movies, and that they are not really photos at all. They are planets.

Part II

SOUTH TOWARD HOME, 1981–2013

ATCHAFALAYA RIVER

Louisiana, 1982

I had no intention of moving to Louisiana. I knew where it was but it did not seem like a place I particularly wanted to be. In 1971, however, I left the U.S. Attorney's Office in Washington to work for the Wildlife Federation and, as fate would have it, the first telephone call I received was from a Louisianan with a Cajun accent that left me groping, telling me that I needed to "get on down here." If I heard him correctly, the Corps of Engineers was going to drain the Atchafalaya. I didn't dare ask him what that was. Then he added, "There's an ivory-bill in there," and I knew right away what that was. The ivory-billed woodpecker had not been seen for half a century, anywhere on earth. I said, I'll come on down. Nothing has more altered my life than that call.

The Atchafalaya is a treacherous river. In the 1920s it nearly abducted the Mississippi, taking it on a western course to the Gulf of Mexico and leaving the City of New Orleans with about an eighty-mile walk to the water. Fifty years later it tried again and undermined a man-made control structure at its mouth like a toy. It is not the sort of river you play on.

Over its banks and into the trees is another story, a million-acre cypress and tupelo gum swamp that takes you back to the Jurassic and thoughts that a dinosaur could come creeping by, something large in its mouth, perhaps you are next. The main Atchafalaya is for barges and tankers but these backwaters are remarkably peaceful, as I discovered on my first trip down, days before an encounter with the Army Corps, which had other plans for them. I went into the swamp with Vic Lambou, where the motor on his flatboat conked out. He jiggered with it for an hour before turning it over again, cursing softly in fractured French and mortified that he had ruined my day. Far from it. I sat there sipping a soda and soaking in the dark, clear waters studded with cypress knees, erect as little gnomes, shafts of light coming from the canopy above. For me, a little time without a motor was just fine. Lambou, a fisheries biologist, would be one of our experts in the mano a mano with the Corps to come.

The voice that summoned me on the phone, so thick it seemed filtered through tobacco, turned out to be exactly that. Charlie Bosch, head of the Federation's Louisiana affiliate, lived with an unlit cigar in his mouth at what seemed to be all times, laying it carefully next to his plate while eating. Lord knew what he did on more personal occasions. A hard-drinking, fish-killing, duck-stomping, gumbo-cooking outdoorsman with a perennial three-day stubble—decades before this look made television specials—he was also deeply green and, by necessity, a wheeler-dealer who began conversations with whiskey and ridicule of "environmentalists" as persons whose masculinity was in question. Charlie wanted to keep the Corps from draining the Atchafalaya swamp, which it was set on doing. Not fully appreciating that the project had been authorized for fifty years, was bringing in millions of construction dollars each new budget cycle, and was important to keeping New Orleans dry, I bought in.

Charlie picked me up at the Baton Rouge airport which looked like a landing strip in Panama, steaming hot after the rain, and escorted me to New Orleans for my inaugural meeting with the Army Engineers. To my surprise the room was chock-full with Corps employees curious to see this new phenomenon, an environmental lawyer, parlay with the District chief. The three of us sat at the front like fish in a bowl, me talking about laws that might tangle up this project unless of course we worked together, Charlie chewing silently on his cigar, and he, the District Engineer, head down, wordless, drawing small squares on a notepad and then filling them in. The thought of how arrogant it was for me, barely thirty years old, a complete stranger to Louisiana, who had dropped physics in college as incomprehensible, to be telling these engineers how to do their business occurred to me only after the fight was over.

The issue was clear. The Corps was dredging a ditch down the river that would drain the swamp, ostensibly for flood control. Char-

lie's people were fishers and hunters, they lived for environments like
this and there is a reason the state license plate read "Sportsman's
Paradise": they were a force. They also saw the dredging project as a
real estate scheme, drying out the swamp for development. Resolu-
tion of these differences would take, on and off, the next ten years.
Charlie would later describe that opening round with the Corps in
cinematic detail, the poker faces around the room, the silent Colonel,
me talking and talking, and he would finish, as if he'd witnessed a
trick of magic, "there was no notes in front of him!"

As the Atchafalaya controversy grew, an application surfaced for
an oil refinery at Krotz Springs. It seemed an improbable location.
The town sat in the middle of the Corps' own floodway, smack dab
where the Mississippi River would be routed at high water in order
to spare Baton Rouge and New Orleans. Charlie and I had nothing
personal against refineries but we were not trying to save the Atchafalaya only to lose it to an industry that already owned the Mississippi,
and to the tank farms, pipelines, and service operations that would
certainly follow.

For its part, Krotz Springs saw gold. In better days it straddled
the main road from Baton Rouge to Texas and had enjoyed a steady
business in gas stations and the quick-food trade, often the same
buildings, their signs reading "Gas . . . Fresh Boudin." Then a federal
interstate came west on concrete pillars and bypassed the town completely, speeding on toward Texas. Huddled behind its levee, cut off
by the new highway, Krotz Springs was a community in decline. Now
came the oil industry with a multimillion-dollar proposal for new
cracking units, storage tanks, and docks, right here on the river. The
only hitch was that a Corps permit was required and, in turn, a public
hearing. We decide to go.

We drive out from Baton Rouge in Charlie's truck to the Corps'
permit hearing, the rattle of an ammo box and plastic decoys in the
rear. It is early May, already summer and dark storm clouds backdrop
refineries along the Mississippi that are flaring gas and ablaze with
lights like ship disasters at sea. We have no expectations here. Corps
hearings are foregone conclusions. One of the first I attended, deep

in the marshes of Terrebonne Parish, opened with a local priest who asked us to thank the Almighty for delivering the project at issue, a $50 million canal through coastal wetlands to benefit two oil-rig manufacturers. I had arrived late, after missing both plane and bus connections, in time to hear a woman at the microphone declare that "when God made environmentalists he should have had an abortion!" The audience went wild.

The Krotz Springs refinery hearing unfolds at city hall, hard by the ring levee, a flat building with the look of a grammar school. Vans and pickups are in constant motion, pulling in with a jerk of the brakes, pulling out with bursts of gravel, carrying shouts to deputy sheriffs who are lounging near the entrance wearing Levis, boots, and sidearms. Some are drinking beer. The room is packed with townspeople sitting in rows of folding metal chairs. At the front sits the District Engineer wearing his service medals, and a battery of lawyers and consultants for the refinery in suits and ties. The town is in shirt-sleeves, the windows are open, and people lean in to pass beverages back and forth and catch the goings-on.

The applicant leads off with a rapid-fire presentation by its attorney that lasts close to an hour, and concludes by equating the project with a body blow to the Ayatollah Khomeini. There follows a parade of "local interests," which is Corp-ese for persons who support the project. Opponents are called "other interests." A surprising statement is read from the mayor of Baton Rouge saying that the refinery would "jeopardize the hydrologic integrity" of the flood scheme protecting his city. At this point the mayor of Krotz Springs rises to say that he knows the mayor of Baton Rouge very well and is sure that his good friend has never said "hydrologic integrity" once in his life, so somebody is putting words into the man's mouth. He goes on to talk about the need for jobs and how he has no intention of hurting the environment, and then he is finished. A short, stocky man with white hair and a face as honest as Spencer Tracy, wearing a faded sports shirt, putting his hands on friendly shoulders as he makes his way through the metal chairs to the door.

A few speakers later I borrow a cigarette, although I don't even like the taste of them, and retreat to the lobby. A trophy case features a silver bat and a golden glove, the sport of baseball is still number one here. Above the water cooler is a map showing a town far larger than today, spread up and down the Atchafalaya with hundreds of private lots and a commercial center. On the right of the plat is the inscription:

> Buy Lots in Krotz Springs
> The Coming Health Resort of the South
> In this town Krotz Famous mineral water
> well is located. The water from this
> well flows from a depth of 29,000 feet
> and will cure all kinds of Stomach,
> Kidney, and Bowel Disorders and
> Indigestion. The finest bathing
> water in the world.

The mayor walks by, exiting from a group of well-wishers, and I ask him about the plat. In the 1920s, apparently, a man named Krotz discovered mineral water here and promoted the town as a health spa. The promotion failed but Krotz sent his famous water "all over the country." Of course that was before the Corps built the Atchafalaya floodway. Looking at the map I ask, truly curious, what he thinks will happen to the town when they open up the floodway and send half of the Mississippi River this way. He shrugs. We're already here, he says. That's a lot of water, I say, but smiling.

Back inside the hearing room the politicians have left the stage, the local television crew is packing up, the last newsman is making for his car. A man in a short-sleeved polo shirt with a pack of cigarettes tucked by his bicep, tattooed with what appears to be a length of chain, rises to speak from the floor. He is a member of the town council and he doesn't remember voting for this refinery and he doesn't want it. What about the next refinery, and the next? When is it going to stop? After the hearing we run into him at the Quick Stop on the edge of town, the only place with lights on at that late hour. He lives out near the river. His and his boys go hunting right where the refinery will be. The weekend before, he tells me, his oldest shot fourteen woodcock there.

I finally take my turn and tell the Corps that if it is going to spend several billion dollars to make the Atchafalaya a functioning floodway then it is going to have to keep things like oil refineries out of it, or it will have an acute headache on its hands. Refineries can't run to higher ground. Going back outside, in shadows on the lawn, small groups are in earnest conversation. A construction job is starting up in Opelousas. The soybean crop looks good, but cane is down. A white-haired man looks my way. "Think you did any good?" he asks me. For a moment he looks like the mayor, the same open shirt, open face. I shrug noncommittally. "A shame," he says. "They no purpose to put it out there," with shake of his head toward the night beyond the levee. "Why cher," he goes on, "they crawfish, they all the job we need." I see him later with the mayor on the lawn, arm in arm. They could be brothers.

The last address of the evening. The sign-up list is exhausted, the Colonel is winding up things quickly with a pro forma invitation for anyone else to speak who has not done already so and, lo and behold, a hand is raised and to the platform steps a middle-aged black man. The only black in the audience. He winds around his subject. He concludes by saying that God gave us the right to work and he hated to work and spent most of his life avoiding it, but if God was going to send this oil refinery then we ought to accept it and go to work, and if God sends a flood through next year well that's God's answer too. Let that be up to Him.

The Corps permitted the refinery, of course. The outcome was never in doubt. The controversy over draining the floodway went on for a very long time, however, and was clinched in the end not by the Atchafalaya's preternatural beauty but, instead, by a dawning awareness that if the Corps drained it then subsequent development in here would make the project unusable. When that light bulb finally went on we cut a deal, the landowners, the environmentalists, the Corps, the governor, and last to the party, the congressional delegation, ever loathe to change course on a bonanza that brought large dollars into the state, whatever for. The big ditch was scrapped. The Corps bought no-development easements instead. We all won.

In the spring of 2010 a large bolt of water came down the Mississippi threatening the city of New Orleans. The Corps opened the Atchafalaya floodway for only the second time in history, unleashing a torrent of water twenty miles wide safely toward the Gulf of Mexico. Almost safely. Some people from Krotz Springs had moved out into the floodway anyway, and the media played them up as tragic figures, sitting in stuffed couches on their bungalow porches with tall cans of beer, waiting to be evacuated. Not wanting to miss the high water, I took some students and old friends and floated it through the treetops where raccoons were hanging on for dear life along with swarms of hornets and fire ants. You can't pick and choose in nature. You save some, you save them all.

The Atchafalaya is a treacherous river. It is still trying to capture the Mississippi and, with enough time, some day it may. Meanwhile it rises and falls with the seasons, flooding and receding, spilling into its overflow swamp. It ferries barges loaded with drilling muds and soybeans. Every once in a while one slams into the highway bridge at Krotz Springs, killing people. It's not the sort of river you play on. Whether you build oil refineries out there, well, it's a Louisiana thing.

SHELL BANK BAYOU
Louisiana, 1985

Robert is in the stern. I have stopped paddling because there are strange objects in the water ahead and I do not want to spook them. As it turns out I need not have bothered because they are dead, their legs and plumes stretched out on the surface as if they were just getting up in the morning. There are quite a few. The nearest is a snowy egret with slim black legs and golden feet. The next three are white ibis, their orange beaks long as scimitars and at this moment quite useless. Oddly, their legs look broken.

East of New Orleans a series of lakes sit on top of each other like a set of bags, first Lake Borgne along the Gulf, then Pontchartrain which borders the city, and lastly Maurepas, named for the euphonious Jean-Frédéric Phélypeaux, comte de Maurepas and advisor to King Louis XVI. People who live here know Borgne for fishing and Pontchartrain for sailing; those who come this far up know Maurepas for its cypress trees. Local artist Julia Simms says it, "I don't know what it is . . . I get lost, but I mean that emotionally. I feel absolutely right." Which I suppose is why we're here too in this morning light.

A neck of land stretches between Maurepas and Pontchartrain, cut by connecting passes. The Tangipahoa Indians and the later Choctaw settled these passes for hundreds of years, camping on their banks and feasting on small clams from the lakes whose shells accumulated by the thousands into large middens and sunk twenty feet deep into the soft, biotic soils. The water we are now paddling is called Shell Bank Bayou. We have decided to go toward Pontchartrain this time, which neither of us has done before. Robert says that there is supposed to be a large midden back there.

There are a couple of things to know about Robert. The first is that he was about to become a state fish and game agent at the time, a job he would take seriously. Shortly after he got his badge he told me about seeing a lady in a car ahead of him throw a soft drink can out the window. It bounced on the road toward his vehicle which in his words "wasn't right," so he came alongside her, asked her to pull over, walked up to her door, and asked her to go back and pick it up. Whether he had the authority to do this I've no idea. The only reason I feel free to tell it is that he is now retired. Nonetheless, that is part of Robert and it plays a part in this story. He believes in the law.

We drift up to the dead birds, Robert just feathering the boat forward, me quiet in the bow, speechless. A fallen tree lies nearby and a half-dozen dead birds float around it like a macabre flower display. These are the signature birds of south Louisiana, the ones whose flights sweep the sky above morning and evening commuters and land on the levees, playgrounds, and even roadside ditches, probing for food. State plaques, oil industry logos, commercial signboards, and environmental group newsletters all feature these species, large, stately, able somehow to live with us and thrive. Only here they are dead and, worse, most have broken legs, down by the feet, it makes no sense at all. Looking more closely, Robert says with wonder in his voice, "This one's been shot."

The second thing about Robert is that he has a heightened awareness in the out of doors that seems to come from another time in history. I have been out with paddlers who know rivers, who can read chutes from fifty yards and floods by the debris on the bends, but this is different. Robert is an animal-whisperer. Walking with him on a Gulf island one day we came across a deep track as if someone had dragged a log through the dunes. It led straight into the water. "It's an alligator," he mused, finding a claw print along side, "but where was it going?" Then he spotted a turtle shell, chewed open by the creature as if by pliers. We could find no others. "He probably fished them out of the surf and took them back into the dunes," Robert said, and sure enough we found a litter of little carcasses back there. Things touching on wildlife reach him deeply, which is also part of this story.

We decide to paddle on, a narrow route winds through the trees, but taking the next bend we see another cluster of bodies ahead. There are some new species this time, a little blue heron and a common egret, some shot, most with broken legs, floating on the water, next to a large log. Having seen enough, I dig my paddle into the water to move us forward but Robert, whose stern seat is just passing the log, says, "Look at that," and I turn, and on top of the log is a steel leghold trap, jaws open, set for prey. We are both struck with the same thought. The traps might explain why so many of these creatures had broken legs, down by the feet. But who in the world would trap large wading birds and then shoot them and leave them here? It makes no sense. "Let's see if there are any more," says Robert.

I am paddling in the bow; Robert is in the back and thinking out loud. "He's not in the plume business," he says, "or he'd have taken the birds with him." A pause. "And he's not out for grosbeck," referring to the legendary appetite of Cajuns for night heron stew, "or he'd have taken them home." I stay quiet, hearing him think. "With traps like that," he goes on, "placed on a log, he's looking for animals, mink and nutria. Maybe an otter." I cannot keep from asking the obvious: "So why is he killing the birds?" Another pause, and then Robert's computer spits out an answer. "They are messing up his trapline," he says. "They are walking on the same logs that the animals do, they are stepping onto the pans and springing them." I can take it from here. The trapper comes up in his motorboat, tending his line, and instead of finding a furbearer that he can sell for pelts he has a dumb bird, maybe already drowned, maybe still alive and squawking and carrying on as he comes into view. Naturally, he kills it. Naturally, he kills every one he sees out there, whether in his traps or not, because each one costs him money.

"He's simply doing his business," says Robert, philosophically, in the same way he understands the game poachers he would bust down in the marsh for the next twenty years, each one of them trying to make a little extra to get by. This guy is also breaking the law, I point out, this many kills would make a felony. Robert knows this too, of course. But what do we do about it? Sit out here and wait . . . and what then if the fellow comes back? He is obviously armed, he shoots the birds. The only arm we have is my pocket knife, which has a very limited range.

The sight of the traps brings back childhood memories. I know about these things. I reach out sideways and draw us into the log where the jaws lie open, ready to spring. I tap the pan lightly with my paddle and they leap up to snap it, fast as a pistol shot, latched on to the blade like a vise. Robert says nothing. For one thing, he said later, these traps were somebody's personal property. For another, he added, if the fellow came up and saw us he might shoot; that happened down in parishes, it could happen here. All I say at the time is, "this guy's killing birds, Robert." Robert thinks about it and then says, "Oliver, he'll just come back and reset them and kill more birds." Which is obviously correct. Which pushes me to the next step, which could be called over-the-line.

Unwilling to put the trap back onto the log I tug at its chain, which is fastened by a large nail. There is no getting it loose. I then, idly, finger the pan which, the trap sprung, is free-moving and hanging like a leaf in winter. Without premeditation, as if someone else were doing it, I begin to work the pan back and forth on its little arm, which is stiff at first but then weakens with the pressure, then cracks and breaks off. I hold the pan between my fingers for a moment and then scale it like a coin out over the water where it hits lightly, floats for a moment, and sinks out of sight. Gently, I replace the trap on the log. Robert is quiet the entire time.

We never agree to do this. We just paddle on to the next location, the next group of dead birds and their killing ground, a log. I can feel Robert with me by now, having finished what was obviously a difficult debate in his head—you don't mess with other people's things out in the marsh—he comes out on my side. The new site adds yet new birds, cormorants, it looks as if an entire family went down. I spring the trap, break off the pan, and replace it. We are moving more quickly now because the day is heating up and we do not want to get caught out here by whoever it is, whether red-handed or no. We are also as aware of our own culpability as his. It feels right and wrong at the same time.

We find about a dozen sets in all leading to Pontchartrain, and there by the lake is the large shell midden Robert had spoken of and had been at one point the object of our journey. We beach and walk up it to speculate for a moment about how it must have been living here, where did they camp, did they set up on the shells or away from them, it must have smelled like the very devil, what else did they eat, maybe wading birds like the ones we were seeing, and then we get back into the canoe and paddle back. Fastidious to the end, we stop at the log we'd seen first and neuter that trap as well. In all, a very different day from the one we'd planned.

Our car is parked on the berm of the road. As we are pulling out our canoe, a truck comes in hauling a motorboat on a trailer, which is not at all unusual. Lots of boats put in to fish the bayou on the other side. To put in toward Pontchartrain is harder because a set of pipes blocks the water, under which you have to manhandle your canoe. To say nothing of a motorboat. But this boat is putting in this side. It has to be our man.

Which panics us. I do not understand why we did not at least write down his license tag or the registration number on his boat. All we are thinking at the time is let's get out of here, and so we do. We do not even take time to tie the canoe to the roof, me holding on to one side from the window while Robert has a death grip on the other. We do not stop until we reach La Place, laughing with relief at the absurdity of our getaway. As if we are leaving the scene of a crime. Which we are.

Exactly what the crime is and who committed it is for others to say.

RIO GRANDE
Texas, 1986

Driving across Texas in the dead of the night, our headlights on the road look small and ridiculous, a spaceship in the infinite black, only distant stars. We last saw our lead car two hours ago, when mine began to sputter. We have not seen other lights, not a store, not a habitation, for the last hour, not even a side road leading away. If there is a jackrabbit out there it must be lonely. Vickie is in the backseat bopping to a tape of the Bee Gees and syncing in a high falsetto, "dancin', dancin' in the street." She has me doing it too. My boy Cyprian is asleep back there and Eric, drunk with fatigue, is in the passenger seat looking woodenly ahead. We have been on the road since yesterday noon. Our immediate target is a town on the Rio Grande called Del Rio.

The car coughs again and begins to falter. My gas gauge broke several months ago so I am only guessing what is in the tank but that wouldn't matter now because the last gas station we saw was way back there, and it wasn't open. We have been climbing a rise and so I have been reluctantly stomping on the accelerator, urging us up, but this might be the last straw. The motor chokes as if expiring and now I know that it is. By good fortune we seem to have topped the rise. Way in the distance, and way below, is a patch of lights. It may be an oil refinery. Or it may be Del Rio. Vickie leans over the seat, grabs my shoulder, and says "no brakes . . . just don't use the brakes."

By some unseen communication, Cyp wakes up to ask what happened to the motor. "We're saving gas," I tell him, me leaning into the curves like the Tour de France, Vickie digging her fingernails into my shoulder and repeating, "no brakes, no brakes." It turns out to be Del Rio. We glide in as if part of a silent movie, cruise through a red light, and stop, gently, in front of, of all things, a Mobil station, open all night. All we have to do is push the car up the little fan. It was that kind of a venture. Everything went wrong and turned out fine.

This was my first trip from New Orleans over to the Rio Grande, and besides Cyp we had eight of my students on an early spring break, all of them swearing oaths that they had canoed and camped before. Perhaps in their fashion this was true, but not true enough for a week in the Mariscal and Boquillas canyons which were ruggedly isolated and had some serious riffles from time to time. But those challenges lay far ahead. Our next one, past my car which not only needed gas but a new water pump, was that, from yesterday to today the temperature had plummeted from the eighties to below freezing, which in New Orleans had been unimaginable. I'd packed some long johns; beyond that, none of us were prepared. These were the days before polypropylene fabrics and synchilla and we stopped in every Texas town past Houston looking for woolen clothing, sweaters, mittens, even scarves. There were none. The salespeople stared back at us as if we were extraterrestrials and pointed to shelves of cotton socks. We bought sweatshirts and moved on. We also bought a frying pan, which the student assigned had left behind. It was a little thing made of aluminum that proved untouchable when hot and even less possible to clean. And moved on.

We were tested again at the put-in, stuffing our gear into wet bags. Vickie seemed particularly challenged and, walking over to help, I saw her unloading a laundry hamper of what looked like all the clothing she owned so we emptied it on the ground, she protesting lightly about the exposure of her underthings, and put much of it back in the car. On the trip, she would prove to be indispensable, enthusiasm you would kill for; ace campers are not always ace companions. After a long day's paddle, her hands wet and raw, Vickie would put on her best Boston accent and say, rolling her words like a vaudeville act, "Glo-ria, oh my gawd, my nails!" I have since lost all trace of her. The thing about having these students is that most of them walk across the stage and out of your life, as well they should. But still.

We took a short first day, it was biting cold, and pulled out with extra time to make camp. Fortunately. One pair of students had forgotten the poles for their tent, and another had forgotten a tent altogether. We reshuffled the deck for sleeping and went hunting for

Downstream: Scouting Owyhee Canyon

Roots: Author's mother (*left and right*), grandfather, and guides in
New Brunswick, Canada, 1920s (*right*)

Early Days: Lisa and the canoe rack (*left*), a typical
eastern run, Virginia (*right*)

C&O Canal: The Peanut run (*left*), and put-in and paddle (*right*)

Potomac River: Buckling up (*left*), and return (*right*)

Barren Grounds: Dragging the Kognak (*left*), and sailing
the Maguse (*right*)

Henik Lakes: Taking advantage of windless evenings (*left and right*)

Red Creek and Potomac: Morning (*left*), and evening (*right*)

Wolf River: Stump jumping (*left*), and ready to go (*right*)

Swamps: Entering the Pearl (*left*), and Grand
River Flats, Atchafalaya (*right*)

Salmon River, Middle Fork: by a feeder stream (*left*), and
running ledges (*right*)

Horton River: Caring for bites and blisters (*left*), and midday pause (*right*)

Southern bayous: Shell Bank (*left*), and Lake Maurepas (*right*)

Grande Ronde: The Narrows, airborne (*left*), and backwards (*right*)

Students: Stream walking (*left*), and the five-tier pyramid (*right*)

McGee's Creek: Lisa and Ms. Bear

Red Creek: South toward home

Grande Ronde: In camp

tent poles in a willow thicket with stems about the right size. Willow stems are not very strong, however, and firmly snugged in their sockets they lifted the top only twenty inches or so into the air. The tent looked as if a giant had stepped on it by accident and then apologized, nothing broken, but quite low to the ground. A good thing about students is that this kind of thing seems not to matter at all.

Mariscal Canyon on the Rio Grande is worth the trip by itself. It is not very long, perhaps twenty miles, but the walls go straight up like a street in Manhattan lined by skyscrapers, their ledges above you as scaffolding. Below them were only the rushing water and, where side canyons came in, small deltas with beaches to spend the night. I was paddling with a tall fellow from Scandinavia who was in heaven the entire trip. He rescued me one night when I was struck by leg cramps, a bane of my life, a please-God-no! moment, followed by shooting pain. Both legs folded like jackknives and I remember calling out to Torbjorn for help. He pulled me from my sleeping bag, folded my legs back one at a time and began to knead them like loaves of bread, saying, "OK? OK?" The cramps finally subsided and we went back to sleep. The next morning Vickie, all vaudeville again, called over in a loud voice, "you two lovebirds are going to have to keep it down in there!"

The surprising thing about the Rio Grande is how long it is. It rises in the mountains of Colorado clear and swift and then crosses New Mexico for five hundred miles before it reaches El Paso, takes a left turn at the Mexican border, and runs another thousand miles to the Gulf. When it has water, that is, which is less and less often. Locals along the border have come to call it "the forgotten river," as if there used to be one here. Drought is a factor, but the reality is that there are so many pipes and diversions sucking water out of the Rio Grande that little remains and what returns is laced with salt, fertilizers and pesticides. The main thing keeping water in the river on the U.S. side these days is, of all ironies, a small fish called the silvery minnow, which is of course endangered. The anger that protecting this fish provokes among real estate developers, irrigators, and other boomers in the desert looking for one last drop, we need not work hard to imagine. It is a distressingly common phenomenon. We are the species with no brakes, and we hate other things that signal us to slow down.

There is more angst along our border with Mexico, of course, and those years it centered on marijuana which seemed to wash over like a river itself and into the insanely lucrative American market. I had prosecuted drug cases in Washington for several years, successfully if one counts convictions, but my colleagues and I did not make a dent in the market or the price on the street. The market came to us this trip on the Rio itself, where a flat on the Mexican side dropped to a ford and was met by an identical flat on ours. As we floated toward it there was a wild commotion and out of the bush came a posse of horsemen with chaps and sombreros, charging into the water and pulling long ropes behind them tied to an old van which crashed into the river and was hauled to the other side, the horsemen yipping and yelling all the way. I whipped out a camera and began snapping pictures of them before realizing how unwise that was. By the time we passed by, the horsemen had dismounted and were untying their ropes from the van, which then drove off into the nothing of the Texas plain. We did the discreet thing and waved.

Canyon rivers are particularly susceptible to the wind, and this time it did us in. The unprecedented cold front that caught us at Mariscal Canyon was followed by a blow in Boquillas so strong that we could scarcely keep a fire lit and paddling against it was like climbing a wall. There was a moment where the river bent into the wind and seemed to go backward, blown upstream. There was nothing for it but to dig in and pull for the next beach but on arriving we found ourselves one boat short. A student and I walked up the bank for sign of our mates but they had disappeared. A point across the river had burned to the ground though, smoke still rising, and their canoe was beached nearby. Up on a ridge we saw what appeared to be the roof of an adobe hut, and starting up toward it, calling, we found our companions coming down. Unable to get downstream, they had made a fire on the point to get warm but the wind blew it out of control and they had to flee for their skins up this bank and into, of all things, a bar. We struggled their boat back to camp, to find the other canoes pinned with large rocks to keep them down. The blow had lifted one up earlier and tumbled it into the water.

The wind mounted through the night. By morning river grit was in everything, underwear, Ziploc bags, and we were eating out of a Frisbee, which at least had a rim to keep food on the plate. The eyes of one student were swollen shut. We didn't have to talk about it. Two days into Boquillas we called it quits. We drove out past a ranger station where two couples, in from their Winnebagos, were asking the receptionist, "What is there to do around here?" Vicki would tell that story for months, laughing. "How about eating oatmeal from a Frisbee?" she would say.

The following year several of us went back and ran another section of the Rio Grande, the Lower Canyons, which has drops that are more open and easier to navigate. The weather was perfect, we ate off of actual plates and came home happy. But I remember the first trip better. These students of mine, early-twenty-somethings, had leaped from an academic pressure cooker into an environment they were in no way ready for, except in their heads, and that was enough. Through all of the mishaps there were no complaints, no cross words, none. I would lose touch with them, all but two, over time, but then come new ones. As Lisa says, they rock and roll.

BUFFALO RIVER
Arkansas, 1987

They looked so pretty, a red canoe, a yellow and a blue one, sweeping off into the trees. I could barely see the couples in them, they were way on the other side of the river, but I think the girls were in bow. They were wearing orange flotation. The first canoe struck a willow trunk broadside and bent in two, quick as crumpling a can; then the second one folded; the one remaining dodged a tree or two and then seemed to flip clean over, all within yards of each other. I saw some thrashing in the water, at least one person was hanging onto a limb, no sounds reached me, there was nothing I could do for them, I was a football field away and the current was shooting past me at warp speed.

It took me at least ten minutes to cross the river, round a bend, and pull out below them, maybe a half mile below, maybe more. I rested there for a long time waiting for someone to float down, hopefully alive, but no one came. There was no way to get back up there, there was no bank on this side, and the water was rushing through drowned woods. I had no cell phone. No one did in those days. Finally I turned out into the river again and went on.

I had been invited up to Fayetteville to give an Earth Day talk and discovered that April is a wet month in northern Arkansas. The following day broke clear, however, and I took a notion to float the highly regarded Buffalo River. When we arrived, however, the outfitter announced that he was letting no boats out, the water was too high. I ended up writing him a check for the value of his canoe, new, and leaving my wallet and watch too for good measure. I might have left him my dog as well. I had no qualms about high water, which I well should have had, and my companion was content to hike around for the afternoon and then come meet me below. As I was getting ready I saw three couples drive up on the other side of the river and put in, three cute boats, they looked brand-new, nice-looking kids too.

After the wipeout I made the rest of the trip down with great cau-
tion, like walking down stairs backwards, holding onto the near side
of every turn, ready to escape. The first thing I said to my friend at
the takeout was, that was a stupid thing to do. We went back up to the
outfitter and told him what had happened. He made some telephone
calls. I volunteered to go back down but he said not in his boat. I have
no idea what happened to them. We checked the paper for the next
two days and saw nothing about it, which made me feel better. The
outfitter had apparently closed shop until the water went down. In
my mind, though, for a long time afterwards, I raced over against the
current with gargantuan strokes and hauled those youngsters into my
canoe, all six of them, the girls bursting with gratitude. I sure hope
that someone did.

The thing about rivers is that any one can kill. Then again, so can
a bathtub. The Buffalo is not unusually dangerous, not on this stretch
anyway, this was just an unusually dangerous time to be on it. In
fact, the Buffalo is one of the most beautiful rivers in America and
the first to be included in the national Wild and Scenic River System.
For people from the East it will look vaguely familiar, as if someone
carved out a piece of West Virginia, carried it halfway to the Rockies,
had second thoughts, and dumped it on the far bank of the Mississippi. The Ozark mountains where it rises have an eastern look, craggy,
forested, and studded with names like Hemmed in Hollow Falls and
settlements lost in time. Looking more closely, however, you stumble
across elk, red-shafted flickers, and other western creatures. If there
is a single place in America where East meets West other than the
golden spike that joined the railroads this would be it, which makes
for an astonishing variety of wildlife, much of it aquatic, because the
Ozark streams are the stuff of legend.

Down in South Louisiana, flat as a rice field and cut through with
muddy bayous, the draw of the Buffalo is constant. Despite the scene
I'd witnessed a few years earlier, I promised my older boy that I'd take
him up to white water when he reached twelve years old. I would follow the weather carefully. We'd go when it was low and easy.

Moving water draws other enthusiasts, however, none so impor-

tant as the Army Corps of Engineers which makes its living impounding rivers for other purposes. No state in the East has been spared,
but Arkansas was particularly hard hit because it had so many available rivers and because, lightly populated as it was, there were fewer
people to oppose. The rationales for the dam spree varied but they
always included recreation as a major component, the user-day values of motorboating around man-made lakes apparently dwarfing
those from enjoying these streams in their natural state. One dam
in neighboring Missouri was justified on the basis of "scenic visita-
tion," which claimed large benefits from the number of people who
would park their cars there to look at it. By the 1960s, dam building
in Arkansas was on a tear and the Buffalo was a constant contender
for a major Corps project, several projects, in fact.

Finally Arkansas drew the line, and it drew it at the Buffalo. In
the early 1970s Governor Faubus, sensing a new mood, refused to
approve the Corps' latest proposal to dam the river. Opposition to
the project was fueled by the media and a political cartoonist named
George Fisher who lampooned the Army engineers mercilessly, each
of his Corps officials wearing a "Keep Busy" button that captured
the build-or-die mind-set common to the construction bureaucracies.
Fisher's work was collected in a pamphlet entitled *U.S. Corps of Engineers Coloring Book* featuring two engineer chiefs on the cover congratulating each other on top of "Lake Arkansas," which had drowned
the entire state. The first cartoon inside showed an engineer holding a
large fish called "The Beautiful Buffalo" in one hand while he waved
a knife in the other and exclaimed, "Quit floppin! All I want to do is
GUT YOU!" I have a copy, dog-eared and timeless, to this day.

All of this is by way of explaining how and why the Buffalo River
was still up there waiting for us, one of the longest unobstructed rivers in the Mississippi watershed, when Cyprian turned twelve. I did
not tell him about the wipeout but this would be a very different
river, a fraction of the volume, more a pick-around-the-rocks run,
fun. Cyp was a quiet boy, supremely shy, we had paddled together on
meandering streams and he arrived at the point he could handle flat
water on his own, throw in a few steering moves. He would be in our

bow. We'd have two friends with us who had run the Buffalo several times. We bought new life jackets.

Stopping a dam, of course, on the Buffalo or anywhere else is never forever. The idea of damming something dammable never quite goes away. To the engineering mind it is always an unmet challenge, and to the many boosters who stand to profit from such a project it is money forgone, uselessly flowing downstream. In the 1960s, America came up with two genius ideas that confronted these impulses directly. The first was the concept of wilderness, simply leaving some parts of nature alone, and after a nine-year struggle it became the Wilderness Act, setting aside lands from development of all kinds except the most passive forms of recreation. The act defined wilderness as areas "where the earth and the community of life are untrammeled by man, where man himself is a visitor who does not remain," sheer poetry. To its opponents, of course, it was sheer idiocy: Like we humans do not rule? Upping the ante a few years later, a green Congress enacted the Wild and Scenic Rivers Act, which allowed for compatible riverside development but flatly prohibited the one use that altered them forever: dams. It is some testimony to the public passion for the Buffalo that this one and Maine's Saint John were the nation's first two rivers to enter the system.

Looking back on Cyp's trip to the Buffalo, it is anomalous that what I best remember is what he ate on the long drive up, and how we built a fire. Everything about this run was a surprise. Come late spring, water levels on the Buffalo were down to ideal, no longer pushy but enough volume to float over its rocks and ledges. The weatherman said fair skies through the weekend. The red bud trees had gone into leaf but pink rhododendrons and white dogwood blossoms stood out from the edging woods like wedding gowns. We packed on a Thursday eve, picked up Cyp from school that Friday, and began the drive North. We'd arrive early the next morning and sleep in the woods before putting in.

It actually took a bit longer because we were pulled over around midnight for going forty-five miles an hour in an unmarked speed zone, but there is no contesting the law under circumstances like this so we pooled $180 together and went on. If that's the way small towns in Arkansas made their living, it seemed preferable to robbery by force. We stopped at the next diner we found open and sat down at the counter, Mike and Tuffy ordering hamburgers. Cyp was next in line. He had never eaten meat in his life, rejecting nearly all foods but yogurt and cheese, but asked what he would have in the presence of these three grown men, he being one of them now, doing a grown-up thing, he said in the barest of voices, "hamburger." I froze, not daring to disturb the equilibrium in any way. I said hamburger too, although I really wanted something else. He ate half of his. Tuffy helped him finish, trading bites. The earth moved.

The last surprise came the following night. We'd had an easy float that first day, the river winding past bluffs, caves, and waterfalls that shot down from height into deep pools, small rapids adding their own little pleasures as if playing along with us. I let Cyp take the stern at one point and he did fine, me steering a few times from the bow. We set up camp at a bend and Mike and Tuffy took the low ground by the river, next to a tiny creek, very pretty, very near the boats. Cyp and I went up to a ledge with a slight slant, but tenable. The stars were clear when we went to bed. The rain woke us a few hours later. It was so unexpected I thought it might be insects, rain was not in the playbook. Looking out, the sky was black dark and the patter of drops was thickening. A little while later I heard Tuffy hauling the canoes up to higher ground and Mike moving their gear to join us on the ledge. The Buffalo was rising.

By morning the trip was looking grim. The river had turned from shallow and clear to high and brown, wiping out the small drops but turning others into lions whose hunger we could hear well ahead. The weather had settled into one of those steady rains that promised to last all day, perhaps the week. You can keep dry in these conditions for about twenty-four hours, taking good care, but we were wet already and had another full day ahead. We decided to abort. Tuffy and Mike would go back for the cars. Cyp and I would stay with the canoes and gear, and soon found ourselves wet, cold, and alone in a campground that had been stripped clean by previous parties. Puddles swamped much of the site and any hint of firewood had long been eliminated, tree limbs cut, not a twig on the ground. Cyp was shivering in the way that hugging cannot stop and we could only jog around for warmth for so long before running out of gas. I had one book of matches in my dry bag, a couple of receipts from the diner, and the toilet paper roll. Anything else to burn we'd have to find out here in the rain.

It may be the best fire I have ever made. To be sure, I have made bigger ones. When I was young my brother and I nearly burned down the local gasoline station with a fire we'd started in a field nearby and somehow leaped up into the pines. This one, however, on the Buffalo, was both urgent and seemingly impossible. We went back to first principles, the dry stuff would be under the wet stuff, so we would have to go out deep into the woods, tear off wet bark, lift rocks, reach into crevasses, and dig it out, piece by piece, and stick it under our clothing for safekeeping, right next to the skin. Cyp enjoyed the hunt, it was like finding Easter eggs, and he slowly accumulated a little nest of leaves and sticks that could, in pinch, maybe, catch fire. I concentrated on step two, slightly larger sticks that would cover the first like a teepee, and then larger sticks yet that, even if wet, would provide more shelter and eventually dry from the heat below.

We found cover along a rock face and I strung up our tent fly soggy and low over us, kneeling below, constructing our little twig house. At the last moment, I crumpled in the cardboard toilet roll and the diner receipts and got out the matches. The trick, I told Cyp, was keeping the matchbox dry; a couple of drops on the striking board would end the game. The first match puffed out. The second took, and lit the receipts, then the cardboard roll, which flared up steadily for long enough to catch some leaves, which caught some twigs and it was magical, it was like in a book, it was the way engineers must feel when something they build goes up in the air, it worked. When Mike and Tuffy returned we waved them over to the fire, which was something less than roaring but terribly friendly. I still feel proud of that one.

The Buffalo remains a protected river, the leader in a network of more than 150 Wild and Scenic Rivers to date. The security they enjoy, however, will hold only so long as people want them to. Congress can take a river out of the Wild and Scenic System whenever it wishes, for whatever reason it wishes. It can also authorize a dam on whatever river it wishes, protected or no. It can open up protected wildlife ranges in Alaska for oil and gas development, and is under continuing pressure to do so. The Buffalo and all rivers, and all wilderness, and entire ecosystems, and an increasing number of living things at this juncture, are as safe as we let them be and no more. Some find that a comforting thought. We are the species in charge. Some find it proof of our proximity to God. I do not find it either one.

HORN ISLAND
Mississippi, 1988

I tried writing about this trip one night but it fell into fragments, nothing pointed the way. I lay in bed the next morning aware that sunlight was coming in the window but still dreaming. A man dressed in black stood at the foot of the bed, barefoot, holding an oboe and surrounded by water, facing away. He was playing a soft downward scale, holding the first note, over and over. At his feet were a number of children, puffed up and resting on stilt legs and toes like shorebirds. You could hear them rustling. Behind them the sound of waves.

Suddenly, the man came rowing toward me, no boat, no oars, but he swayed between his knees and his arms pulled hard. He had jettisoned his jacket and his white shirt was blowing in the wind, as was his hair, unkempt and out of control. Reaching the beach the man stood up, raised one arm, and made flapping motions while unfastening a watch from his wrist. Still following the arm in flight, one barely saw him toss his timepiece into the sand, gone. He lifted both arms to the sky, now exultant. I realized by now that this was Walter Anderson and that he had come to Horn Island.

Anderson was the most famous painter of the American South, and is much of the reason we still have Horn Island and not a private resort called something like Beauregard Estates. This small spit of land, separated from the mainland by a narrow sound, was his refuge and the inspiration of his life. His love, really. Even his wife would tell you that and she loved him as deeply as any mortal could through tumultuous years.

Anderson had died, swiftly and unexpectedly, about twenty years before Robert and I paddled out here. In the meantime, with pressure mounting to develop every square inch of sand on the Gulf Coast, a few dogged environmentalists, invoking Anderson's memory at every turn, lobbied hard to put Horn and sister islands into the national park system. This done, Horn became the site for an experiment to reintroduce a badly endangered species, the red wolf, into the wild. Here on Horn it would be away from the human species, except in the least intrusive ways. Which is also what drew us out here.

We kayak the six miles from Biloxi to the island, guided by porpoise who emerge in front of the bow and then race us forward, casting a playful eye from time to time. Who knows what they are thinking. That they are thinking something to do with us is undeniable. In the late 1950s, a Frenchman named Moitessier was engaged in a race of solo sailboats around the world. Rounding the reefs off New Zealand, he had set his rudder on a course to avoid them and dropped below for a bite to eat. He was brought back up by loud squealing noises and found himself surrounded by a pod of porpoise, frantic in the water. Seeing him on deck, they formed a perfect line, swam ahead of the boat, veered sharply right, and dove out of sight. Resurfacing, they repeated the maneuver, time after time. Puzzled, worried, Moitessier checked his bearings and found that the wind had shifted and was driving him straight toward the rocks. He made a quick adjustment and, instantly, the porpoise gathered around him, playful this time, one leapt into the air in a full somersault, and then they departed. All but two, who stayed with him, leading, just in case, until all danger was passed. What we do not know about the life around us is stunning.

We land on Horn Island without incident and are joined briefly by a reporter doing a story on winter camping. The sun is out and a photo shows us smiling. That is the last time we see sun for five days. We have only the gear we could stuff inside the kayaks and we will end up wearing every piece of it to stay warm, even to bed.

To Robert, the out of doors is a detective story. The following morning he stands outside our tarp in a light drizzle, staring at the flat, wet sand.

"It's a wolf," he says.

"Or maybe a dog," I say.

"There are no dogs out here," he says. "And look at the claws, very sharp and deep."

I have to admit, they do not look like dog paws. But I say that they look pretty small. And he says, red wolves are small too.

"And look at this," he adds with excitement, already walking beyond the perimeter. "Here is a circle. This one is casing us out."

Maybe there are two, I suggest.

"No way they'd send two into a situation this dangerous," he says. "Even if there were two, they'd send one in to check it out."

Wolves are a mystery of their own. Not as an animal, all creatures have their secrets, but in the way they trigger human beings. We did not eliminate them casually, while hunting for something else, or as with other wildlife by razing their habitats. We set out to exterminate them and nearly succeeded. A recent governor of Alaska claimed to have shot more than three hundred of them in a single month, from an airplane. It was considered an accomplishment.

It was also a war. We put bounties on their heads, laid out poisoned sheep for them to eat, trapped their trails, fumigated their dens, stomped their puppies under our boots, and hung their bodies on road signs and barbed wire fences. We hung their pelts on our office walls. We did some of these things to eagles, too, before it became a federal offense, but the wolf killing has been far more personal, else why all the display? It is said to protect calves and lambs, but the numbers killed by wolves are miniscule and have been compensated by the government for decades. It is said they reduce deer and moose populations, the first of which are so numerous they constitute a nuisance and the latter of which, as populations, are doing just fine. Even if one finds nothing wrong with killing one wild animal so that we can enjoy killing more of another, that cannot fully explain what is happening here. Whatever it is, it is profound and it drove the red wolf, like its cousins, to the brink.

Of all the paintings of Walter Anderson, I have seen none of wolves. That is probably because he painted what he saw and we had eliminated them across the South before his time, but it is interesting to speculate what he might have done with the subject, so charged with its own testosterone. Anderson's works swim with pelicans, fish, crabs, and alligators . . . so stylized that they seem almost Egyptian, but always recognizable as nature. After a few days on Horn Island Robert and I begin to enter Anderson's world, the pelicans float motionless as cutouts in the sky, the waves are triangles of light. Anderson would row out here in a small boat with his own tarp and a handful of food, meeting storms that might last for days and other stretches so placid he must have been lulled into dreams. That is the Anderson we know. The other one was possessed.

Agnes Grinstead Anderson, his wife from early years until his death, has written a memoir of their marriage, one of the most bipolar experiences imaginable. A daughter of privilege, she was swept away by the fire in this young man and remained that way for life. They had several children, he loved them all, but he journeyed in and out of the rational world increasingly erratic over time, leaving for Horn Island without warning, then leaving the state without warning, never unfaithful but more and more alone. Early in their years together, when he returned unannounced from Horn smelling of muck, marsh, and guano, she asked "where in God's name" he had been, to which he replied, getting unwashed into bed, "in heaven!" Years later she went up by train to extract him from an asylum on the East Coast and was persuaded to join him on a return trip down the Ohio and Mississippi to New Orleans, by canoe. It was after all, he told her, all downstream. She was game. He nearly killed her.

They camped an evening along the Ohio, the water cold as ice, and he took her into the water. Forcing her below the surface until she began to drown, he only released his hold as she stopped struggling and went limp. He was wildly excited, asking her how she felt. She said, struggling, that it was as if she were melting. "Rot!" he screamed at her. "Stop thinking! Can't you feel at all? . . . It was like finding yourself, your primal self, knowing exactly where you come from!" The primal Anderson had something in kind with the primal wolf. The question is whether we can live with either.

We skip breakfast that first morning on the beach, Robert and I. He is hot on the red wolf trail. The drizzle has slackened. Down the sand, on the Gulf side of the island, we find more tracks in a single line. Then they begin to stretch out.

"He's running now," says Robert, "he's onto something."

The tracks merge with other tracks, clearly a different animal, tiny front paws and large rear prints, a rabbit. There is a scuffle in the sand so wide it touches the water but we can find no tracks leading from it, as if both animals either went swimming or were lifted up by skyhook. We are left with the mystery.

"I say he got it," says Robert. "The fight reached the water, maybe waves washed it away." "Besides," he muses, "once the wolf has seized it, how is a rabbit going to win?"

We go back to eat under the tarp, the fire struggling bravely against the rain. We share a speckled trout caught yesterday, six packs of instant oatmeal, and hot tea, sequentially, all in the same cup. You get less picky out here.

In the 1970s, with few red wolves remaining in the wild, the government started bringing them in to protect and breed them. It was a dicey process. Due to crossover with coyotes and genetic drift they were down to the functional equivalent of eight creatures. I visited a species survival center near New Orleans during this time and passed the red wolf enclosure. A female was lying on top of a low mound, nothing else in the cage. I was told that she had whelped a litter the month before and had since eaten them all. Which is what stressed animals do.

Mixing and matching genes to maximize diversity, the government grew its captive stock into double figures, and then began step two, reintroduction. That too was dicey, the released creatures falling afoul of hunters, dogs, automobiles, and the hazards of a changed environment. In the 1980s, Horn Island became a way station between the breeding cages and the uncontrolled wild, wild in red wolf terms meaning places where humans ran free. Here, they had the island to themselves. It worked and several young adults were eventually released in the Carolinas, but after a few years the Horn Island operation was shut down due to "the likelihood of encounters" with people. Horn itself was becoming a hot spot.

In a way, Walter Anderson died at the right time, when his beloved island was still wild and rarely accessed by the people of the Mississippi coast. That phenomenon ended with recreational motorboats that grew ever larger and made access to the island a matter of forty minutes and a half tank of gas. Spring through fall, and particularly in high summer, Horn began hosting a lineup of motor craft anchored a few yards out into the sound and sending country music into the sky. After a full weekend of partying, with the wind calm and the wave action down, the waters smelled of motor oil, and trash was floating ashore. It was doubtless a good time, and innocent enough as well, but Horn was no longer ideal for a reclusive creature on the edge of extinction.

Years later the BP oil spill also visited these same beaches and teams from all over the country arrived for cleanup and to assess the resource damages. The first thing they remarked on was not the oil slick, which sank largely under the sand, but the trash. They might of course say the same of New Orleans or the country roads north of Lake Pontchartrain. People are not a Mississippi thing; they are a people thing. Down here, though, they can seem more people-like than usual.

Robert and I move camp several times that week, driven by the weather. When the wind is up we go to the shelter of the trees, which is easy to do, we have little more than a tarp. When the wind dies, which can be sudden, we move back to the beach to escape the mosquitoes and catch whatever breeze remains. Wherever we string the tarp we find wolf tracks in the morning. We stay up at night hoping to see them, but they seem to know that too and stay away. In the morning Robert rolls out of his sleeping bag, heads for the perimeter, and returns saying, "Darn it, Ollie, they did it again!"

But I do not think that he was in the least displeased. He was happy that they were here and equally glad that they didn't come in, didn't even allow us a glimpse. "If they avoid us," he said, "they will avoid others," and that is the only hope they have. As of this writing, red wolves are hanging on in North Carolina, perhaps one hundred in the wild. It is the only relocation of a wolf so far that does not face a human population wanting to make them extinct again as soon as possible. Even if the Carolinas are less hostile it is still risky to have all of these eggs in one basket, but so far that is as far as we have come. Hopeful and at risk, it is the new state of nature.

HORTON RIVER
Northwest Territories, 1993

In 1845, Sir John Franklin set sail from England in search of a passage across North America. His two ships carried the force of empire behind them and were outfitted with the latest in steam engines, armor plating, retractable rudders to avoid iceberg damage, and an ingenious new heating system to accommodate the crews. One hundred and twenty-nine men died. Not one survived. The Franklin voyage and its mysteries have prompted more search and scientific expeditions than any other in history, to say nothing of dissertations, poetry, theater, television specials, and the song "Northwest Passage," known as the unofficial anthem of Canada. In Bathurst Inlet, where the Horton River meets the Arctic Ocean, lies Franklin Bay.

In 1993, several of us paddled the Horton to its delta through some of the most dramatic scenery on the continent. Rising in a small interior lake of the same name, it flows across rolling tundra, enters a canyon with turbulent drops and finicky routes around them, then opens broadly, slackens its pace, and winds past hills that slough toward the water. You can see these hills a long way coming because they are on fire. They have been on fire for at least hundreds, and perhaps thousands, of years. The trouble we would run into up here, however, unlike Franklin's, came less from the elements than from ourselves.

The Franklin expedition was driven by a single objective, the Far East, and a single problem, a route through this confounding landmass in the way. Like Jacques Cartier, Christopher Columbus, and Henry Hudson before him, then the redoubtable Captain John Smith, even Lewis and Clark's Corps of Discovery, his mission was to discover which waters linked to the Pacific and to spices, silks, and porcelain so fine it took china for its name. The Portuguese captain Giuseppe Veranzano had raised expectations centuries earlier by reporting that, no sooner had he probed the Atlantic coast, than he spotted a large body of water to the west. It had to be the ocean. It was probably the Chesapeake Bay instead. From then forward, the "Bay of Veranzano" became the mythic passage, its putative location shifting slowly northward as southern routes came up dry. "A protean body of water," wrote the historian Bernard de Voto, "as extensible and as migratory on the map as it was illusory, was called the Western Sea. It was not far away. It was only a few days journey farther on." Logic and desire demanded it. Imperial designs demanded it. This faith-based geography retained its grip on the Western mind well past the Renaissance, great leaps in science, and the onset of the Industrial Revolution. Franklin was sent out to clinch it, once and for all.

Franklin Bay today has little to catch the eye. We made our last camp up high on the shore. An Inuit village nearby had long been abandoned, although the outlines of their stone huts endured. Inhabiting these dwellings for a weekend would be challenging enough; for an eight-month winter was unimaginable. Next to them lay an old Canadian radar station, part of the Cold War warning system of the 1950s, disintegrating slowly in piles of rusty equipment. We walked over to the station together and, uninterested in the wreckage, I continued up the coast. I welcomed the solitude. It would be an easy walk, jolted by a moment when whether I lived or died did not depend on me at all.

The end came for Sir John Franklin in the summer of 1847, after spending two hard winters with his ship locked in the ice at the same location, unable to move. He was an experienced commander. He had fought in the Napoleonic Wars, ruled over British-held Tasmania, and even managed to make it to the Battle of New Orleans. He was no stranger either to the Canadian North, having undertaken a brutal exploration on foot that cost the lives of half his men and led to the nickname, bestowed by his Indian guides, "the man who ate his boots." He led another expedition down the Mackenzie River, running parallel to the Horton only a few days' journey away. The reports and diaries make gripping reading. He and other explorers, approaching the Northwest Passage from both west and east, had narrowed the unknown down to a stretch of a few hundred miles. He would sail through and complete the map.

It was, withal, a strange quest. The Northwest Passage would stake no claim to resources and set no stage for colonies. No resources were then known to the Arctic beyond snow and ice, and the prospects for Europeans living in these climes had winked out with failed settlements on Greenland centuries before. Finding a way through neither assured control of the passage nor even a legal basis for claiming it. Nor was it a year-round Panama Canal. Any ships using it, from either end, could anticipate a full winter frozen in the ice in between, hardly a business plan for trade. The quest was basically about glory. It was the space race of its time, equally costly and in the end more deadly. For the individuals involved, though, it was also about another impulse that wells up from the accounts of Franklin, Scott, Shackleton, and so many others who went to both wintry poles, repeatedly, and even died there: the harsh magnetism of this frozen water world.

The anomaly of our brief Horton paddle was that it started so well. We were four men and two women, which kept the testosterone level down. We were well led and organized for contingencies, there were no mistakes. Using other names here to avoid the suggestion of offense, my diary contains entries like, "We played pipe and harmonica after dinner. Daniel and I did the Cajun two-step"; "Patricia and Steve made dinner this evening, a tortellini with wine sauce and a rum cake for desert"; "Allan told a shaggy dog story about a farmer and an elephant; it took quite a while." The diary notes eagles fishing, peregrine falcons stooping, jaegers that passed over our heads at one campsite screaming like jet fighters, then turning to do it again. One morning I listed the wildflowers within reach of the tent and ran up a baker's dozen. A week and a half into the venture an entry reads, "When does this thing get hard?" In a physical sense, by comparison with others, it never did. We all got tired, I lost a tooth, others fell ill for a day or two, but physical was not the issue.

Had Franklin approached his last bite from the west he'd surely have wintered over at Franklin Bay. Several ships did just that, one on a search for him in 1850 noting that "on the 4th [of September], large fires were seen on the shore, and at first supposed to be lighted by the natives to attract attention." Realizing, however, that such firewood was not available, and certainly not likely to be squandered, a party was sent to examine them and found smoke "strongly impregnated with sulphur" emerging from rents in the ground "resembling lime-kilns." When the sailors returned to the ship they placed a sample of the smoldering rock on the captain's desk. It burnt a hole in it. These were the Smoking Hills, the unique and defining features of the lower Horton. A deep layer of lignite ignites of its own accord apparently and burns rain or shine, fanned by constant winds, for one can only guess how far back in time. The hills run for nearly fifty miles. We canoed by them into the wind and a thin drizzle, there was little alive on either bank, the water was turbid with ash, the last living fish were miles behind or ahead in the Arctic Ocean. My diary reads, "It is like paddling through Mordor."

Franklin approached from the east, however, as was only natural. That was the European side, and the eastern approach through Baffin Bay was well-known and oft-traveled. The trouble came beyond Baffin because the waterways narrowed and froze solid in winter. Franklin's problem, unpredictable, improbable, was that for the entire summers of '46 and '47 these passes never thawed. He had provisions for three full years, this expedition sailed fully equipped, but the food was hastily canned and the seals did not hold. Worse, they were made of lead and samples from bodies found years later showed high toxic levels. Lead piping was also used in the vaunted heating system. Lead poisoning has its own pathology, which includes wing-droop in the limbs and the impairment of brain functions. The last notes recovered from the expedition were bizarre, jumping from "all is well" to chaos in a scant few weeks. When Franklin expired from unknown causes, his body never found, the surviving crews left their ships for a desperate run inland toward outposts that lay hundreds of miles away. Inuit histories report the sight of forty men stumbling forward in a blizzard. They sought no Inuit help. None was given. There is evidence, knife marks on bone, of cannibalism. Perhaps it is better we not know.

The breakdown of our Horton paddle faced no such obstacles, not even close, not even for a moment. Small differences simply got bigger, when we would set out in the morning, how we cooked, hot rinse or cold, routines that on extended ventures act as pacemakers, the order of our lives. Personal quirks, who snored like a chain saw, who stayed up late, began to hiccup and get in the way. We all tried to keep it together but there were times when one of us would walk by without speaking, take a dinner bowl, and move away. Playing "Dixie" on the harmonica didn't do the trick. Nor did a chocolate cake. Up on the Horton, even the canoes seemed at a loss. It had never happened to me before, nor has it since, but in environments like this it does happen.

Some years later I read an account of ten robust Americans who traveled to the north woods to winter over, in isolation. They built a solid cabin, the snow set in, they hunkered down, and then the gremlins appeared, all the small grievances magnified as if under a great lens. They began bickering and when, of all misfortunes, a Russian sputnik crashed nearby, bringing out Canadian air force helicopters and an invasion of engineers, they fell apart. It doesn't take a sputnik to do this. Their group was on its way out anyway. The miracle of Shackleton's survival off the South Pole, saving each of his men under the most harrowing circumstances, is that he kept them together. The same seems required for life in submarines or travel in space, next said to be slated for Mars. As for me, I will decline that trip in advance. So long as I get my daily walk in the concrete yard, I'd rather go to jail. I could not hold up.

The Franklin debacle prompted a frenzy of search and rescue. For a few years it was funded by the British government, and later by his widow. Her photo survives, wide eyes, soft smile, a décolletage so deep it would frown foreheads today in the American heartland, all hiding a steely determination to find and vindicate her husband. Many more died. Still, expeditions continue to this day. The Franklin legend is that powerful.

Scientific expeditions also continue to the Smoking Hills. All are struck by the phenomenon, of course, and by their curious role in the lives of the caribou nearby. One venture reports that in 1975, 1979, and again in 1984, "when the weather was hot and the air very still," the "entire herd, led by a number of old bulls, streamed towards the fumigations, running hard." They ran among the expedition's tents, "young and old together, into the dense smoke plumes, and stayed in the smoke for several hours, during which their grunting and coughing were quite audible." They were seeking relief from the black flies. The Inuit did the same. We built smudge fires too, and they worked.

That last evening, my walk up the coast had a healthy breeze. The insects were down. I carried a small camcorder to film the wildflowers, which would be the most pleasing features for Lisa. Sometimes I think that being alone in the wild, just the fact of it, brings marvels. When I turned away from the coast to return cross-country I came on a valley, flat as a table, through which a stream ran to the bay. The valley was in peak season, when everything living is eating, breeding, and rearing in a frenzy because there is so little time. We had seen a few caribou along the Horton, single or in pairs, but the floodplain ahead was suddenly crawling with hundreds of these big animals in motion, thin-legged and elegant, some with outsized racks on their heads, the sound of distant bugling, all moving toward the sea. I was witnessing the fabled migration. I did not even think to film them. I just stood there saying "thanks," although there was no one near me for miles.

An hour or so later, walking over the tundra, I fell into a broad patch of Indian paint brush and Labrador tea, bright red and white, and began to film them intently, seeing nothing else. Topping a hump I looked up to see the largest grizzly God ever made, deep brown, in a depression no more than ten yards away, facing away, feeding. Its neck rippled with strength. I'd only seen *Ursus horribilis* once before in my life, through binoculars, on a far mountainside and ambling away. I could smell this one. The wind was coming directly at me which could have been my salvation. I dropped ever so slowly to my knees, and then flat on my stomach, burying my head in the grass. I stayed there for an eternity, not moving a muscle, thinking about grizzly advice I'd heard, do not run, do not face it down, the options seemed extremely limited. I waited another eternity. I dared not lift my head for a look. I do not remember saying a word but that would not be accurate, because in my panic I had pressed the camcord recorder button and until the film runs out I can be heard whispering "oh shit, oh shit," over and over. Thinking back, I would hate for that phrase, among all the others possible, to have been my last words on earth. I have no yen to go back today. The Horton River like many sub-Arctic runs has become a popular adventure catered by outfitters with table stoves, satellite communications, and camp stools. Better this, I tell myself, than pipelines and open pit mines although these, too, are booming up here these days. With a warming climate the Northwest Passage is opening for navigation the year around and multinational corporations are vying with each other to claim everything above the earth and underneath. I am grateful to have seen it before, in the last stages of its before. I feel the same way about Louisiana, where I now live. There are times I feel the same way about the world.

But other days are brighter.

PEARL RIVER
Louisiana, 1993

Hugh has his boat off the car and wanders over to where a man is fishing, white, thin beard, baseball cap, whipping the water with his lure. He is looking pointedly away from the other side of the landing where a black family is fishing as well, their truck door open and the radio on high. They are in lawn chairs and are drinking sodas, letting their plastic bobbers float out and do the work. The white fisherman is nearer and I hear Hugh say, "What are you catching?" before he is out of earshot and I go back to unstrapping my canoe.

Hugh returns a few minutes later and I ask him how the fellow was doing. Hugh looks me in the eye, all poker face, and instead of answering my question says in a low voice, "There's a meetin' tonight."

"A meetin'?" I ask.

"That's what he says . . . there's a meetin'." Just a hint of a smile. Hugh never overplays his hand. And then it comes to me.

We are out here by the Pearl River about an hour from New Orleans and in as different a place as you could find without taking the plane. It is a broad, forested swamp, fast currents braiding through on their way to the Gulf. It is also the still-beating heart of the Klan.

Two years before this trip Edwin Edwards, a former governor of Louisiana and an all-but-convicted felon—the conviction came later—was running for reelection against David Duke, the Ku Klux Clan leader and a fan of Adolf Hitler. Absurdly improbable, but there you have it. Such were our ballot choices that bumper stickers in New Orleans read VOTE FOR THE CROOK, ITS IMPORTANT! The bumper stickers and lawn signs over toward the Pearl read quite differently, and all the same name, DAVID DUKE. Some remain to this day. But for the New Orleans vote against him, The Grand Imperial Wizard would have governed the state.

It is this mix of the beautiful and the menacing that haunts the

Pearl. You are never that far from either one. It is one of the longest, unspoiled rivers in the United States, nearly 450 miles on the main trunk and five times that in tributaries, with only one dam upstream and very little encroachment. This is wet country and water levels can come up ten feet in thirty hours, flooding out close-by communities too slow to get the picture, unprotected to their apparent surprise by names like River Ridge and Highland Park. The very volatility of the Pearl has allowed the wildlife to flourish and on the opening day of hunting season bodies of white-tailed deer lie draped over the fenders of local trucks at country gas stations, waiting their turn to be skinned and dressed inside. The Pearl also harbors one of the most ancient and least abundant fish known to man, the Gulf Sturgeon, which is where Hugh comes in. He wants to bring the sturgeon back.

Putting your boat into the Pearl from the west side you cross a canal built by the Army Corps of Engineers many decades ago. Although quite unintended, the canal has become a paddler's dream because at any point you can canoe up the canal, pop into the swamp, meander down its passes, and come out where you left the car. You can do it alone and I have come to do it that way often, not counting my dog, whom even this day, at fifteen years, I would not think of leaving at home. Her eyes have turned glaucous and her hearing requires something near a gunshot to get her attention, but out on the Pearl she perks up like a puppy, ears up, nose twitching, sensing the air and things out beyond my sight that I cannot not even imagine are here.

Unfortunately, the canal has nearly exterminated the sturgeon. The project was dubious from the start. As early as the 1880s the Corps was dredging the main river in an attempt to turn the small town of Bogalusa, eighty miles upstream, into an inland port. In 1935 Corps engineers were authorized to build this artificial waterway alongside it, armed with three locks to handle the expected shipping boom. Which never came to pass. The myriad small businesses that were said ready to use it ran out of product or closed their doors. Then came a rail line, faster and on dry land, clouding, one would think, the canal's future. In the 1950s, however, undaunted by sinking economics, the Corps built several large sills across the Pearl and its lower tributaries that steered a steady flow of water into the canal for the hypothetical and still-hoped-for boom in navigation. The barriers succeeded in diverting the water but provided no new customers and by 1970 the entire project was abandoned, but left in place. Including the sills. Which reduced the living space of the Gulf sturgeon from more than two thousand miles of water to fewer than fifty, all in the main channel. A gigantic, reclusive, and bottom-dwelling species, it couldn't get by the sills.

Paddling down the main Pearl or poking through its backwaters you are unlikely to see a sturgeon. They are way down deep. Even the people studying them rarely see them unless one gets snagged in a trawl. They did see several recently when a pulp and paper mill in Bogalusa spilled a flood of toxins and killed out the river for miles. Thousands of fish died, there is no real count, but the dozen or so big sturgeons floating dead on the surface were hard to miss, and more than most biologists would see in their lifetimes. All this fish requires is deep holes, clean water, and a little peace, but those demands seem very hard for humans to meet.

The Gulf sturgeon is threatened all along the Gulf coast, and a sister species, the Alabama sturgeon, is so badly endangered that we are not even sure they still exist. No one can find them. The government captured six of them in the 1990s for breeding but they were all males, and they all died. What the sturgeon in the Pearl need, and badly, is to remove the sills. You would think that would be rather easy. Hugh has been banging on the Corps over this over the past ten years without success. There are always other priorities.

Going into the Pearl invariably brings surprises. This particular weekend, as if sprung from thin air, three-inch banana spiders are out in force and stretching their webs between standing trees, the water swirling below. How they get from one tree to the next across these currents to string their traps is a miracle of acrobatics, but there they are ahead of us, head-high, the heavy fibers of the webs catching the light like fishing nets. Striking one face-first is unpleasant enough, throw in that the guarding spider will be rushing toward your head to repair the breach. Lisa and I were paddling through here the previous year, her birthday in fact, I believe I told her the trip would be idyllic, and ran into a wall of webs that had her slashing wildly with her paddle to break them and me struggling to keep the canoe right side up. I didn't, we flipped, and the only thing I could think of saying as we tried to right it in the water was "happy birthday." On the instant trip, Hugh and I each paddling solo, he pauses before a grid of webs and says, "after you."

Farther down we pass a cutoff toward a lake that I found once and have not been able to since. Nor do we this trip. I had paddled in alone that earlier time, winter was waning and the big wading birds, egret and heron, were beginning to choose mates and construct nests high in the trees. Poking the canoe toward the west, trying to feel my way back to the canal, I entered a promising current that wound back and then slowly lost its verve. The warning sign in a river swamp is still water ahead, which means that nothing is flowing out of it, which means that you won't either. I had emerged onto an interior pond ringed by downed limbs and debris that at lower water stages lay on dry land. We stayed quiet, Ms. Bear and I, looking for an opening and at that moment were greeted with large shrieks overhead. The entire canopy exploded with large, flapping birds, rising and falling from half-built nests of sticks and branches, surprised, panicked, their droppings raining down around us. We sat quiet as stones and, after a while, they started coming back. There were several dozen of them, white, slate-blue, green, gray, four in this tree, seven in the next, one guarding its territory while a mate flew in with new building supplies. I could have stayed the day. Somehow I knew that once we left this spot we'd not see it again. I had no good idea how I'd wandered in.

I've come across these mystery places all my life, completely unexpected and now completely gone. A dance hall south of Baltimore that played live polkas over illuminated tiles on the floor. A hollow covered by rhododendrons with a tiny waterfall, someplace off the Appalachian Trail. This rookery joined them. I suppose that a GPS device would have answered the question had they been around at the time, but there are things in life where finding them again is not the point.

In the late 1990s, pushed by Bogalusa again and a congressional delegation only too willing to treat its constituents to free federal water projects, the Corps proposed once more to dredge the main Pearl for, as if no one had read the previous scripts, a projected boom in navigation. The Engineers came up with figures that purported to show that the benefits from all that new traffic would exceed the costs. Hugh and another attorney brought a lawsuit to spare the remaining Pearl River sturgeon on the bottom of this stretch and about to be scooped out by bucket dredges the size of steam shovels. It turned out that the Corps' figures were based on telephone calls to businesses in the area asking how many tons they would like to put on the river were it dredged, for free. As could be expected this method produced some wild numbers. Hugh had a chart for the trial showing current tonnage, about a quarter-inch high, and projected tonnage at nearly a foot.

The Pearl project was hardly alone in this regard. Many Corps navigation canals throughout the South—the Red River Waterway, the Tennessee-Tombigbee—predicted staggering benefits that never materialized, hardly a trickle. They carry the names of proud congressmen who rammed them through, the Bennett Johnston Waterway, the Tom Bevill Lock and Dam. And they kill rivers. Ultimately, the Pearl dredging was stopped not by its humbug numbers, which should have done it in, but by the endangered sturgeon, which of course took the heat. Headline: Fish Stops Progress.

Hugh and I come out of the swamp at Lock 3 near an island where the local Klan killed a young woman it had recently enticed over from Texas for an induction ceremony. They must have been desperate; I didn't even know the Klan accepted women. According to the newspaper the woman was mentally disturbed and easily persuaded but once here, apparently daunted by the dark of night, the bonfire, the men in hoods and the awesome isolation, alarm bells went off in her head and she began begging to leave. So they shot her. Then they dug a hole and buried her, and left. That very night, though, one of the younger members, himself mentally challenged as it turned out, told a friend about it, who told another friend, and they all ended up on trial. Very few people up here are Klansmen, I would guess. Very few. But there is an undercurrent that speaks its language and it cannot be denied. And yet. Coming out that evening Hugh is in a kayak and well ahead of me, smelling the barn. I have caught the slows and am enjoying the late day light, my dog up in the front like a statue and surveying the scene. As we pull into the landing a small fishing boat is putting out, white guy, ball cap, gray hair, and skin that has seen a lot of weather. He idles his motor, letting us go by, Ms. Bear just off his bow. We are alone here, the three of us. He examines the dog passing before him and then turns to me and says, deadpan, "Don' he paddle?" Just the hint of a smile.

This is also the Pearl, and it cannot be denied. It is sometimes difficult to carry both of them in my head at the same time.

GREEN RIVER
Utah, 1994

Maj. John Wesley Powell and his tiny expedition were in trouble. They had lost half of their rations, all of the sugar, and had begun sifting bugs from the flour through a mosquito net and setting out spoiled bacon to dry. The water roared by like an animal. Canyon walls stretched above them to the clouds. "We have an unknown distance yet to run," Powell wrote in his diary, "an unknown river to explore. What falls there are, we know not, what rocks beset the channel we know not, what walls ride over the water we know not." They went on down. They had been battered upstream on the Green. They were now on the Colorado. As late as 1870 this was all terra incognita, a huge blank spot on the map of the American West. He was commissioned to fill it in.

The Green's canyons, still unspoiled, are one of the most stunning runs in the country negotiable by open boat canoe. Float maps show more than one hundred rapids in as many miles, some of them walks in the park, others requiring a good look no matter what the guidebooks say. And so it was that on a week in late summer when the water levels had dropped and commercial rafting parties had left in search of bigger prey, we went as a family with some former students and a copy of Powell's diary to take a small taste of his historic run. It remains a lovely memory and I mean no disrespect to the river or to the memory of the intrepid Maj. Powell when I say, however, that the most indelible moments of our own trip were the blunders. Like most mistakes in my life, they seemed so logical at the time. I have to conclude that had I been in charge of outfitting Powell's expedition I might have lost them all.

I erred on the rental car before we even arrived. A neighbor had recommended a second-hand vehicle as the way to go, he used the term "rent-a-wreck" which I assumed was a euphemism. On the telephone, the price for a used van in Salt Lake City certainly seemed right. Once at the airport, however, no one seemed to recognize the address. I ignored the warning sign. Leaving the family with Eric, who had driven up from Albuquerque, I hired a taxi and went looking. As it turned out the rental office was not in Salt Lake at all. It was in a trailer on a dirt lot some twenty miles out of town. What appeared to be my van was parked by an old station wagon, near the door. As I entered the trailer a family speaking Spanish was signing papers and receiving their key. They went out past me, entered the van, and drove away. I asked if that wasn't my van. The manager said not to worry, he had an even better deal on the station wagon. I looked doubtful. He said, the deal is even better than what we just told you. It was. In fact, it would cost less than the charge for a cab ride back, which had already cost me a fortune. I ignored this warning sign as well.

We were staging at the University of Utah. The recreation department would rent us the canoes. The day was shimmering hot, and by the time I finally pulled into the campus the rental wagon was boiling over. Blue coolant spread over the asphalt and surrounded the car in a pool. Lisa came out with both boys, for whom it was a good joke. Dad's done it again, said Gabe, and I saw his point. As it turned out the boil-over was a Godsend. Tomorrow's drive to the Green was about eighty miles and the last stretch dropped over rocks and ledges. We would have lost the rent-a-wreck within yards of the highway and abandoned it like furniture on the trail. We arranged for a Utah student to drive us out in his pickup instead.

That night the Utah football team arrived for fall practice. They came in driving motorcycles and Mustang convertibles, roaring at idle in the parking lot. Within minutes they were surrounded by young women in tank tops, heels, and what might have been shorts—members of a welcoming committee, I suggested to Lisa—appearing out of the night like moths and pairing off in twos, threes, and fours. The dorm halls were made of echo-box linoleum and tile. We didn't miss a beat. I dozed off into nightmares about the station wagon and at first light I was driving it back to the rental trailer—at least they hadn't relocated yet—the motor red hot, radiator water gone, its working parts about to seize. At least I hoped so. Then I spent another fortune cabbing back to campus.

We crowded into the back of the pickup for the ride to the river, holding onto the canoes so they wouldn't fly off into the subdivisions that stretched east from Salt Lake behind a series of exotic facades, Runnymede, the Hacienda, and a cluster with small mansard roofs called something like Equantine. When the houses finally ended there was rock, dirt, an endless decline, and, finally, the Green.

The very names of the canyons ahead, Desolation and Gray, give some idea of the impression they make. In places they seem to join overhead. The sun reaches down late in the morning and its glancing light turns the rock walls on and off throughout the day, bright reds and yellows sliding back into shadow. For most of the nineteenth century, even after railroads had joined the Atlantic to the Pacific and conquered the high plateau of the Colorado, no one had gone down these rivers; no one even knew where they went. The falls were daunting and required Powell's men to rappel their dories forward as down a cliff, hauled in by lines below. Lugging a heavy telescope and barometric equipment, the Major scaled the walls one-handed to take his sightings and shout them to a scribe. His maps remain accurate guides today. His diaries rival any in American history. Unfortunately, his recommendations for keying western development to available water were buried by their opponents, surfacing again only recently like a letter overdue in the mail.

Our first evening we set aside Powell's writings to study the owner's manual on the use of our portable latrine, in river language, the groover. On previous trips west we had used a dry bucket with plastic sacks within sacks, layered in lime, and although the container became heavy it was easy to use and it worked. This year, however, the government required a chemical waste system so Eric rounded up a loaner, second-hand. Which became our third error.

The days were beautiful, the sun shining through occasional sprinkles of rain, evening stories around the fire pan, but as time went by odors from the chemical groover became a presence of their own.

Mike, who had played football at UCLA, cinched the lid until the plastic groaned but every day more exhalations leaked out into the high desert air.

The fifth day ended on a beach below Gray Canyon. Opposite rose a rock formation carved by wind into the head of an Egyptian queen and we slept there happily, open to the breeze and stars. At some late hour, however, the skies clouded over, the air hung low, and the groover, beating like a malignant heart, seemed to crawl over to join us on the sand. I woke up early, anxious to off-load it at a KOA Campground in the town of Green River. That is what the manual recommended: go to a commercial campground, pay the hook-up fee, wash out the groover, and finito. None of us had done it before, but how hard could that be?

First thing off the river we headed for the KOA, its triangle sign at the edge of town. The campground was a pretty place with green grass and bright trim, even the rocks were painted white. It looked like a miniature golf course. Eric, Mike, and I would rent a site, vacuum out, and be on our way in twenty minutes, max, while the others waited for us at the Dairy Queen. We found our site, number four, halfway up the drive under a cottonwood tree. It was perfect. Mike and I unloaded the groover and set it carefully on the cement pad. Eric found the hoses, the smaller for water in and the other for sucking the contents away. We attached them. Eric turned on the switch.

What happened next is a little hard to describe, and to this day I get different views. I remember feeling something swipe across my legs like a whisk broom, then go away, and then whisk me again. I looked down to see a stream of brown liquid shooting sideways from the top of the groover like a farm spreader, coating the campsite, rocks, table, and all. There are those of us who rise to a crisis and others who simply stand paralyzed and wait for the crash. Mike, a clear Type A, leaped to the top of the groover like King Kong, squeezing down the stream to a fine mist. Eric managed to reach the vacuum switch and turn it off. Dead silence on the campground. Campsite Number Four had become Blowout at the Mustard Factory. We examined our surroundings. Some visitors in an Airstream were lunching on the far side of what appeared to be the restroom. No one had come out of the office shack. There was still time.

We reacted as one. Lifting up the groover we ran to the latrine, slammed the door, and emptied the entire container into the first commode. Yet another error. The bowl quickly overflowed, spilled out onto the floor, and moved straight toward the door. Our communal brain still not functioning at peak, we took off our T-shirts and began to mop the slop toward the central drain, a three-inch-diameter grate that clogged within seconds and belched when we pried it open to jam more down the hole. In the distance we heard a door slam. It had to be the office. He would be coming over to take a look at Campsite Number Four. What else did he have to do that day, and why else would he leave the office?

Again, no one said a word. Like a beast with six legs we ran to the truck, threw the groover in the rear and were in third gear before reaching the highway, Eric pounding the steering wheel and saying, "Damn, they've got my credit card number!" The groover rolled around the back of his van all the way back to the University of Utah's football dorm, where we were to spend our last night and divvy up the gear. Which presented our final challenge.

Eric had to return the groover to its owner. He could not return it smelling like that, so we smuggled it into the shower room where he and I began to wash it out with Lisa's shampoo. It was like perfuming roadkill. As the hot water hit the groover, shampoo or no, the odor filled the room and attacked the walls. Grabbing wads of toilet paper we began wiping off the condensate but the stench was winning. We had to get out of there before somebody came. We won the race by a hair. Just as we were leaving a huge man, odds on a lineman, came in, buck naked with a towel over his shoulder. We sped up the hall and disappeared.

Eric slept in his van that night. Some weeks later he called and explained what had gone wrong with the apparatus. The fellow he'd borrowed it from forgot to include the seal. The lid was gapped the entire trip. Then again it didn't cost us anything, Eric added, so he guessed we couldn't complain. It seemed pointless to contradict him.

That last night on the river, below the stone face of Nefertiti, we stayed up reading the last chapters of John Wesley Powell's great adventure. They did not end well. Two of his men jumped ship in the Grand Canyon, climbed up and out, and were later found murdered on the rim. Rumors blamed the Hopi, others a Mormon wagon train. Yet others blamed Powell but their reasons were never clear. Based on his expedition, the major was appointed chief of the newly formed U.S. Geological Survey, which he used to advance the radical notion that the West, so naturally dry, would do well to organize development around water sources rather than the reverse. "I wish to make it clear to you," he told a body of legislators, "there is not sufficient water to irrigate all the lands which could be irrigated, and only a small portion can be irrigated . . . I tell you, gentlemen, you are piling up a heritage of conflict!." They would have none of it.

Powell was of course correct, and of course he was crucified for it. Western land speculators, railroads, and other boomers were enraged, called for his scalp, and soon got it. He retired from government service and, on a tiny pension, all but forgotten, his vision for the West defeated, he died alone. Which would have ended the story, but Mother Nature has thought otherwise.

The evidence of a warming climate is nowhere more dramatic than on the western plains. As the region's droughts deepen, reservoirs turn to mud, aquifers run dry, and forests go up in flame, the notion of planning lives around available resources is gaining new respect. Like the rivers he explored and thought about so prophetically, Powell's life continues to flow and may yet help us learn to live in a bountiful but finite world.

GILA RIVER
New Mexico, 1997

There are six of us under the tarp, the rain pattering down like gravel, the fire at our feet trying bravely to dry out the wood on top of it before it expires. The drizzle had started this morning and, unbelievably, seems to be increasing. This is southern New Mexico in October, when rainfall is said to be zero. How long could it possibly last? I sortie out for more dead branches, looking for a dry underside, something that might burn.

We have come into one of the cradles of conservation in America, the Gila National Forest, through which pass the headwaters of the Gila River, also called the Apache de Gila, the Brazo de Miraflores, Akee-mull, Hela, Hah-qua-sa-eel, Cina'ahuwipi, Keli Ami, Rio Azul, Rio de las Balsas, Rio del Nombre Jesus, Rio de los Apostoles, all the same river over time. To the Hohokam and Pima peoples and, judging by the very names they gave to it, to the Spanish as well, these were holy waters, sources at the right hand of God. It wasn't until the Americans that western rivers were stripped of their connection to the spirit world in favor of other deities. None of this means much to us right now, huddled under the tarp. The water seems more curse than blessing. Worse, Turkey Creek is beginning to rise.

This was a fishing trip to a tributary of the Gila nestled high in the forest, along the Aldo Leopold Wilderness. Leopold, like John Muir before him, held a religious view of nature that has persisted against all odds and confounds the pragmatists among us. While Muir came roaring out of nowhere like a prophet ("God's First Temples: How Shall We Protect Our Forests?"), Leopold grew into his belief more gradually, but he would impact not only the American soul but our way of managing nature as well, decades ahead of its time, still ahead of its time and in a race with exploitation to the finish line. In an essay called "Thinking Like a Mountain," Leopold described shooting

an old she-wolf and watching the "fierce green fire dying in her eyes."
He realized, he went on to say, that there was something in those eyes
known only to her and the mountain, and that his notion that "no
wolves would mean a hunter's paradise" was one with which "neither
the wolf nor the mountain" would agree. He had shot the wolf right
here in the Gila. He worked for the Forest Service; killing predators
was his first job. In one sense, what he wrote was simple poetry, a
nice sentiment at best. But it contained the spark of revolution. The
mountain and the wolf "would agree"—what the hell did that mean?

Back under the tarp, Leopold is very far from mind. The afternoon
is waning, the rain is steady, and we have run out of the usual tall
stories, finished speculating about how we would advertise this experience to commercial clients, and begun an attempt to list the presi-
dents of the United States in order, foundering somewhere before
Andy Jackson, picking up again with Lincoln and Grant, and then losing it entirely for the next forty years. In the silence that follows, only
the hiss of wet wood burning, Dave Snyder begins to hum a song, I
forget just what, but it is one that some of us happen to know and, furtively, we join in. Which would soon end, but I then remember "Oh!
Susanna," and we muddle our way through two verses and the chorus,
and then try it again, everybody in this time. Not bad. It seems a little
embarrassing, adult men with three-day stubble singing a song from
childhood, but here we are warming out hands over the halting fire,
each of us trying to reach back to somewhere and find another. We
sing the rest of the day, off and on, untutored voices challenging the
dropping sky. What I remember most about this trip and this campsite along Turkey Creek was the singing. I think it saved our bacon.

We had come to this spot because it was wilderness. Right where
we were standing, way back in 1924, at a time when things like the
word "wilderness" were unknown to the federal ear, Aldo Leopold
made it happen. He had the clout: he was by then supervisor of the
Gila Forest, and, with no explicit legal authority, he set this unique
region of high ponderosa and savannahs of yellow grasses off-limits to
roads and permits. The Forest Service, still in its early romance with
the resources it was charged to manage, went on to establish more

"back country" areas in other forests, a chain of them, which would be incorporated well after Leopold's death into the Wilderness Act of 1964. Few good things in history do not have someone like Leopold at the bottom of them. Offhand, I can't think of a single one.

Day two under the tarp begins hopefully; the sky is a lighter gray. We'll have sun by noon, says Dave, who enjoys some credibility among us because years earlier he had floated the length of the Mississippi to New Orleans in a canoe, alone. We dig out ropes and leave the shelter with the ambition of building a hand bridge across Turkey Creek, which at this point is ripping. Our intended hiking route enters the wilderness on the far side. We make some halfhearted efforts to carry the rope across for the first tie, but without something like it already in place to hold onto, it seems like a good way to drown and so we abandon the mission. By noon the sky is dark and, Dave notwithstanding, it is raining again, hard. I break out a harmonica and try "Little Red Wing," not a singing kind of song. We dig up others and find that we know the first words to a good many songs, sometimes the first stanza, and then go belly up. "Home on the Range" we get through, several times in fact having scored with a common script, and someone knows "When the Caissons Go Rolling Along." I add "Oh Shenandoah." They pass the time. They more than pass the time; they make it funny, friendly, a bond in the rain.

Looking down from above, the Gila Forest looks like a rumpled napkin with its deepest folds cut by tributaries that join each other in a parade that, forming the Gila River now, lead west across Arizona, join the Colorado, and flow south toward Mexico. Once a major waterway and still so marked on the charts, the Gila has long been sucked dry by agriculture and urban communities that are now locked in a death struggle over the remaining drops. The difference between the charts and reality surfaced in an account of three World War II German prisoners of war who escaped their compound in Arizona, constructed a kayak, and, armed with a gas station map showing the river as a clear blue line, started to float the Gila to Mexico and freedom, only to find it a dry gulch before the border. Less water yet is left in the mighty Colorado by the time it reaches its Mexican delta, now bone dry most of the year, some measure of the success of the use-it-or-lose-it nature of western water rights, and of raw American power.

Come the third day under the tarp it becomes clear to the most optimistic of us that our fishing trip is over. We caught few nice ones the first day, all catch-and-release, which was easy for me because I'd spent most of my time untangling my line instead, but this water is going to take weeks to clear. Besides, we are wet through and seemingly out of singing fodder.

On the hike out I find myself thinking about the nature of songs, which for all human history have supported no end of adventure, some good, some bad, but with stunning consistency over time. Did Caesar's legions sing? His famed memoires do not say, but every army since has sung its way forward, the Crusaders, American revolutionaries with "Yankee Doodle," opposing camps of Rebs and Yanks along the Potomac, calling over the river with requests for favorites, German troops in the world wars with "Lili Marlene," the French with "La Marseillaise," a common fabric, and here is the astonishing part to us today . . . they all knew the words. So too the songs of the southern chain gangs, negro cotton pickers, Canadian voyageurs, sea shanties, Scott's men singing to the Adele penguins on entering the Antarctic toward the South Pole from which none of their leaders would emerge alive. It is said that one of Shackleton's few questions of the men to join his polar expeditions was a simple one: did they like to sing? He had good reason to ask. I have asked myself many times since Turkey Creek on the Gila, what songs would my boys now have together were they out in the rain, or out anywhere, just for fun or to lighten a load. Exactly what do we do these days for glue?

I think about the Gila too, and Leopold, and his old she-wolf and the mountain. Throughout that scene, down in the wrinkles of the napkin, run streams toward a river that bind this place, its veins and arteries, so much of its life. Which became a momentous legal issue only a few years following our trip, whether the Gila Forest had rights to these very waters for these natural purposes, or whether they and the trout, bear, cougar, and other wild things that they nourish would be at the mercy of whatever enterprise wanted to come and siphon them away. New Mexico opposed the Forest Service claim. It wanted the water.

The case tore the Supreme Court in half, a majority holding that, no, the national forests of this country had no inherent rights to water because, in the water-short West, they would swallow it all up and deprive local communities of their life blood. If there has been a more ignorant opinion in this field I do not know it. It got the facts wrong: forests do not eat water like some Pac-Man monster, they store it, they save it, they distribute it clean and evenly over time for humans to use downstream. They are the very antithesis of consumers; they are the bank. A tiny group of justices from eastern law schools didn't have a clue about how, physically, western water worked. They also got the law wrong, beginning with the very act that, back in 1897, created the national forests "for the purpose of securing favorable conditions to water flows, and to furnish a continuous supply of timber." Securing water led the list. I'm reminded of a line from Leopold's *Sand Country Almanac*, his most well-known writing, phrased as a question: "Is education possibly a process of trading awareness for things of lesser worth?"

But there is a final line of Leopold's that takes me back to the Gila and to the sheer poetry of his vision that remains as revolutionary now as it was then. "The good life of any river," he wrote, "may depend on the perception of its music; and the preservation of some music to perceive." Some day I may put that statement on exam. I used one like it some years back, a poem by Borges that goes:

There is an hour approaching dark when the desert seems about to speak, but it never does,
  Or perhaps it does, but we cannot understand it,
  Or perhaps we can understand it, but what is says is as untranslatable as music.

We are back to the idea of music again. As a final question, a toss, I asked my students to describe what the poem had to do with natural resources law. I told them later that I gave everyone who tried an answer the same grade, which was true, and that there was no one correct answer, which was untrue. The answer to me was very clear. It was about the wolf and the mountain.

BAYOU SAUVAGE

Louisiana, 2005

Driving east from New Orleans, leaving its fringes, you have the impression you are sinking into the Gulf of Mexico. Off to the left is Lake Pontchartrain, a monster, and to the right lies Lake Borgne, even larger and wide open to Gulf tides and storms. Hurricane Katrina blew through here a few months ago and there is not a tree left standing. I am riding out with Cyprian and alongside the highway is a wide ditch coated with algae and tossed trash. Some time ago, as in five thousand years ago, incredible as it seems, this used to be the Mississippi River. Then the river turned west. Ours is a landscape in motion, which has been a painful lesson for humans to learn, if indeed anyone here has learned it. What remains of the old riverbed is now called Bayou Sauvage.

Our timing is not good. A cold front moved in last night and the temperature plunged. This morning the wind is blowing like a truck and any sensible creature out here would be burrowed deep in the bushes or en route to the Florida Keys. But once you get an outing like this in your head it is difficult to punch the kill-switch. Cyp and I are going birding, come what may. We end up with a fish instead.

Lisa and I discovered the Sauvage quite by accident, driving back from Mississippi. A long pond stretched off to the south and a flock of coot was rising, their little feet pounding on the surface to get airborne in such numbers that they roared into the sky. The next weekend we came back with the canoe, early in the morning, and met a man hauling an alligator out to a truck on the road. It was not alive. I didn't say anything and he didn't say anything. We paddled in and the waterbirds, thick this spring, rose and fell in layers. We went back many times with our young boys in tow and enough treats and comic books to make it a party on the bottom of the canoe.

Sometime later I was shown an official-looking map with our

pond on it colored in orange. The map key said that orange stood for "light commercial." Nearby ponds were in yellow, for "residential." It seemed an unlikely notion, except that the three people behind the real estate venture were Clint Murchison, who owned the Dallas newspaper as well as its professional football team, and the President and First Lady of the United States. Odds were they could do pretty much anything they wanted.

Cyp and I exit the car on the other side of the road under a metallic sun that casts no heat and a wind so bitter we have to turn our heads sideways to breathe. There is not a soul in sight. I sling a spotting scope over my shoulder and we begin to hike the levee top toward Pontchartrain but within minutes the metal legs are freezing to my hands and we leave it behind in the grass. The chances of someone coming by and taking it are nil, like everything else today. According to the map we are entering a zone colored red for "industrial." I keep a copy framed in my office. It is captioned "New Orleans East, A New Town in Town."

The ambition was to build a Houston version of New Orleans out here, low-rise, on slab, with shopping malls and acres of parking. I have no idea whether they had seen this swampy landscape but it was undeveloped and probably cheap, so what else was there to know? Putting the map in motion, President Lyndon Johnson had the Federal Highway Administration build three access ramps from Interstate 10 to his New Town. Abutting the interstate rose a great block of polished granite reading NEW ORLEANS EAST. It still does, along with the three off-ramps leading to nowhere. No one seems to know what to do with them.

The go-go years ended abruptly, Murchison went bankrupt, and his major investor, Merrill Lynch, was caught holding the note. It proposed its own development in Bayou Sauvage, only to discover that it would be operating in two feet of water and four feet of shoe-sucking mud. This was an unlikely place to site a new city, which ultimately became apparent to all. Or rather, to almost all. Yet another improbable dream lay ahead.

As the New Town idea was collapsing, the *New Orleans Times-Pic-*

ayune published yet another map for the Sauvage area. Where Cyp and I were standing that morning would now be an airport terminal, an access road, and the end of a runway. Out of the blue, the mayor of New Orleans announced plans for a new international airport right here, bordering Lake Pontchartrain. I may have used the word "nut-sos" to the newspaper, which brought an invitation from the mayor for a sit-down that weekend to explain.

This was not about an airport, the mayor began, or even needing an airport; it was about attracting a billion dollars of federal money. If, the mayor's point man went on, the Sauvage wetlands were a problem, the runways could be moved out into the lake instead. To demonstrate, he moved a little plastic plane across the map onto the blue water. I asked what they might do if a big storm came along and they said, as if it disposed of the issue, not fly the planes. My actual concern, though, was for the health of the lake itself, which we were trying to bring back and did not need to have its wetlands paved and a daily slug of airport runoff and spent fuel. I did not want to be impolite, but I saw a second battle of the Sauvage looming.

In the end, the mayor's proposal went the same way as that of the Texans, and for similar reasons. These unstable marshes south of Lake Pontchartrain were going to be even more hazardous for runways than they were for slab housing; better to leave them to other uses that required less capital and lower maintenance. And no hurricane protection. After some negotiating Merrill Lynch sold the property for its sunk costs in the venture to the Conservation Fund, which resold it to the government for a wildlife refuge. And so it is that we are out here, Cyp and I, freezing to death on a winter day.

What keeps us going is the shine of a pond in the distance, which means the possibility of ducks or wading birds sheltering on its lee shore. Wherever the birds are, though, they are not here, only two killdeer on a mud flat and on this particular day their piping call, which is sad to begin with, like something about to expire. Nothing else is in view and, having run our luck, we turn to go back and the adventure begins. Right behind the killdeer, on a squishy-looking shelf covered by a thin layer of water, there is an explosion. A large body heaves itself up and then flops back down into the muck, still. My first thought is nutria. Or maybe another, which would be a coup. We put the binoculars on it.

Large scales and a fin on top. The head is below the waterline, as is the tail, but the middle humps up in a parabola like the back of a raccoon. Filing through the note cards in my head I come up with alligator gar, the long front snout harboring real teeth, about as primitive a fish as there is and one whose prehistoric cousins made it onto dry land, and then into the air. It is struggling and out beyond I can see the tip of another fin, a sister, also blown in by the wind which comes across that shallow water like a shovel, pushing everything toward shore. But my gar—by this time I am starting to feel proprietary about the near one—is in serious trouble. Half of its body is out of the water and it is going to die out in that muck like a statue, sucking its last life out of the thimble full of muddy water in which it can hide its head. I tell Cyp I am going down to take a look. Later he tells me he had a premonition.

What happens next was logical every step of the way. Even examining it later, knowing the outcome, each move had a rational basis and an exit strategy should a worst-case situation arrive. Cyp is saying, "Dad, I really wouldn't," but I see few alternatives, the fish is out there and it is going to die. I step off the levee and onto the edge of the flat. It looks chalky, which I take for dried salt, and when I put one foot out it holds my weight. This is good. I can go one step at a time and if the next foot starts sinking I can pull back. Beckoning me forward is a washed-up tree branch about eight feet away. I can creep out to it, grab one end, reach out to the gar, and flip the creature out into the deeper water. Even if Cyp and I took the time to sit together and develop a plan, this would be the one we'd come up with.

Treading carefully out to the tree branch, I notice that the soil beneath my feet is beginning to quake, the consistency of old pudding. It will support my weight if I keep moving but it smells faintly of oil and rank vegetation and is already rising over the soles of my sneakers and seeping inside. Nonetheless the branch is now within reach, another six feet or so to the fish, and a few feet farther what looks like deeper water, our destination, my fish and me. I grab the branch, raise the butt end, and it breaks. I am left holding a four-foot piece of a stick so rotten it could not even lift out of the mud without, gently, parting in two pieces. This begins to change the contingencies. Cyp's voice comes in from the levee at this point, a check from ground control, "I'd come out, Dad," he is saying, but he apparently doesn't get the picture from where he is situated. I cannot come out and still reach the fish.

As I am calculating the next move, a strong gust whips the flats and the stranded gar lifts a mighty heave, as if raised by the heavens, as if pleading with me to finish the job. I conclude that the water is so shallow that I can walk out a little farther to it and then flip it with my shortened pole to the far water and safety. All it will cost me is some wet sneakers, which are already wet although my feet are so cold I barely feel them. Sure enough, arriving at the fish I slip my stick into the mud below it and flip it out, and it works, only not too well because all I have done is turn the poor thing onto its back where it lies belly up, dorsal fin stuck deep into the mud, a sure goner now whatever its prospects had been only seconds before. At this point I am morally stuck. A bungled rescue that puts its object at yet greater risk is a form of homicide. Besides, now that I know the flip maneuver works, in concept, all I have to do is execute it a little better. I take another step and try again.

The next flip is, I'll admit, a disaster. I do manage to get the fish over onto its belly again and a few feet closer to open water but at a huge cost. It is no longer a fish. It is a large tube of ooze from snout to tail, not even its thick scales showing through the brown coating, there is no way this creature will live even a few more minutes unless it washes off. I rethink the contingencies. The stick solution has run into unexpected difficulties and there is no other useful instrument within a thousand yards. Except my hands, which have always been Option Z because I have no wish to get bitten by those alligator jaws and if those fins are anything like those of a hardhead catfish they can go through the palm of my hand and send me to the emergency room trying to explain just how such a nasty-looking wound came about.

Granting all this, the fish is still before me and whatever happens to it is on my watch. As I make toward it, Cyp's voice comes more urgently this time, he can see that the water is deeper and that I am at this point without tools of any kind. I do hear him, but I still figure that the operation is salvageable, potentially quick and clean.

I am ankle-deep at this point, no pretense of solid footing. My movements are correspondingly slowed, but I remain optimistic, conservative even, able to retreat at any time if my next step forward drops into the abyss. The fish is now at my feet looking like road-kill, its fins flattened against its sides and its head a tapering piece of slime. Instinctively I reach down under its belly, no jutting fin there to cut me, no twist of the jaws to reach my hands, who knows, maybe not a breath of life left in the creature either at this point, and I lift it as easily as I would a wounded dog, swing my arms back to gain momentum, and then forward and away! the fish spinning out over the flats like a football, a small flash of scales where a patch of mud tears off, and into the deeper water, where it disappears. I remain leaning forward, looking for a sign, fully concentrated on the spot where the gar landed, hoping that it will not reappear, belly up, my unintended kill. It does not and then I am toppling over like a falling tree, flat to the ground, only of course there is no ground, just the liquefaction of Bayou Sauvage.

The water is shocking and when I finally struggle to my feet I resemble a larger version of the gar just a few seconds before, encased in muck that seems as durable as a rain slicker. I wade ashore, Cyp appalled on the levee top, the only way home will be in his car which he keeps fastidiously clean. So it is with mixed emotions that he greets me on the berm, he having advised me not to go in a crescendo of warnings, and we begin walking back to the car, rapidly, because the temperature has gone from chilly to meat locker.

A flooded ditch lies on the side of the levee and, already wet, I hand Cyp my unrecognizable wallet and drop in, scrubbing off as best I can, rediscovering that on a winter day cold water does not feel so cold at all, in fact it does not feel anything. I emerge less like a dead gar and more like a human who has been rescued from a plane crash in the swamp. Back at the car we jack up the heater, throw my wet clothes in the trunk, Cyp lends me his coat and drives us home.

If I were still trying to save the Bayou Sauvage today, out on the eastern rim of New Orleans, this might not be the story I would tell. It certainly would not inspire anyone to go there, or the U.S. Fish and Wildlife Service to buy it for a refuge, even at a bargain price. For many, it might be a good reason for draining the place and topping it with human conveniences instead. Who knows, they may yet do it. Nothing saved is forever.

I still think about that gar fish when I come out this way, though, past the large monument reading NEW ORLEANS EAST and the three exit ramps to nowhere. I wonder if it made it that day. I've come back along these ponds after cold winter blows and a lot of fish lie dead by the shores. It is the way nature works. The kill from Katrina itself was stupendous. Why developing this area is a worse outcome than that seems obvious to me. But I'll admit that it may be hard to explain.

DESCHUTES RIVER
Oregon, 2006

I have dreams about the Deschutes from time to time and they do not
end well. Cyprian is caught in a hole behind a large rock, arms out-
stretched, swirling around like a sack and I am unable to help him.
Only, this part actually happened, it was no dream. Weakened by
shock he was calling, "help me, help me," but I could barely hear him,
much less reach him. We had no business being on the Deschutes in
open canoes at these water levels in early spring when they were all
snowmelt in the coldest kind of rain. When a river this size is named
for its waterfalls, including a great drop where it joins the Columbia
and thunders on toward the Pacific, that is at least a warning. I still
think about the rapids that wiped us out on this trip, and how we
could have run them differently. When I mention this to Cyp he tells
me that he has these dreams too. They are not about how to do them
again, however. He is still trying to get out of the water.

There was another warning. As we parked the truck for our first
look at the river we saw several Indian teenagers standing on the
bank. A few yards below them a large plastic net, bright-orange, was
tethered to a tree and stretched across the water to the other side.
Only the top of the net was visible, the rest bulging like a stomach
below the surface. My first thought was that they were seining for
salmon but the net seemed too bulky for that and entirely too visible. One of the boys came up, unsteady on his legs, and asked us for
money. We gave him a couple of dollars and asked him about the net.
He said that another boy fell in yesterday, upstream, and they were
trying to find the body. He was casual about it, as if this were not the
first time. He returned to his group waving the bills in triumph and
was given an open pint of liquor to pull on in return. My guess was
fourteen years old, maximum. It was two in the afternoon.

Western rivers are different. That particular season several boaters would die on this stretch of the Deschutes alone, all wearing life jackets and on professionally guided trips. Apparently they just popped out of the raft at the wrong moment and the water took them. Rafts are to open canoes, however, as barges are to bars of soap. Driving up to a put-in out here with our canoes on top drew comments like, "You really use those things?" At a local diner, our last commercial meal for a while, the owner came over to the table, solicitous, shaking his head. We said we had two solo rafts going with us and lots of floatation, we'd be fine. As a practical matter if the fellow had told us about fire-eating dragons around the first bend and a floating mine field we might have said the same thing. We had come a long way. Second thoughts at this point were not in the cards.

I do not want to demean the Indian boys we saw. They were part of the Warm Springs Confederation whose tribes have been undergoing a human tsunami for nearly two hundred years. These youngsters are part of the fewer than four thousand who have survived, only sixty or so still speak the language, none of them under the age of fifty. The first white push into their territory was driven by bizarre accident. Lewis and Clark had brought back from the Pacific Northwest two natives with highly unusual facial features, perfectly flat on the top. These Flatheads, as they were quickly called, were obviously rejects from God's chosen few and stirred deep sympathy in evangelical Boston, which promptly organized relief expeditions to take them the Word. Once on scene, however, the brave missionaries discovered that the Flatheads did not have flat heads at all, nor were they eager to adopt European farming practices or a religion based on killing martyrs on the cross; they had a functioning culture of their own. The next white wagons to come kept their Bibles to themselves and focused on taking the land. When the inevitable frictions arose they called on Washington for help.

In an 1855 treaty for which the word "negotiated" would be highly misleading, the Wasco, Walla Walla, and Paiute ceded ownership to ten million acres of land and waters that they had occupied for perhaps ten thousand years, in return for a postage stamp to live on and the promise, almost immediately broken, of fishing rights at all accustomed places beyond the reservation. These treaties-of-no-choice, imposed through the Army on orders from the White House, extended to all tribes of the region, most memorably the Duwamish, whose chief, named Seattle, made one of the most moving speeches in American history, beginning with the lines, "The Great Chief in Washington sends word that he wishes to purchase our lands. The idea is strange to us." Strange or not, we did it and have perpetuated the chief's name in a thriving city all our own.

Back on the Deschutes, we launch onto fast water. Normal levels in May run a little over 2,000 cubic feet per second, and the latest gauge readings we saw were at 3,800, nearly twice the push. River runners are of two minds about water this high. On the upside, it washes over the rock gardens that otherwise require quick maneuvers. On the other hand, it is so powerful that the boulders remaining fly toward you like oncoming trucks, and the holes behind them are enormous. For rafts, they pose little problem so long they keep their line; they are made to bounce off objects and to surf tall stacks that will swamp an open canoe, even one packed with flotation. What we would discover in canoes is that riding the big trains was preferable even if we loaded up with water; we were still together and off the rocks. This said, schooled on eastern water, I remained leery of high waves and kept trying to dodge down the sides which had dangers of its own and would leave Cyp swirling in that hole, and later in his nightmares.

Cyp and I have drawn a Blue Hole canoe that is flat-bottomed and easy to maneuver, but which has little defense against getting slapped around in big water. After we flip several times, Adam, who believed none of it, switched in for Cyp and we dumped the next rapid down. This said, there were some we simply shouldn't have tried at all.

The first two days are relatively calm and, as the Deschutes is known for spring salmon, it has attracted catered parties to fly-fish the shallows. We pass them from time to time, strung out along the banks like sentinels and dressed in the latest gear from outdoor catalogues including identical rain jackets with the outfitters' logos on the breast. They need the jackets because it is raining lightly and will for days. Looking at them I tell myself that getting people with lots of money to like the out-of-doors is a good thing, but I'm just as glad to leave them behind. On our way past their guide, sitting in a raft, says simply, "Canoes don't belong out here."

The fourth day brings Boxcar. Cyp and I had gotten wet one rapid earlier and come into it cold, while Gabe and Adam had not only stayed in the wave train but paddled backwards to stay in it, remaining dry. I should have learned. The Boxcar rapid curves right at the very beginning, so it is difficult to see your way down. It is also nearly a mile long so whatever is seen on scouting does not stick in the brain.

At the top of Boxcar is a cluster of rocks that seems to eat boats for the fun of it. The remains of one are pinned to the side. The right chute drops precipitously onto a tongue, slides left of a triangular boulder and toward the center, where it crashes into the surge from the left and, together now, descends over more rocks into a deep cleavage of foam. Cyp and I never get there, the backwash from the bank wallops our bow like an angry parent and flips us instantly, down the tongue and out to claw our way downstream. Gabe and Adam, in turn, stay upright as far as the cleavage and disappear from view. Gabe pops up first and then the canoe but there is no Adam, who is undergoing a transcendental experience. He finds himself squatting on the bottom in a boiling column of bubbles that will not float him out. Slowly realizing that nothing is leaving this hole on its own, nor will he, he braces his feet and leaps straight up, snapping his legs like a frog, thrusting his face out of the foam for a gulp of air, and then stroking his way to the side. He describes it matter-of-factly. I doubt I could have done the same.

We leave the Deschutes fifty miles before the really big rapid, the one for which the river is named, its epic junction with the Columbia at Celilo Falls, which no longer exists. The falls lie buried under a hundred feet of water by the Dalles Dam. The Warm Springs Indians had been promised that they would be able to fish at all usual and accustomed places off of the reservation but not, apparently, that the fish or even the places would be there. Salmon were both food and religion to these people, and Celilo Falls had been their temple. Native tribes had constructed a spectacular network of ladders and scaffolds that hung over the raging chutes to catch their salmon, one run following another each spring. They snared them in hand nets on long handles as artfully as scooping butterflies, only the fish went twenty pounds–plus and that weight by itself could pull a man over into the cataract. They did this for years beyond memory. They needed little more to survive, indeed to thrive. Eighteen dams the size of the Dalles now stunt the Columbia and Snake Rivers from Idaho to the Pacific, eliminating some salmon runs entirely and reducing their numbers to the point that the government now ferries the remnants around in barges and pays the tribes off with hatchery fish instead. It is a good thing that I am not a Native American or I'd be eternally angry.

I cannot really write about Weminuche, the rapid that wiped out Cyprian. I erred early on, trying to skirt a current that dumped us like a bug from the windshield, we washed over the first drop, and he could not get out as I sped by. Denny came up in a pontoon raft, grabbed Cyp by the collar, and towed him in. Ed, in a small raft downstream, did the same for our canoe, his hands like meat hooks and as reliable as iron. Had those little rafts not been with us, the boys and I might still be walking out from someplace way upstream.

That evening we loosen up. It is our last night on the river and Ed breaks out a box carton of wine. A pair of Canada geese is on the water, struggling against the current toward only they know where, leading a string of goslings that appear to have no chance of making it at all. Ed, into the carton at this point, announces that he is going to rescue them and launches a canoe furiously across the river. I'd never seen him in a canoe before but he is a large man and the bow rises on a steep angle. We yell helpful comments to him, laughing, while Gabe and Adam ready a second canoe to pick him up should he lose control. Somehow Ed stays afloat, and somehow he herds the goslings toward shore where the water is calm and they have a chance to get out. You can swap the rapids on any river for scenes like this and come out ahead.

I remain afraid of the Deschutes. The water was too high for us, although stronger paddlers might have made it. On other western rivers since, the Owyhee, the Chama, I have come to trust my boys to read the water now, what we should run and what we should just let be. I still wonder about Weminuche on the Deschutes, though, had we not tried that crossing, whether we could have ridden the wave train instead.

Then I remember the Warm Springs boys on the bank of the river, passing the bottle around, drowning in their way the drowning of a friend, or perhaps a kid they did not even like but who was tied deeply to them by DNA, and I sense the pain. Had I lost Cyp that day I'd probably have gotten drunk too at some point following, maybe often, maybe regularly. Maybe I too would feel lost in a world I no longer liked a great deal, in a body I didn't like very much either. It is a terrible thought and I try to let it go.

OLD RIVER
Mississippi, 2006

Many rivers across the Deep South are called Old River, and for the same reason. They used to be the river but then got left behind. They are frequent here because rivers in the Delta meander through soft soils that they have deposited ahead of them in broad fans of land. Spring floods tear at these soils like fangs, making new channels and abandoning the former ones. Only pockets of the old riverbeds remain, shaped like teardrops and prolific in wildlife and beauty as progress passes them by.

Not all Old Rivers are idle. Louisiana's version is a relic channel between the Mississippi River and the Atchafalaya which, as a shorter route to the Gulf, has threatened more than once to capture the main river and swallow it whole. The threat is, like so many, of our own making. For centuries this Old River was blocked by a mile-long raft of logs and trees so enormous that it grew its own vegetation and formed a bridge for driving Texas cattle to Baton Rouge and New Orleans. Seeing the raft as nothing but a nuisance, however, navigation interests had it blown up, which was hailed as a great success. Mississippi flows into the Atchafalaya, unblocked now, began to swell and then to boom, presenting the Port of New Orleans, six river parishes, and one hundred miles of petrochemical plants lining the Lower Mississippi with serious freshwater problems. The Corps of Engineers was rushed into the breach to build a dam across Old River, in effect a new raft, and when a flood in 1973 came within an ace of flushing this structure away, the Corps rushed in again to build a superdam, stemming the force of the Mississippi we had, in retrospect, so unwittingly released. The odds are good that in any given year, over any time frame measured in decades, the new structure will hold. No one thinks it will hold forever.

The Old River of Mississippi is a very different creature. It is part of the Pearl River system about fifty miles east of New Orleans and a shifting piece of the state line. This Old River was the main Pearl at one point but was forsaken as new branches threaded west, leaving a chain of lakes lined by cypress trees. They are a favorite haunt of people looking for fish or a few hours of peace.

Several months before this trip, National Public Radio broadcast a report on the ivory-billed woodpecker, a shockingly beautiful bird said to have been recently seen in this vicinity. The report was something like an Elvis sighting; the ivory-bill had not been seen alive for seventy years. When Jay and I floated into a relic piece of Old River that spring, however, I thought I heard the sharp rap of its beak, as heavy and delicate as an axe, and then answering raps from far away. No other bird did that so loud and so slow. Something large was communicating with something large, and the ivory-bill was the size of a hunting dog. If Ms. Bear up in my bow had not woofed at the wrong time, I might have seen whatever it was doing the near-side rapping but I never did, which is perhaps just as well. The thrill of imagining an ivory-bill far outweighed that of discovering the truth. Still and all, whenever I think of making the run to Old River I get a momentary chill. The prospect is impossible of course, but still.

The Old River run is not easy to reach from New Orleans. Either we drive around the base of the Pearl for a couple of hours, or we start from the near side and paddle straight across it, an adventure in the best of conditions even if what you are reading on the map corresponds with what you are seeing around you, which is rarely ever the case. Maps are not particularly helpful when the topography changes so quickly and water is running free through the trees. We bring compasses to track our direction, but if darkness catches us beforehand that is another story. This story, in fact.

We brought three canoes, solo, Jay and I and Ty. Jay raises bees for a living, with great care. He uses no chemicals and has eschewed wearing gloves ("I don't want to crush them picking them up") until recently when the more aggressive African bees arrived. Ty tends to trees, young cypress mostly, throw in a recent trip to the Florida panhandle to look for the ivory-bill that a sketchy report had placed there. They are both used to the out of doors and to finding their way. At short breaks in the paddling, Jay spooning down raw pollen, Ty opening satsumas, me fingering out peanut butter from a jar, we may chat about the latest on Formosan termites or the local football team but once in motion, looking at the drowned forest around us as if we were still and it was moving, we might as well be mutes, even my dog who is up on point and testing the air.

Crossing the Pearl basin to Old River this time was relatively easy, once past the main river that was ripping south like a conveyer belt carrying full trees. We followed a winding bayou and caught our first sign of trouble. Hurricane Katrina had made landfall just south of here and mowed down mile-wide swaths of forest to the northern reaches of the state. Here in the swamp the cypress and the tupelo gum trees, rooted widely in deeper water, made it through unscathed but on the elevated banks the pines and hardwoods fell like checked kings, which would complicate things enormously. The blowdown at this point, however, was well off to the side and we drifted instead through carpets of bright yellow-top, early red maples, and cypress needles of the lightest green, under a pure blue sky. Vivid primary colors, in a way much too pretty, and we swung into a pond and stalled. We broke out some lunch. We lay back in the sun. Noon came and went.

Crossing back began easily enough as well, cruising down the Old River chain with a light current behind. Even the side channels were running ten feet deep, although come fall you could walk them in dry shoes. At this water level, post-Katrina, few markers scribbled on our maps as "cluster of sweet gum," or "board nailed to tree" remained visible. The board might be gone. The entire tree might be gone. We poked and parried our way back to the main river, a bit late, but still with adequate time. Ahead to the west lay a patchwork of bayous leading to the levee, our car and home. The first of these was Hog Bayou, where things began to fall apart.

Hurricane Katrina had wasted it. A naturally narrow bayou to begin with, Hog was crisscrossed by fallen trunks, huge root balls, and tangles of debris. On a normal day this leg of the journey might take twenty minutes to negotiate. This afternoon it took more than an hour, much of it spent crouching on logs and hauling the canoes over them, or standing in shoulder-deep water to shove them under, and then on to the next abbatis. The water was stunningly cold. At one point, me standing with one foot on a log and the other in the boat, Ms. Bear leaped out from the bow, pushing it away and giving me an extra dunk. Exiting Hog at last, the sun was low in the western sky. We would soon be working on residual light for as long as it might last.

Late as it was my body was shaking and I had no choice but to stop, open the wet bag, and change into dry clothes. This took a while because my numbed fingers would not work the clips, and that was a while we did not have to spare. Fortunately the next stretch, Big Creek, was wide open and we paddled it swiftly as the day shut down. We found the turn up Smith Creek by braille, feeling it push back at us full force. We struggled up against it on adrenaline, there was no choice, shadowy stumps appearing suddenly ahead, our three canoes, green and blue and yellow in the sunlight just shapes now in the void. It was pure dark when we arrived at Chapman, but at least we would have the current behind us again. There were no stars and the moon must have been lighting up some other part of the world. We navigated down by watching the opening in the canopy above us, a lighter sky against the caps of towering trees. Only one more leg remained, Devil's Swamp, but we could not find it.

It seemed impossible. Chapman runs directly by Devil's Swamp, either you turn into it or blow past it. In the dark, however, everything looked like Devil's Swamp. Our flashlights showed only a few yards in any direction and all we saw was trees, roots, and underbrush. We decided to probe by compass straight west toward the levee, hoping at some point to spot the current coming in from a levee gap and trace it backwards, and out. So far as we could see, however, the currents were drifting every which way and, poking doggedly east, we ran into barriers of logs and mud. We could not tell whether we were still north of the swamp, had gone past it, or were in fact in it. Wherever we were did not lead home.

Jay was for spending the night. There had not been a patch of dry land for hours so we'd sleep in the boats. I did not see myself sleeping in a canoe out here, I do not even sleep on airplane flights, to say nothing of the cold and of Ms. Bear who was also shivering in the bow. She got her last nibble of food, a gob of peanut butter, about seven hours ago. Or we could go out below, said Jay, farther down Chapman, up the Bogue Chitto River to the canal, up the canal to the car. It sounded easy. He'd done it once with his brother. Only he had done it in daylight, and at low water, and he didn't mention the sill dam along the way.

So we floated down Chapman, skirting stumps that popped up out of the gloom like targets on the firing range, and met the Bogue Chitto, which was in a flood of its own and running dead against us, whipping around the near trees with an angry sound. It was around 8:00 p.m. We went upstream for an eternity, me switching sides every few minutes because my shoulders had been rebelling all afternoon. We did not stop, we could not stop without going backwards, there was no bank to the river, and we did not dare get trapped in the trees. My bladder was aching. My right shoulder had caught fire. Then in the distance came a dull roar and Jay said, "There's a sill ahead."

Jay mentioned the sill so casually that I thought it would be a nonissue but the sound it made had very large issue written all over it. The low dam stretched entirely across the Bogue Chitto, there was no finessing it. Jay was plowing straight forward toward it, however, evidently figuring that with water this high the drop on our side would wash out and we'd meet at worst an incline of faster water. He was half-correct.

I came up next to Jay. He knew this obstacle; whatever he did I'd do. I had lost sight of Ty. Whether sensing the danger or not, Ms. Bear had moved up from her perch on my wet bag to put her paws on the rim of the bow point, the most unstable spot in the boat. I shouted "BEAR!" to call her down but she seemed entranced by the huge, unseen rush ahead. At this moment I saw Jay's bow begin to rise and felt mine do the same, we were on the incline now, the water was even faster, roaring past us as we tried to maintain our momentum and the bow straight into it. If the current caught any angle we presented to it the canoes would roll like toys. I might be able to swim out, but there would be nothing I could do for Ms. Bear; it is not likely I would even see her go. We were gaining ground, though, Jay and I, more slowly with each stroke, until we felt ourselves on the cusp of the sill but powerless to top it, our paddles stroking through the water as if they were going through clouds. It wasn't going to work.

Perhaps the best canoeing I've ever done came next, given the circumstances. We had to back down that same sluice, side by side, very slowly, without swerving a jot, the bows under close control, against an incredible push that was all black and impossible to read. Its noise was overwhelming. I wanted Ms. Bear to come down off the point in the worst way but I dared not shout at her again or even turn her head. And so, it seems almost fiction now, I would not bet on being able to do it again, we slid back down the slope straight as a die, back-paddled through standing rolls at the bottom and then out to the side, looking for a place to angle out of the river. Since there was a sill here there had to be an anchoring abutment on the bank as well, at least something to hold onto. It turned out better than that, a block of concrete and behind it, Lord be praised, a patch of high ground

Ty was in first and waiting for us, Jay followed. I came in last and Ms. Bear jumped clear but my legs, kneeling for the past several hours, refused to function. Finally I just rolled the canoe on its side and lay in the shallows, the relief of the water opening my bladder which felt so good that I started laughing. It seemed to go on for an hour. Then I crawled out and we built a fire and a blaze so warm that I went off to the side and relieved myself again. We inventoried the remaining food, two satsumas, Jay's pollen, and the bottom of my peanut butter jar which we mixed together and shared with Ms. Bear. It was delicious.

The final leg up the canal to the car had no facing current and it passed as in a dream. Stars had come out, but no moon. The constellations were as bright as Christmas. Ty and Jay ran the shuttle to the other car that we had left above, but they missed the turn coming back and did not return for yet another hour. I'd built another fire in the meantime and just lay by. I was as content as I can remember. Ty told me later that he had hung back below us at the sill with his flashlight between his teeth and pointed upstream, ready to act in case one of us turned over. He was particularly concerned about saving Ms. Bear, he said, as she floated by.

It was near midnight now. A bar was still open on the access road. Several rough-looking characters were hanging around outside but at that point we looked pretty much like them. I went in to look for a telephone to call Lisa and discovered that the one at the counter didn't work; it didn't even have a receiver. Driving out of the lot Jay was pulled over by a local trooper who was apparently staking out the place for driving while intoxicated. Jay was not intoxicated. He said, "I'm going drinking with a canoe on the top?" He started to explain our trip to the trooper and, granted, the story seemed a little incredible, but he let Jay go.

I got home too late to describe, left the boat on the car, walked in the house, and met Lisa still up and wide-eyed. I hadn't tried to call again. I figured it better to just put the pedal to the floor and get there. That was a mistake. I went out and bought large sunflowers the next day and they looked very nice in the house, but I should have called.

Perhaps I should have taken a cell phone with me, or a GPS. I could have stayed in touch, and even located where we were in the dark and how to get out. Paddlers today do this routinely. And more. I read an article in the dentist's office written by a fellow who'd paddled a northern river that I too had paddled, quite remote. He described coming out of a rapid so exhilarated that he dialed up his wife in California on a cell phone and described it to her. He was still on the water and on the phone. I have since come across an advertisement for something called the ECO-TERRA BOOMBOX: "Listen to your favorite tunes while you swim, float or raft down a river." In the water, the device rotates to point the speakers upward. I'm not sure where any of this stuff ends. Nor do I know how to escape it.

I have to admit that there is real utility in knowing where you are at times, most times even. Commercial fishermen have come to depend on these devices, so do drones, and we have automobiles now that tell us how many blocks before we take a left turn. It all seems quite handy and equally so, apparently, to thumb out a tweet as you are walking across the street oblivious to the world around you. But to be alone is useful, too, to actually be able to be alone, and to figure things out for yourself. When I teach classes these days I ask my students to unplug completely, no laptops or phones, just us and the ideas of the class. I feel the same way about the out of doors. Come to think of it, though, perhaps my notion here is an Old River of its own.

As the new river moves on.

RED CREEK
Mississippi, 2009

This was an odd place for an airplane tire. It was on a beach that slipped into the creek like a fan, the current curling around it in a loop that was transparent near the shore and then dropped off into darkness. Sandy streams cave in the banks that contain them, along with trees and the fronts of weekend cottages that press too close, so eager are their owners to dominate this piece of Paradise they have purchased to be theirs and theirs alone. For protection they line the banks with old tires, rubble, whatever might keep nature at bay. Come the next high water, however, these objects tear loose and drift downstream like spill from a dump truck, to be replaced by new and bigger ones. So it would not be unusual to see an automobile tire along Red Creek. It was more unusual to see an airplane tire but, when you think about it, whoever it had belonged to was probably just going his neighbor one better.

For the most part, though, this stretch of Red Creek was junk-free. Shallow bars and tangles of downed trees deterred motorboats, four-wheelers, and rental canoe runs. This was as close as you got around here to the wild, a term that at least promises few humans and their sign. It is all relative, of course. A chewing gum wrapper on the top of Mount Katahdin can feel like a stick in the eye; so, too, an airplane tire on the bend of a small river in southern Mississippi, its treads gleaming in the sun as if they had never hit a runway. An unlooked-for reminder of the mechanical world. Then it began to move.

I am describing the first time here, because it happened twice. Exactly the same thing. On the first occasion I was out with a few of my students, we had camped the evening before on a bluff upstream, made dinner in a pot, and told stories until I turned in and they continued until I've no idea what time, distant voices around a flick of fire in the night. The next day we reached the place they'd left their cars, loaded their canoes, and they were on the road back to the city. I took some of the remaining food and my dog and we continued to float on down. Ms. Bear sat as always on top of my pack in the bow like a hood ornament, sniffing the air. She knew what was out there but she rarely told me. This time she did, though, albeit a bit late. She was as surprised as I was.

You have to realize that Red Creek is not the open marsh or deep swamp of this part of the world that reeks with possibilities of getting lost or confronting an unexpected creature. What we have here is a clear stream winding through mixed pine and hardwoods, the sound of distant vehicles occasionally on the wind. We'd sometimes seen snakes and Ms. Bear got nailed by one while snuffling through the leaves along the Hoblochitto, her head swelling within minutes to the size of a melon, stupid with pain for the hours it took me to get her out and to a local doctor who told us that the strike had hit mostly bone and she would live. So things can happen. And so when the airplane tire up on the beach began to move I simply looked on in wonder, Ms. Bear scenting the air furiously and shifting her feet.

When you round the bend of a southern stream you want to stay off the inside where the water is thin, and away from the far bank as well where snags lurk to grab the hull. So we were perhaps ten feet from the lip of the beach, in less than two feet of water, the sand shelf angling across us toward the deep. I kept our nose pointed in, contouring the curve, examining this huge object that had begun, if I could believe my eyes, to unfold.

The back part moved first, unpeeling like the tread of an eighteen-wheeler, deeply grooved. Then the front part started up, a huge piece of tire swinging heavily out of its mold and showing what seemed like one large eye and an enormous grin. It was the biggest alligator I had ever seen in the wild, as thick through the middle as a willow tree and as long as the canoe. It was recomposing itself from dead tire into live organism at a distance of perhaps twenty feet. Ms. Bear gave it a small woof of warning. From deep in her genes she was confronting the situation in the way she fended off ancestral enemies and the postal delivery man, on whom she practiced daily. Her response here was a bit tentative, though. That was one hell of a big thing out there.

I back-paddled slowly, breaking our momentum, not wanting to do anything sudden to anger the beast, although I have no idea whether anger even plays into the responses of alligators to a small dog perched on top of a red duffel like a snack on a plate, or to the larger but fully edible creature behind it. Whatever happened was entirely in this creature's hands. Fully straightened now, the alligator squatted down on its stumpy legs like a sumo wrestler and then leaped in the air, all four feet at once, the whole body levitating and then landing in the shallow water, a boat length away. I was still back-paddling and saying either holy cow or please God under my breath, I remember both, which cannot be correct.

The alligator swung its head toward us and leaped again, straight up out of the water and into the deep like a glacier and gone. As luck would have it, we were also out deep by this point and floated silently over its wake, the ripples crashing against the banks. Floating on, I knew I had been privileged to a great and private wonder. If another canoe had been with us we might have been making noise, talking to each other, or paddling single file so that only one of us would have seen it, perhaps neither. I felt like thanking someone but there was of course no one else around. Which would soon change.

My car was in the woods several miles below. The dirt road in had been trackless, no sign of traffic. The day was still warm so when I had pulled the canoe out and taken my gear to the car, Ms. Bear rolling happily in the sand, I stripped off my clothes and went down to rinse off for the long drive home. I came back up carrying my bar of soap and nothing else to another surprise, a truck slowly picking its way down the road toward me, two heavy heads silhouetted behind the windshield and a little red light on the top, the cops. My head raced with doubts, this was a closed road, going naked in Mississippi was a public offense, where was the car insurance. As they came up I could see a man behind the wheel and a woman beside, their faces nearly identical, pleasant, curious. I looked down to see what they saw, a naked man, rather skinny, mostly bald, dripping wet. I did the only thing I could and said hello. And then, still pumped up by the upstream encounter I did a terribly foolish thing. I said, "I saw the biggest alligator in my life out there."

Which got their attention. He told me that he was the local sheriff and alligators were not welcome around here. People came down to the creek to get baptized, they didn't want no gators, no sir. He had a rifle in the back of the cab. It struck me that I had just signed the death warrant for an animal that had lived here, apparently peaceably or it'd have been shot long ago, for decades, and whose lineage went back beyond the powers of human comprehension. So I did the reasonable thing under the circumstances and began to lie. I said that I had seen the alligator the day before, way up the creek, maybe twenty miles ago, under the I-49 bridge. That is what surprised me I said, rambling on, what it was doing around all that highway traffic, right under the bridge. He said he'd look into it. Ms. Bear and I drove home.

But the memory haunted me. As well as the idea that I might be responsible for the death of this awesome thing. So a month later, the water still up, I went out with Ms. Bear again, just us this time and some papers to grade. We paddled more quickly and by the second afternoon we were down about where that beach had been, only the beach was nowhere in sight. I paddled on, thinking that perhaps I had missed it, there were similar little sand spits along this stretch, and then like a movie from childhood the banks began to look familiar, the trees looked familiar, and down below was a hook to the left and a telltale gleam of white. That had to be it.

We approached it as before, Ms. Bear up on the red pack, me feathering lightly in the stern, just keeping our bow straight, peering intently as the beach grew larger, my throat tightening with disappointment as it showed up empty. There was no big tire, only pebbles and an edge of sand. Unlike the other beaches, however, this one looked as if it had hosted a prize fight, scuffed all over with deep tracks leading to the water. The tracks were recent. Whatever made them was big and still alive. I could feel a burden lifting from my heart. I whispered to Ms. Bear, this could be it, but she was all sniff at this point, she could have told me that and more.

We rounded the bend in the same way, midpoint between the banks, the current carrying us gently over the spot where the alligator had crashed what seemed like just a few minutes ago. It was glassy, calm, I did not paddle, just steered us quietly, glacially, into the turn. Suddenly I heard a loud slap behind us, sharp like a rifle shot and then cascading water. By the time I'd whipped my head around, the surface was roiling and a wave was beginning to move to the banks, washing both sides, rocking our canoe. I wrenched the bow around but there was nothing left to see. The surface had returned to a dull gloss, underneath which was this great secret, still alive.

I am sure that the alligator was talking to us that second trip. It was barking at the mailman in its own enormous way. It was saying, this is my place, be gone, which, come to think of it, was the same thing all those property owners were saying with their riprap and tires upstream. Why do I respect the one so much and not the other? I suppose it is because wild creatures do not have much of a chance in this fight. Our side has earth movers, firearms, and second home mortgage deductions and it is going to win, it has already has won, there are few creatures like this remaining and, like Indians off the reservation, we cannot tolerate them. Not the really wild ones.

I can, though. I can almost talk to them, if that word can be used for such a phenomenon. I do not mean pray to them for miracles or messages. I mean another kind of feeling that says simply thank you for being. I am only sorry it may not be for long. As for what I said and didn't say to the sheriff up there on the creek, lying about where you were and all, I regret nothing.

BAYOU SORREL
Louisiana, 2010

A man named Stanley rescued me one afternoon in the Atchafalaya, the sun dropping and no route leading out. Some friends and I were paddling from Bayou Sorrel to Pigeon, where the flanking cypress stood like old warriors, their tops torn off by hurricanes, their trunks charred by lightning, green shoots sprouting impossibly from their shells. It felt like another planet here, two other planets if you counted the soybean fields we passed while driving in, three if you included the refineries. Four if you counted New Orleans. We heard the man before we saw him, roaring away in the distance, a short burst, a stop, another burst, making his mysterious rounds. We were totally lost.

Years back, I made this run with a dozen canoes and, in order not to lose them, I asked each to keep the one behind in sight. It was a nice theory and it had actually worked before, but each trip is different. This time we realized a boat was missing toward dusk when we found a campsite and counted noses. We were one short. We counted again. Peter Brown and his girlfriend had not come in and they were carrying the dessert.

In the failing light two of us lit out over the lake, through an isthmus and back up Cannon Bayou where we found them, chatting quietly, holding onto a tree. When he had gotten to that point, Peter said, he saw two routes and did not want to risk choosing the wrong one. Instead, they opened the wine. They knew we'd be back for the food, he added. The faith that students can have in us is frightening.

Camping that night was also a challenge. High water had flooded the swamp save the spoil bank of one pipeline canal covered in mud and vines. There would be nothing better for miles. We took it, pitched tents, and started a tiny fire of sticks and snags from neighboring trees. Dinner came in installments over a tiny flame, a spot of light and a circle of us on upturned canoes, small conversations, a little somber with the setting, and then Orinze, my Nigerian student, appeared. He had gone into his tent following dinner and when he emerged he was dressed head to foot in an embroidered robe, tall as a spire, face blacker than the night, firelight sparking off his eyes. He came to the edge of the circle, raised his arms, and said that he would lead us in song, a story song from his country about the lion and the monkey. We would sing too, he told us, as if we were children under his care.

I still remember the chant, three descending notes, em-a-way, em-a-way, em-a-way. Sometimes it comes to me in the shower and I feel a great sadness because Orinze died three years later, I never learned how. For my boys he had been a magician, tricking with the soccer ball while they tried to kick it away from him, while they and several others tried, while their whole little pickup team tried, it couldn't be done. When Grandparents' Day arrived at Gabe's primary school we had no grandparents available, so he asked for Orinze, who showed up in his magnificent gown, and they all learned the story song as well:

> Once upon a time in the deep jungle lived a lion
> Em-a-way, em-a-way, em-a-way
> And a monkey who liked to tease him and take his food . . .

Out there in the swamp below Bayou Sorrel this young man from Africa recomposed our evening, drew us together, spinning out his verses into the dark. We woke up the next morning to see signs plastered along the far tree line reading: "NO TRESPASSING, VIOLATORS WILL BE PROSECUTED, Atchafalaya Landowners Association." They were the first such signs I'd seen, but would not be the last. At one point during the legal skirmish that followed I pried one loose and put it on my shed. We were in the middle of the Atchafalaya crawfish wars.

The first cash crop of the Atchafalaya Basin was cypress timber, leveled in a few decades as if the trees were the enemy. Small lumber towns popped up along interior waterways like Bloody Bayou, whose bar won its reputation the hard way, and Bayou Chene, where the bateau of Longfellow's Evangeline crossed unseen in the night with that of her lover, as near to each other as they would come. Little of that virgin cypress remains. Second-growth trees, however, have replaced them and down around their massive knees lives the ignominious mudbug, countless numbers of them as attuned as the cypress are to the rhythms of the swamp. Low water is family time, their daubed chimneys poking up from the ground, but with the arrival of spring they venture out to fatten up on fields of yellow-top, crawling below waterline on roots, trunks and stems.

Originally scorned as trash food, crawfish became the staple crop of the Atchafalaya and ready cash for hundreds of bayou dwellers whose small shacks hugged the levees with a flatboat in every yard, parked there during the dry season when the men went off to weld on the oil rigs and rushed back to the swamp come spring to start the harvest. No one made a fortune on mudbugs but together they made a $12 million a year industry as renewable and certain as the seasons. The Atchafalaya fed New Orleans. It fed East Coast cities as well, and other parts of the world. Which is when basin landowners began posting the trees and demanding rent for a fishery that had been open to everyone with a boat for all time. The fight was on.

For some of us trying to save the Atchafalaya—to keep it, as we said, "wet and wild"—leaving landowners with property rights was a given; there was no way we were going to persuade the federal government to condemn a half million acres of swampland, not in this state, probably not anywhere. To be sure, others of us aimed for just that and in my heart I would certainly have preferred it, but I saw the goal here as retaining the water regime and preventing its conversion to soybeans, trailer parks, and the long good-bye. We finally hammered out an easement with the landowners that kept things wet and wild, limiting even the timber cut, but that the basic attributes of private property, minerals and the right to exclude others, in their hands. To the landowners, this settled it. The crawfishers were trespassing on their property.

We, however, didn't see crawfishers as being on anyone's property at all. From early spring into the summer they were floating on water up to twelve feet deep, lowering their traps from the boat, coming back to haul them up, empty the catch, put in fresh bait, return them to the water, and on to the next set. They came by boat, left by boat, and never set foot on bottom. They were, to us, within the rights of Americans before we ever *were* Americans. You could float navigable waters to fish in England from the time of the Magna Carta, and by the same token you could do it here. An attorney who defended the crawfishers when they were arrested by landowner-friendly sheriffs refused even to use the word "landowner"; he referred to them as "water-bottom claimants" instead.

Hence the NO TRESPASSING signs. Eventually a federal court ruled that the boats were not really navigating because they weren't in transit but rather simply going someplace to fish, which sure sounded like transit to me. Opinions like this do serve to enliven the law, however. Consider the ruling of Louisiana's Supreme Court that betting one's money at casinos was not "gambling"—an activity specifically prohibited by the state constitution—but, instead, only "gaming" and hence perfectly proper. The crawfish wars, nonetheless, continue today. I have been stopped several times in the Atchafalaya by men in boats with large motors and long guns, heaving up close to look into the canoe and assure themselves that I hadn't been stealing their creatures. Most of the encounters were friendly.

Yet another crawfish war carries on out here and it involves our man Stanley up on Bayou Sorrel. Poaching is alive and well in these parts and in no activity more than fishing. Simply spotting another boat near your lines or nets is enough to have you reaching for the pistol tucked under the console because the other boat will probably carry its own and may feel under attack. Particularly when it actually is poaching. Out here with students and coming across an untended crawfish trap I may raise it out of the water to show the catch, but not before I look first, very carefully, in all directions. All of which explains Stanley's reaction when we ran into him up on Sorrel, late and lost, as the day was about to disappear. Looking back on it, he could have been emptying someone else's crawfish traps . . . he had quite a few of them in the boat. I wouldn't even have suspected it but for things I heard later. All we knew at the time is that he was the only other human being for miles.

Hurricanes had changed the Atchafalaya landscape. The year before this trip a monster storm called George barreled out of the Caribbean headed straight for New Orleans, putting thousands of residents on the highways out of town. At the last minute George veered to the west instead and up the Atchafalaya River, crushing everything in its path. And so this particular spring, putting in at Sorrel for the usual run, we were soon blocked by downed trees, thorn bushes, and thickets of poison ivy. We improvised. We would bypass into a set of lakes and travel west toward Cannon Bayou, which should be open, a few miles ahead.

The lakes too were unrecognizable. New sandbars stood waist high in willows, forming a maze. We would skirt one, meet a dead end, backtrack, try up to the right, searching for a pass. We were making slow progress, an indecipherable distance from where we came in because we had no good idea where that was. I remained glued to the notion that we could break through to Cannon. Which was when we heard the motor.

It was hard to tell where it came from, the sound just filled the landscape, bellowing , stalling, bellowing again, coming closer, then ear-splittingly closer. I poked around a corner and into a giant of a man standing on the bow of an aluminum flatboat stacked with sacks of crawfish, its big outboard at the other end churning water and deafening us both. I gave him a Cajun shout, hay-yee! which was not wise because it took him by surprise, he looking up, seeing me so close by, reaching toward his console for what he knew and I suspected was there. What saved me was Endre's canoe, his wife in the bow really, who was wearing a bikini and pulling up alongside. I could see the giant relax. He was a vision, standing above us in cutoffs with a face hammered out of iron, nose wrenched to the side, a neck that would repel an axe, massive chest, dripping sweat and saying nothing, looking at us as if we were just as strange as he appeared to us. A pretty girl in a red canoe? Out here?

I tried to shout to him, he cut the motor, dead still, and I told him we were lost and looking for Cannon Bayou. Groping for a connect, I added that I used to come in here to see Alcide who lived off the Teche a few miles below. It was a lucky strike. Alcide was his uncle. His name was Stanley, he was a kickboxer, he never lost a fight, and there was one coming up in New Orleans in October. I told him I'd be there. There was no route to Cannon, he said, but we might go down the pipeline canal instead to the lakes below. He waved his hand to the west. Can't miss it he said and went back to hauling traps.

We missed it for the next hour or so and we might still be out there missing it but, on the verge of turning back, we heard Stanley zigzagging toward us again, stop and start, and then he was on us, puzzled to find us still here. I explained that we couldn't find the way. Follow me! he yelled, and we were off in the boiling wake of his Evinrude, immersed in its fumes. Soon, however, Stanley too ran into jams at which point he seemed to take it personally, or maybe it was the radiance of Endre's wife, and he revved up the motor, turned his boat into a battering ram, and went slamming over vines and logs, blazing trail. Finally the pipeline lay ahead. He pointed to it over the roar of his motor, backed out, and was gone. We hauled our boats to the pipeline spoil bank, topped it, and saw a canal so choked with vegetation that no creature larger than a snake could pass. Our day was done. We'd turn back.

Out into the maze again, all I knew was that our exit was to the east and through the same jumble of islands and false passes that had stumped us twice before. Withal, it was lovely, the time of day when light slants in sideways and the birds begin their final feed, sandpipers on the flats, lines of ibis kiting in, chattering blackbirds, heron scaring up fish with stomping feet and flapping wings. It would go on like this for about another thirty minutes before darkness fell, mosquitoes rose, Stanley would be hauling toward home, and we'd be stuck here until dawn. I nosed forward left and right, probing for openings. When I found one I'd call the others forward. The second time that happened Endre and his wife came up. What was that little strip of tape on the tree, they asked. And that one out ahead? The tapes had not been there coming in. They were there now, tied low and crudely, a single twist, not meant to last like a trap marker, meant to mark something else, like the way out. It had to have been Stanley. Nobody else had been in here. We emerged from the swamp at dark, crossed the intercoastal canal by starlight, and ground the canoes onto the gravel lot. I was dizzy with relief.

I wrote Stanley a letter but I didn't know his last name and only faintly recalled the route number he said he lived on. Some weeks later it came back undelivered. Endre and I kept our eyes out for a kickboxing tournament in New Orleans but never found it either. We enjoyed thinking about it, though, trying to imagine who could possibly defeat our man Stanley in any kind of a fight. Which is when I was told a little more about him.

I have a friend who lives just over the levee here, one street and a strip of small houses, and I'd trust him with anything I own. He is a completely honest man. I told him about my rescue out here some months before, but when I mentioned the Stanley part his face clamped down hard. That's a bad man, he said, the family too. There was a story about a brother who beat a coworker over the head with a shovel for his Friday paycheck and then buried him in the levee. There was Stanley himself, whom he caught stealing his crawfish traps and stashing them up the bayou. It was not pretty. Small towns everywhere look charming passing through, innocent even, and then come the stories, some of which are true. The Atchafalaya is many things but like the rest of this earth it is not heaven.

I never tried to find out more about Stanley, though, what was said about him that is, some corroboration. All I know for a fact is the way in which he treated a group of city folks from New Orleans who were out there that day, who were in his way really, and that he went out of his own way to guide them out. It could be that everything said about him was true, and that this was too. Not knowing is fine.

GRANDE RONDE
Oregon and Washington, 2013

Lisa is standing by me, frozen in place, but my mind has already been captured by the current as if I were a child on an escalator. There is no way I am not going to do this. Below is a rapid called the Bridge where adjacent cliffs pinch the entire river, running at more than 4,000 cubic feet per second, into a drop and nine-foot waves. The good part, I tell her, is that there are no holes, no rocks in the middle that could jam the canoe and me with it. Worst case, I just float out. A couple of friends below have just made the run in solo rafts and are standing by with throw ropes. I'll be fine. This is why I came.

It wasn't why I came of course, not all of why. Western rivers have turned out to be things that I chew on for months afterwards, even years. There are memories of light and space that seem like dreams of their own, was I really there? There are old friends whom we have paddled with a long time and former students who have caught the fever. Each year it is a little harder to come up out of the kneel for the lunch stop, slowly, one joint at a time. We may not have many of these left in us. This, too, was running through my mind as I pushed off toward the rapid. In all probability I would not be back this way again.

Lisa's anxiety goes way back. Forty years ago she was pinned in our first real rapid and that kind of thing lingers. She is braver out here than I am because she has more fear. Brave is about doing something while scared as hell, which I know about too. I can be paralyzed by high ledges, deep water, other things. Even now.

Then there was the Owyhee. Three years ago we ran the Owyhee Canyon with much of the current group in this same high desert, a smaller river than the Grande Ronde but it drops into a gorge for sixty miles. There is little room to cheat the rapids by sneaking them on the side. In places, there is no side. Lisa and I lined three of them entirely and dumped in others, twice on the last day alone, nothing life-threatening, but still. That Lisa agreed to go back again and try the Grande Ronde says a lot. I was fortunate she was out here at all.

The Grande Ronde rises in high forest and joins other swift tributaries to enter a more open canyon which turns slowly into hills already brown in late spring. This was the heart of the western fur trade in its heyday, named by French trappers for its sinewy curves that loop back on themselves so completely they seem to make circles.

It was also the heart of the Nez Perce nation spanning 17 million acres, with sorties as far as the Great Plains for buffalo and to the Cascades for salmon, the largest civilization in the Pacific Northwest. A peaceful one as well, Nez Perce saved the Lewis and Clark party at one point from failure, until the whites who followed wanted their land . . . why does this story sound so familiar? . . . and brought on the U.S. Army. Part of the tribe led by the legendary Chief Joseph resisted and, seeking sanctuary, began a 1,700-mile trek to avoid capture. Some two hundred men, women, and children evaded American soldiers ten times their number, cavalry, howitzers, and Gatling guns, winning no fewer than eighteen skirmishes until, forty miles from the Canadian border, they were finally corralled in the snow. Promised a return to their Grand Ronde homeland, they were instead sent off to Kansas and Oklahoma, where no more than a thousand survived. The United States quickly opened the region to a land rush, first come, first served. This, too, surrounds us.

So do rattlesnakes. According to *Soggy Sneakers: A Paddler's Guide to Oregon Rivers*, there are more rattlers on the Grande Ronde than anywhere else in the West. It could be a tall claim but Ed, who floated it decades ago, tells of lunching on a bluff overlooking the river, reclined against a log, and when they got up to go an enormous sidewinder slid out from under and paraded across the bluff with the careless grace of an athlete, which of course it is. I thought about bringing my old snakebite kit along with us, a wicked plunger to make the incision and a suction cup to drain the poison, only to read that this approach is now passé. The best thing was to elevate the wound and call for help, which you can do these days. One bleep to the satellite for emergency rescue and they send in a helicopter. I hate to confess that I was sorry to learn this.

The first day or so we all tread carefully, whacking the brush with sticks or paddles ahead of us, but that soon abated, until the fourth night when Gabe went to set his tent under a tree and was greeted by a telltale, rattling noise. He jumped a foot in the air and brought us running and there it was, coiled on itself, snug by a root, its tail tingling. We left it in peace and it left us in peace. Which for things to worry about left only the rapids.

The last day brought a large drop called the Narrows. It had a bluff on the right to scout from and we stared at the water for a long time, Gabe saying to himself, "I'm scared of this one" and then, "I'm going to run it," back and forth, Adam saying, "I hear you" and then, "When I take my eyes off it the whole landscape moves," me saying, "Lisa will want to walk it," and then, "Anyone want to try it twice?" Adam's canoe went first and then Gabe's, right down the middle, and they both swamped in the stacks. I decided on a practically nonexistent eddy line along the right bank bordered by pointy rocks. Adam came back to join me and we started out fine, right on plan, hugging the bank when it caught the bow, spun us in an instant, and we paddled the rest backwards as if on a tightrope, the flume boiling alongside perhaps a foot away. Later Gabe said, smiling wryly, "You could never repeat that move," and he was entirely correct. Luck matters.

Now the last rapid, the Bridge, and I am headed out solo with the old West Virginia feeling, the river dropping ahead and sending up bursts of spray, the route, so clear from above, at canoe level lost in the jumble. Cautiously, kneeling straight up, back-paddling a little to buy time, I am completely free. There is no one else to coordinate with. There is just this one paddle. Back on the bank I had turned the canoe around for more control of the front end, the singles position I'd learned back East years before, and it flows back into my veins like a forgotten language. I remember how slowly I can go, so light in the boat, I can turn us forty-five degrees with a stroke, the question is whether in the mishmash below we can hold a line. The fear is gone too, even if I dump my feet are not pinned under a seat but free beneath me, there is no way I can not eject, I am invincible.

I have no idea how long this run took in real time, it couldn't have been more than a minute or two. I cannot hope to feel exactly that way again.

WOLF RIVER
Mississippi, 2013

I'd not seen a vehicle parked down here in thirty years. Out a country road, under a bridge only half-repaired since the last flood, then down a rutted pitch so steep we just let the canoe slide ahead of us. But on this day a huddle of trucks was waiting, nosed up the slope at a sharp angle, rear gates open, beer cans and food boxes on the ground. No one was in sight. I checked the trucks more carefully, none had a boat rack, maybe they brought four-wheelers out here instead. My heart sank. I'd rather encounter wild boar.

The mystery cleared when we reached the water rimmed by a thin sand beach. The marks of a large boat tracked out into the water. Here instead was a single family with fishing poles and a stack of cans reading LITE on the sides, several of them empty. The cardboard case they came in bobbed in the shallows, disintegrating into the current. Several youngsters were stoning a LITE they had tossed in upstream, an enemy ship passing by. Their father was looking out at Lisa and me from under the brim of a baseball hat curled so narrowly it seemed a tunnel, his eyes way back in the dark. His wife warned the children to "stay away from that dog . . . he'll bite your hand off!" It was hard for the kids to escape Ms. Bear, however, who smelled their Doritos bag and was trailing them like a mosquito. I told them the dog'd never bitten a thing but then again that is what all dog owners say, even about the monsters straining at the leash and eyeing your throat. Better we put in right away, Lisa suggested.

Cyp called this our honeymoon trip. Lisa and I had not been out alone for decades. We had always gone with friends, students, the kids and their friends, all of whom tended to buffer us and provide the conversation. We came to assume that we needed them. This time our friends were elsewhere, my students into exams, and both boys into their own lives so we were down to two again, which felt new.

Back in the day I'd simply assumed that Lisa wouldn't mind wet feet, sudden rain, biting insects, and a thin pad to sleep on, and she never did complain. By now, though, we had arrived at a little more clarity; these were not her favorite things. This weekend was going to be hot with a good chance of showers, water levels were low, and mosquito conditions were excellent. I wasn't sure how we'd do. I tucked in some books just in case.

Lisa also remembered our last trip here. We had come up to the Wolf with the boys and two dogs after a heavy rain, intent on paddling this section, but one look told me that it would be washed out. I talked us into running a narrower, faster section upstream that was normally too thin to think about. Before long we were dealing with overhanging branches, barking dogs, one turnover, and increasing signs of discontent. We finally found an early pull-out on the property of a couple who offered to give Lisa and the boys a lift to our car, bless them. I went on down solo, coming in well after dark. It was a costly indulgence. To this day we see that trip with different eyes. This was the same river.

Wolf has a small watershed, and a dry spring had reduced it to small passages and pools. I prayed we had enough water to slip by and we did, just, and it soon became the old game again, picking our way, cut to the left here, then over there, the choreography returning in a slower tempo. We skimmed over bottoms of yellow and gray, tiny canyons tufted with green grass that bent under the current and nodded at us floating by. I felt us getting younger, happy not to need other people, happy in our skins.

I have my own misgivings out here: four-wheelers. With miles of woods and countryside to choose from, these machines seem drawn to sandy rivers like bombs to a target. The first beach we came to was marked by the ruts of truck tires, a spread of LITE cans, and a pile of charred tree limbs lit no doubt, and why not?, with gasoline. It was spectacularly coherent, all of a piece. We floated on past three more beaches, each one similarly wasted, me fantasizing about digging a Malaysian tank trap or better yet finding a vehicle buried in water ahead of us, hopelessly stuck.

Instead, we found peace. An unmolested site. The rises and falls of this small river sculpt the sand in layers, a flat top where last flood came by, white as ice cream, and driftwood scattered about as if someone knew we were coming and laid in a carefully random supply. We hauled up the canoe, turned it over for a table, raised the tent, gathered the firewood, lay out the cooking gear, all the steps of the dance we used to dance when we were younger and did these things by instinct, missing only the sounds of the boys. Night was kept at bay by a rising moon. Out in the distance someone let off a final volley of gunshots, an automobile motor faded, and in the quiet the Wolf came alive, the shuffle of a distant chute, a stick rippling by. Our books never made it out of the dry bag. We sat against the boat, talking lightly, trying to guess constellations like the Crab and Cassiopeia's Chair that we never knew in the first place, as if we had only forgotten them. We felt young and old at the same time.

The next day was as easy until we missed the takeout, completely. We'd left our car at the place of a friend downriver whom we'd visited several times before, only this spring the vegetation had grown so thick along the bank that we never saw it and floated right by. The first sign of something wrong, other than time passing, was a large beach that I did not recall, occupied by two supersize women whom we saw intimately because they lay like tuna on towels near the water's edge, whatever they were wearing hidden in folds of flesh. Above them thirty or so teenagers loitered ankle-deep in soda and beer cans. What was going on here was about as harmless as kids get these days, but I found myself wondering if they saw the cans at all. Perhaps the trash was their mark, we have been here and made this place our own, which come to think of it is what Ms. Bear did on her outings too, a very primal impulse. Or perhaps they simply knew that come next high water it would all disappear.

We floated the last bend and there ahead was the highway bridge, which I recalled from long ago as the takeout from hell. It still was. The clay banks went up forty feet, slippery as soap. First, though, we had to reach the bridge, which is where, as if heaven-sent, we saw a four-wheeler foundered in the river, buried to its handlebars, helpless. An equally helpless young man stood on top trying to start the motor, which wouldn't budge. I started to grin and then saw the problem. The machine straddled the only channel deep enough to pass our canoe. I was not going to be able to savor the moment. I was going to have to help out.

I waded in, quick to my waist in the current, no purchase on the bottom, useless. The boy, bare-chested and muscular, was now tugging his vehicle against the flow, which wasn't going to work either. We got up on the bank and reversed course, rocking the machine with the current, picking up momentum, the front wheels rising, then a rear one, then the other, and it was out. The boy jumped back on immediately, grinding the starter, evidently expecting it to burst into life. He was still at it when we glided past him and down to the bridge of doom. Somehow we needed to get our gear up that cliff and then hitch back to where we'd left the car.

At which point another Mississippi thing happened. A different age set, young families, lounged on the sandbars just up from the bridge, surrounded by more LITES, Coke cans, lawn chairs, stereos, coolers, used diapers, and a raft of toddlers. Ms. Bear leapt from the boat to make friends, alert for the possibility of food. Going to retrieve her, I told a woman she was pestering that we'd missed our takeout and were going to have to go back for the car. It was only an explanation for why we were about to attack the wall but as I was walking away she caught up with me and offered to give us a lift. I did not ask her, I did not mean to ask her, she just came up. People out here do things like that.

Lisa and I began to haul gear. We saved the worst for last, the canoe, which I used to carry on my shoulders like a child but now seemed made of concrete and it was all we could do to inch it up, take a break, and inch it again, crawling like a dying reptile. Lisa had every reason to say something about my missing the takeout but she saved it. In fact she never did say it. Instead we grunted along together, one, two, heave, until we had the final ascent in sight, straight up. As I went in front for a different grip and raised the bow the whole canoe suddenly lifted and pushed me forward like a ram. I looked back and the boy from the sunken bike was carrying the stern, not saying a word. I gave him a smile and a handshake. How could I not? Hello, Mississippi.

I still do not like four-wheelers. They intrude on the reason I am out here, a dream, an illusion, really, and they attack a landscape I love. They have now begun attacking the stream bottoms themselves in trucks mounted high on monster tires, mud rallies posted on the Web, more than a hint of pride in being able to muck up something so pretty. In their way these youngsters are as guiltless as soldiers, there is nothing mean about them, and they are as programmed to do what they do as I am by another program whose roots I understand only faintly better. Whether there is a modus vivendi among us I have no idea.

I keep telling myself that these rivers are very old, that they will always be coming around the bend, that they will endure. Having said this, though, I feel grateful to have lived in a time when the Wolf is still here with its beauty and its freedom, as if the entire scene might end. These thoughts are not fully compatible, but they are the best I can do.

POSTLUDE

I continue to go. I have a lighter canoe now, lent to me by a friend who simply said you keep it, I'll come get it when I want to use it. My shoulders aren't good but I am able to mount it on top of the car, find water nearby, and enter this second world I have been living with like a double marriage for so long. Lisa and the boys come when they can. Ms. Bear would too but she has just gone to the other side. The morning she died a great white egret landed on our lawn and stayed here for several hours, back and forth, stalking. No such bird has ever visited us before, not even the neighborhood, nor has one since. I'd say it was a coincidence, but still.

I try not to go to the same river too frequently, and I try not to remember them lest they become known by markers along the way. What I've come to see is that these are largely trips of the mind, or perhaps trips away from the mind because I do very little thinking out here, I just am. So were all of the places I've described in this book, just themselves, along with people who have arisen from the sleep of our mutual past to parade by me as in carnival, each in costume, throwing me a memory half-lost.

There are times I would like to talk with them about these trips, some of them quite extended, because I'm not sure that any of us made the same journey, not exactly the same, perhaps not even close, which strikes me as beautiful. I'd like to thank you for joining us on this one. This book was a journey of its own and, as I was writing it, I had no sure idea of the route or how it would end. That too has felt right. It is the way I feel about my life.

Oliver A. Houck
New Orleans, Louisiana
August 2013

ACKNOWLEDGMENTS

There is no way to thank or even identify the many people who have introduced me to rivers and then enjoyed them with me, at times in a cold rain. Bill Per-Lee, whom I mentioned early on, was my lead on the Potomac, stronger than I and more skilled. Perrin Quarles organized many of our expeditions into Virginia and West Virginia, and, going west, it has been Ed Chaney and Denny Hanson, both of them rafters, stalling patiently while we scouted a drop, waiting below just in case. My trips in northern Canada were led, sequentially, by John Lentz and Ed Richardson, both made for the role. My canoe mate on the Barren Grounds, Joe Lederle, pulled us out of several jams and infused us all with his enthusiasm; a partner like him is pure gold. Coming south, I was brought into the Atchafalaya by Chuck Fryling of LSU and the photographer Clyde Lockwood; to the streams of the pine belt by Mike Osborne, who defended several of them in court; and to the Pearl by my friend Byron Almquist. I am often accompanied these days by Jay Martin, who is into the same scene for the same reasons, and by a running cast of students who, like the rivers themselves, are always moving on and renewed by the classes that follow. They too, in sum, are magical.

It is hard to place Lisa here because she has been with me on so many outings, has tolerated my absences and surprises (once I came in very late, with a dog), and has her own take on rivers, the mist in the morning, the rush of what she calls "busy water" ahead. I've watched my boys Cyp and Gabe come into their own to the point where they now advise me, get the boats up, load gear, take charge. And then there has been Ms. Bear. I would no more than start to the shed for the paddles than she sensed the adventure to come, bopping up and down, dashing back and forth, showing me that she was ready to go this very minute and I'd be crazy not to take her. And so I did. And was so richly rewarded.

Bless all of you.

LEADS AND RESOURCES

The best way to learn canoeing is to go paddle, and nothing could be easier. Almost every river of size has a rental and livery service, and they tend to favor the easiest runs, you can't go wrong. They make for very pleasant days.

If you want to take the next step and go out on your own, new canoes these days run around a thousand dollars, but the nice thing is that old canoes are just as good and often pop up on Craig's List or in the classified sections of the newspaper. The canoe rentals usually have sales of their used canoes at summer's end, a little banged up but no matter: it takes a bad accident to destroy the aluminum boats or the new breeds of Royalex and similar compounds. Caveat: Fiberglass is more fragile, and Kevlar is superlight but more fragile still: you will not want to run white water in either one. Canoes these days come in different shapes and sizes, and guides to them are all over the Web. Your basic tradeoffs are maneuverability (flat-bottom), carrying capacity (size), and tracking (keel or V-shaped hull), the ability to hold a line in swift current or wind. Everyone who paddles has a favorite. Nearly every vehicle made short of a convertible can carry a boat (and, as described in this book, even a convertible at times though I do not recommend it).

Kayaks and rafts are their own worlds but present the same advantages and disadvantages, one meant for maneuver and the other for carrying loads. Both can handle big water. Personally, I find the canoe a good compromise because you are up high enough to see things and still have plenty of excitement, yet camp with an ice chest at day's end. Kayakers and rafters, of course, will vociferously disagree, and they should. They are each into the scene in unique ways.

If you want to paddle more rapid water then a little training is helpful, for white water it is mandatory, and fortunately there are several books on the subject (see Robert McNair, *Basic River Canoeing*, Buck Ridge Ski Club, for one), and many groups and outfitters offer teaching programs. The Nantahala Outdoor Center on a river of the same name in North Carolina runs intensive white-water classes for both kayaks and canoes, and they are but the tip of the iceberg. Byron Almquist's Canoe and Trail Adventures in New Orleans does the same but at a more basic river-running level. Lisa and I learned from the Canoe Cruisers Association of Greater Washington, D.C., and almost every city in the country has a similar club (often associated with hiking or skiing). The basic moves are not hard to learn but require live practice, including safety and rescue. Flipping over need not be a disaster, it can be a good lesson for next time.

It should go without saying that no one should be out in a canoe without knowing how to swim . . . absolutely no one . . . and wearing a flotation device in fast water should be as automatic as breathing air. I am stunned by the number of people who don't seem to get this. We in New Orleans have spent fifteen years cleaning up Lake Pontchartrain to the point that it is swimmable again, only to read of drownings in a few feet of water: it was a hot day, he went in with his buddies, he didn't even know how to float, so back up go the "No Swimming" signs. What is wrong with this picture?

The next question is where to paddle and, again, nothing is easier to discover. I am looking at eleven river guidebooks alongside me as I write this, a small slice of those available for every state and region. Lisa and I sortied out of the Washington, D.C., area with Randy Carter's *Canoeing White Water River Guide* (Appalachian Outfitters) in the car, covering Virginia and West Virginia, a mini-world of its own. At the state level, there are, for example, Cassady and Calhoun's *California Whitewater* (Northfork Press); Hank Fischer's *The Floater's Guide to Montana* (Falcon Press); and Ray Gabler's *New England White Water River Guide* (Tobey Publishing). Each contains river descriptions, access points, and difficulty ratings. For the New Orleans region, John Sevenair's *Trail Guide to the Delta Country* (Sierra Club) has a good rundown on canoe trips in the area. On a national level, there is also

Richard Penny's *Whitewater Sourcebook* (Menasha Ridge Press), with data on all major runnable American rivers.

A word about the ratings. The scale runs from the easiest, Class I, virtually no obstacles, to Class VI, death-inviting, you have to be crazy or very, very good, think Great Falls. As a rule of thumb, open boat canoes with skilled paddlers can handle through Class III with appropriate scouting, and even the occasional Class IVs, particularly with a spray skirt, extra flotation, and perhaps portaging the gear (or a raft along to carry it). This said, the scales are interpreted differently East and West, because the East sees a majority of canoes and the West very few. A western Class III might be a tricky but relatively risk-free run for a kayak or a raft, but a heavy challenge for an open canoe. Rule of Thumb: open boat canoers should upgrade the western ratings by at least half a step.

The Web has made river scouting yet more accessible, and a simple Google search will pull up river descriptions, photos, trip reports, and outfitters with a move of the mouse. Many states have river websites as well, the Florida Paddling Trails Association's site, floridapaddlingtrails.com, being a good example. Major rivers through federal lands are managed for recreation by the agency responsible, i.e., the U.S. Forest Service, Bureau of Land Management, and each piece of water will have its own website and trip ticket describing the run and identifying obstacles mile by mile. These federal river managers are quite helpful and are very much worth, after doing your homework, a telephone call for updates and details. The U.S. Geological Survey reports water levels around the country on a daily basis; go to usgs.gov/water and then "current streamflow conditions." Amazingly handy.

The popularity of many managed rivers in spring and summer has led to permits on a lottery system (divided between commercials and recreationals), usually open in February. For a high-value run such as the Middle Fork of the Salmon it is not unusual to try for years before landing. Or you can just show up one morning and hope for a cancellation. Much as one may dislike the notion of applying for permission to use a public resource, the lottery system has managed to keep most runs clean and enjoyable; the alternative would be neither.

From this brief rundown I hope you realize that it is all quite doable and within reach. A little learning will go a long way to make it more so, and more fun. The only additional rule out there is a largely silent one: to carry out what you carry in, the same for outdoors anywhere. For some folks this rule seems to be viewed as a challenge—look what we left behind!—but, with regional variations, it is widely respected. Of all the things I've heard people talk about doing, I've met almost no one who regretted going out on a river.

SOURCES

CHARLES RIVER

16 **On the Charles they did cows too** . . . William Marchione, *Allston-Brighton in Transition: From Cattle Town to Streetcar Suburb* (Charleston, S.C.: History Press, 2007), 18–21; William Marchione, "Cattle Trade Was Major Business in Brighton," *Allston-Brighton Citizen-Item*, July 31, 1980, 1.

16 **the river has become a comeback story** . . . Charles River Conservancy, "A Swimmable Charles? Water Quality and Public Access," 2001, pp. 2–7, www.thecharles.org/media/uploads/2013/04/Charles03_web.pdf.

SHENANDOAH RIVER

24 **Stonewall Jackson's Shenandoah Valley campaign** . . . Peter Cozzens, *Shenandoah 1862: Stonewall Jackson's Valley Campaign* (Chapel Hill: University of North Carolina Press, 2008), 1–6.

25 **it would have fallen** . . . Ibid., 37–38; Herman Hattaway and Archer Jones, *How the North Won: A Military History of the Civil War* (Champaign: University of Illinois Press, 1991), 95.

26–27 **where John Brown brought his tiny band to ignite a revolution** . . . For a recent history of John Brown and the raid on Harpers Ferry, see Tony Horowitz, *Midnight Rising: John Brown and the Raid That Sparked the Civil War* (New York: Holt, 2011). See also John Edwin Cooke and Robert M. De Witt, *The Life, Trial, and Execution of Captain John Brown* (New York: DeWitt, 1959), 29–37.

27 **these mills top the nation's water pollution list, year after year** . . . In the 1970s, before the advent of federal clean water requirements, the pulp and paper industry was discharging more than 10 million tons of raw solids a day, second only to the coal industry (U.S. EPA, *Water Quality Improvement Study* [1989]). Even follow-

ing new controls, as of 2010, the pulp and paper industry was
releasing some 17 million pounds of toxins into the water, the
fourth-largest toxic discharge category in the country (EPA, "2010
Toxic Release Inventory, National Analysis Overview," www2.
epa.gov/sites/production/files/documents/2010_national_analy-
sis_overview_document.pdf).

27 **the industry is still fighting** . . . William Boyd, "Controlling Toxic
Harms: The Struggle over Dioxin Contamination in the Pulp and
Paper Industry," *Stanford Environmental Law Journal* 345 (2002):
21; National Wildlife Federation v. EPA, 286 F.3d 554 (DC Cir.
2002) (dioxin discharge standard); "Introduction, Chlorine Zero
Discharge Act of 1995," *Proceedings and Debates of the 104th Congress, 1st Sess.,* 1995 WL 144078 Cong. Rec. (Apr. 1995) (remarks
of Rep. Bill Richardson).

JUNIPER SPRINGS

28 **a jewel of water rising from a thirty-foot well** . . . See Johnny
Molloy, Elizabeth Carter, and John Pearce, *Canoeing and Kayaking in Florida,* 2nd ed. (Birmingham, Ala.: Menasha Ridge Press,
2011), 176–77.

29 **but the largest of all is at Wakulla** . . . Michal Strutin, *Florida State
Parks: A Complete Recreation Guide* (Seattle: Mountaineers Books,
2000), 55–56.

31 **into a dead-end lagoon** . . . Molloy, Carter, and Pearce, *Canoeing
and Kayaking in Florida,* 109–10.

32 **Florida's famed springs have run into trouble** . . . Greg Allen,
"Now Endangered, Florida's Silver Springs Once Lured Tourists,"
NPR news report transcript, April 2013, www.npr.org/templates/
transcript/transcript.php?storyId=177105692; Richard Hamann,
Managing Nutrient Inputs to Florida Springs: The Legal Framework,
in *Summary and Synthesis of the Available Literature on the Effects
of Nutrients on Spring Organisms and Systems* (Gainesville: University of Florida Water Institute, 2008), 325, www.dep.state.fl.us/
springs/reports/files/UF_SpringsNutrients_Report.pdf.

32 **it sets records** . . . Elizabeth Stanton and Matthew Taylor, *Valu-
ing Florida's Clean Waters,* Stockholm Environment Institute–U.S.

Center (Medford, Mass.: Tufts University Press, 2012), pp. 14–16, http://floridawatercoalition.org/wp-content/uploads/2012/11/ValuingFloridasCleanWaters.pdf.

32 **While there are several culprits here** . . . Another major player is phosphate mining, whose open pits contaminate surface and ground waters alike. The water consumption of these operations, at an average of more than one hundred thousand gallons per minute, per mine, makes serious inroads on freshwater supply as well (Adrianne Appel, "Florida Counties Try to Contain Phosphate Mines," *New York Times*, August 4, 2007, www.nytimes. com/2007/08/04/us/04phosphates.html; U.S. Army Corps of Engineers, "Final Area-wide Environmental Impact Statement [AEIS] on Phosphate Mining in the Central Florida Phosphate District [CFPD]," *Appendix D: Surface Water Quality Evaluations for the Final AEIS on Phosphate Mining in the CFPD Jacksonville District* [Washington, D.C., 2013], D-53–D-54, www.phosphateaeis. org/doc_final_aeis.html).

32 **a knock-down with the sugar industry** . . . See United States v. S. Fla. Water Mgmt. Dist., 847 F. Supp. 1567 (S.D. Fla. 1992) (settlement agreement requiring Florida to comply with phosphorous load allocations); Michael Grunwald, *The Swamp* (New York: Simon and Schuster, 2005) (history of the Everglades and legal challenges); and Michael Grunwald, afterword to *The Everglades: River of Grass*, by Marjory Stoneman Douglas (Sarasota, Fla.: Pineapple Press, 2007), 410–31. The litigation pressure produced results, and phosphate contamination is down.

32 **spent decades resisting** . . . Florida began resisting federal cleanup requirements for particular waterways in the 1990s (Oliver A. Houck, *The Clean Water Act TMDL Program: Law, Policy and Implementation*, 2nd ed. [Washington, D.C.: Environmental Law Institute, 2002], 165–212), and then resisted numeric standards for its major pollution problem, nutrients, primarily from agriculture. See Fla. Wildlife Fed'n v. S. Fla. Water Mgmt. Dist., 647 F.3d 1296 (11th Cir. 2011) (requiring state to promulgate numeric standards); see also Fla. Wildlife Fed'n v. Dept. of Envtl. Prot., DOAH Case No. 03-3532RP (2004) (state pollution allocations invalid). After several losing lawsuits, the state has at last agreed to set caps

on nutrients, albeit with an implementation process so tentative they are unlikely to be effective (author conversation with David Guest, Senior Attorney, Earthjustice, January 2013, Tallahassee, Fla.). In August 2013, the Florida Wildlife Federation sued the EPA to force Florida's compliance with related anti-degradation requirements of the Clean Water Act (see T. W. Reese to author, e-mail titled "Notice of Complaint against EPA," August 10, 2013; Mr. Reese represents the Federation in this case).

BIG SUR

34 **the big dog of California's central range** . . . Olaf Domis, "A Pico Blanco Solstice," *Double-Cone Quarterly: A Window to the Wild* (Fall 1998), www.ventanawild.org/news/fe98/olafpico.html.

34 **uncannily familiar** . . . Matthew Holliman, "Pico Blanco: Climbing, Hiking & Mountaineering," *SummitPost*, February 21, 2006, www .summitpost.org/pico-blanco/154509.

35 **a company called Granite Rock filed a mineral claim** . . . Domis, "A Pico Blanco Solstice."

35 **a reasonable proposition for any miner** . . . The Mining Law of 1872 is found at 30 U.S. Code §§ 22-54, and is well-described in Council on Environmental Quality, *Environmental Quality,* 9th Annual Report, 291–92 (December1978). It continues to govern mining on public lands for such high-value minerals as uranium and gold, which are made available to (often foreign) mining corporations without the payment of royalties. For the staying power of this anachronism—cemented in custom and politics—see Marc Humphries, "Mining on Federal Lands," CRS Issue Brief for Congress, IB89130, 4–9 (Congressional Research Service, June 11, 2002); Richard L. Gordon, "Reforming the 1872 Mining Law": *H.R. Testimony before Subcomm. on Energy and Mineral Resources: Comm. on Resources* (106th Cong., Aug. 3, 1999), www.cato.org/ publications/congressional-testimony/reforming-1872-mining-law.

36 **Enter a new actor, the California Coastal Commission** . . . The federal Coastal Zone Management Act, 16 U.S. Code §§ 1451–1466, was enacted in 1976 to stimulate state management of coastal areas and resources. The California Commission was created in response to this act.

36 **The Commission took its task to heart** . . . The Pacific Legal Foundation was formed and funded largely by the California real estate and development interests to combat the Coastal Commission (*see* Oliver A. Houck, "With Charity for All," *Yale Law Journal* 93 [1985]: 1415).

36 **off they went into a legal fray** . . . California Coastal Commission v. Granite Rock Co., 480 U.S. 572 (U.S. 1987).

GREAT FALLS OF THE POTOMAC

51 **to intervene famously** . . . 121 S. Cong. Rec., 94th Cong., 1st Sess., pt. 25 at 32281 (Oct. 8, 1975).

51 **until a government witness showed a map** . . . Conversation with Robert M. Kennan Jr., August 1971. Mr. Kennan was general counsel to the National Wildlife Federation at the time and had formed an organization called Committee of 100 on the Federal City to oppose the highway project; he attended the trial throughout. See also Zachary M. Schrag, *The Great Society Subway: A History of the Washington Metro* (Baltimore: Johns Hopkins University Press, 2008), 136.

51 **wrote an opinion favoring the environmentalists** . . . See D.C. Fed'n of Civic Ass'ns v. Volpe, 316 F. Supp. 754 (D.D.C. 1970), affirmed 459 F.2d 1231 (D.C. Cir. 1972), partially on grounds that the District of Columbia had been blackmailed into approving the bridge by Senator Natcher of Kentucky, who threatened to cut off federal aid unless the District dropped its opposition (459 F.2d 1245–50). The dissent, in turn, dismissed the Three Sisters Islands as "nothing more than three small rocks" in the Potomac River which "at low tide are connected by a small sand bar" (id. at 1253 n. 6). Perspective is everything.

DEERFIELD RIVER

56 **Vermont first passed a bottle bill** . . . Anthony Gierzynski et al., "Bottle Bills," James M. Jeffords Center's "Vermont Legislative Research Service 2," University of Vermont, 2012, www.uvm.edu/~vlrs/Environment/Bottle%20Bills.pdf (scholarly report on bottle bills in Vermont and America).

57 **They killed the program outright** . . . Ibid.

57 **Oregon and Vermont (again)** . . . Oregon's bottle bill came in 1971, The Beverage Container Act, or Rev. Stat. § 459A.700–740 (1971), www.leg.state.or.us/ors/459a.html. Vermont's second bill came the following year, and although subsequently expanded, it faces recurring opposition (id. at 3). Lynn Monty, "Vermont's Bottle Bill, Once First in the Nation, Now Facing Serious Effort at Repeal," *Burlington Free Press*, January 30, 2011, 8www.bottlebill. org/news/articles/2011/VT-1-30-VTsBBOnceFirst.htm.

57 **The first time she went up to lobby** . . . Conversations with Marcia Barber, August 1981. See also Marcia Barber, "Federated Garden Clubs of Vermont, Inc., Activities in Support of Billboard Control Legislation," undated memorandum, on file with author.

58 **29 degrees BELOW ZERO!** . . . Ibid., 3. The memo runs five typewritten pages, small font, single-spaced, and ends: "The Federal Highway Beautification Act and the new Vermont law are like the U.S. Constitution in that they both establish a broad principle, and both (all three) need continuing support and strengthening and eternal vigilance."

58 **it too went on for several years** . . . "Vermont Billboard Law," 10 Vt. Stat. Ann. 21 §§ 480–506 (1968), www.leg.state.vt.us/statutes/sections.cfm?Title=10&Chapter=021; Nathaniel Gibson, "Yes, We Have No Billboards," *Rutland Herald*, March 11, 2012, www.nathanielrgibson.com/yes-we-have-no-billboards-rutland-herald-article/2012/03/13/ (outdoor advertising regulations in Vermont and their application today).

59–60 **which put new development proposals** . . . Act 250, 10 Vt. Stat. Ann. (1970) p. 151. State of Vermont Natural Resources Board, "District Commissions, Act 250" (May 25, 2011), www.nrb.state. vt.us/lup/publications/nrb1.pdf.

60 **went one better to form a larger coalition** . . . See "Group Forms to Defend Act 250 and Land Plans; Mrs. Barber Co-Chairman," *Bennington Banner*, March 8, 1973.

60 **I'd like to see Vermonters decide** . . . Ibid.

60 **after the bill's passage** . . . Conversations with Jonathan Brownell, attorney, June 10, 11, 2012. Mr. Brownell was an assistant attorney general for the State of Vermont at the time and worked with leg-

islators and the Federated Garden Clubs on the enactment of Act
250 and its subsequent defense in court.

60 **which should have ended the matter** . . . Tracy Schmaler et al.,
"Permit Overhaul OK'd by Split House Committee," *Rutland Herald,* March 22, 2003, www.vce.org/changingAct250.html (collecting news stories on Act 250's permit "reform").

60 **I would ask Marcia about it** . . . One of Marcia Barber's last initiatives was the cleanup of the Hoosic River, which flowed directly through her hometown of Bennington, Vermont (see Mary Bell, "Hoosic River under Study," *Bennington Banner,* August 26, 1986). She, too, came to the water.

ROCK CREEK

62 **the pedigree of Rock Creek Park** . . . Timothy Davis, "Rock Creek and Potomac Parkway," Historic American Building Survey, HABS No. DC-697, 2 (Washington, D.C., 1991–92), lcweb2.loc.gov/pnp/habshaer/dc/dc0800/dc0806/data/dc0806data.pdf.

62 **one of the best-preserved examples** . . . Ibid.

62 **some four thousand of them during a good morning rush** . . . Joseph S. Springer, "June 2004 Traffic Study for Rock Creek Park: Washington D.C.," National Park Service Denver Service Center, "NPS Contract No. 1443C2000-99-013," Task Order No. T2000991384, pp. 1–2 (Washington, D.C., 2004).

65 **our pact with the American people** . . . Newt Gingrich, "21st Century Contract with America," 2012 Presidential Candidacy: Republican Platform, Des Moines, Iowa, September 29, 2011, http://firstread.nbcnews.com/_news/2011/09/29/8045194-gingrich-launches-21st-century-contract?lite.

BARREN GROUNDS

67 **The Canadian writer Farley Mowat called them** . . . Farley Mowat, *People of the Deer* (Vancouver: D&M, 2012).

67 **Samuel Hearne set out two centuries ago** . . . Martin W. Sandler, *Resolute: The Epic Search for the Northwest Passage and John Franklin: Discovery of the Queen's Ghost Ship* (New York: Sterling, 2008), 259.

CACHE LA POUDRE

71 **The story goes that** . . . "Cache la Poudre River Origins," Examiner.com, February 9, 2010, www.examiner.com/article/cache-la-poudre-river-origins; Rheba Massey, "Was 'Cache La Poudre' the Original Name of Our Local River That Flows through Downtown Fort Collins?," Fort Collins History Connection, http://history.poudrelibraries.org/archive/poudreriver.php.

71 **In the late 1800s** . . . Enos A. Mills, *The Grizzly* (New York: Ballantine, 1973 1919).

71 **Mills traveled into grizzly** . . . Ibid.

71 **Mills begins his book** . . . Ibid., vii.

72 **To Native Americans a** . . . Joseph Mussulman, "Grizzly Bear—*Ursus arctos horribilis*," "Discovering Lewis and Clark," http://lewis-clark.org/content/content-channel.asp?ChannelID=138; it continues: "Bears are 'half-human' some Indians used to say, 'humans without fire' said others."

72 **Governor Clinton of New York** . . . Mills, *The Grizzly*.

72 **Mills recalls one man** . . . Ibid., 99, 100.

72 **Lewis and Clark's Corps** . . . Gary Moulton, ed., *The Definitive Journals of Lewis and Clark* (Lincoln: University of Nebraska Press, 2002–4), 14:292–93, quoting Captain Lewis, June 14, 1805.

72 **The last track of the** . . . Joseph Mussulman, "Griz in the 'Roots," Discovering Lewis and Clark, http://lewis-clark.org/content/content-article.asp?ArticleID=938.

72 **The watershed moment for** . . . Russell McLendon, "Are Grizzly Bears Becoming Unbearable?," July 25, 2011, Mother Nature Network, www.mnn.com/earth-matters/translating-uncle-sam/stories/are-grizzly-bears-becoming-unbearable. See also Mark A. Hardoldson et al., "From Garbage, Controversy and Decline to Recovery," *Yellowstone Science* 16, no. 2 (2008): 13. After the shakeout, bear numbers are now said to be stable. Defenders of Wildlife, "Got Bears? Keeping Grizzlies Alive and People Safe in the Rockies," *Defenders: The Voice of Defenders of Wildlife* (Winter 2013): 16, www.defenders.org/magazine/winter-2013/got-bears (asserting that about 1,600 remain); "Grizzly Bear Facts," *National Geographic*, http://channel.nationalgeographic.com/articles/grizzly-bear-facts/ (asserting that about 1,500 grizzlies remain).

73 **Since the early 1900s** . . . See "Water Supply," Denver Water, www.
denverwater.org/SupplyPlanning/WaterSupply/.

73 **I first learned of** . . . The attorney Robert Golten represented the
National Wildlife Federation in litigation over the Two Forks Dam.
The Federation had established a law clinic at the University of
Colorado the previous year.

73 **To be sure, the** . . . Ed Marston, "Water Pressure," *High Country
News*, November 20, 2000, www.hcn.org/issues/191/10100.

74 **One Colorado governor called** . . . Ibid.

74 **For their part, environmentalists** . . . Ibid.

74 **The federal government was** . . . Ibid.

74 **Denver still operated on** . . . Ibid.

74 **The legal proceedings meanwhile** . . . Luke Danielson, attorney,
Law Offices of Luke J. Danielson P.C., telephone interview by
author, May 12, 2013 (Mr. Danielson, still a practitioner in Colorado, worked with Golten at the NWF Colorado clinic for several
years); George W. Pring, professor, University of Denver Sturm
College of Law, e-mail exchange with author, January 2014, on
file with author. (Professor Pring was counsel for the Environmental Defense Fund in Colorado, which was deeply involved in
the Two Forks issue; he also represented environmental parties
sued in the accompanying litigation.) For a fuller account of the
Two Forks controversy and litigation, see George W. Pring and
Penelope Canan, *SLAPPS: Getting Sued for Speaking Out* (Philadel-
phia: Temple University Press, 1996), 75–79.

74 **But for a single hitch** . . . The EPA veto is contained in the Clean
Water Act, 33 U.S.C. § 1344(c). It has been used only thirteen
times in forty-one years (see Jeremy P. Jacobs and Manuel Qui-
nones, "Congressional Intent at Issue as Judges Wrestle with EPA's
Clean Water Act Veto Power," E&E Publishing, March 14, 2013,
www.eenews.net/stories/1059977867).

74 **In early 1989 the EPA** . . . Marston; "EPA Vetoes Two Forks Reservoir Proposal," *Deseret News*, March 25, 1989, www.deseretnews.
com/article/39492/EPA-VETOES-TWO-FORKS-RESERVOIR-
PROPOSAL.html?pg=all. The administrator, William Reilly, later
said that his staff had advised him not to exercise the veto because
of the political consequences, but he acted because it was "the

right thing to do" (William Reilly, interview by author, October 12, 2012).

75 **Within a short time** . . . Marston, "EPA Vetoes Two Forks Reservoir Proposal."

75 **consume more fresh water**. . . U.S. Department of Energy, Office of Fossil Energy, National Energy Technology Laboratory, "Modern Shale Gas Development in the United States: A Primer," 2009, p. 64 (citing Satterfield et al., Chesapeake Energy Corp., "Managing Water Resources Challenges in Select Natural Gas Shale Plays," presented at the GWPC annual meeting, September 2008 ("The drilling and hydraulic fracturing of a horizontal shale gas well may typically require 2 to 4 million gallons of water").

75 **The new response here** . . . Northern Colorado Water Conservancy District, "NISP Overview," Northern Water, www.northernwater.org/WaterProjects/NISP.aspx.

75 **Scientists a few years** . . . Daniel Glick, "Grizzlies Take an Important Step Back," *Casper (Wyo.) Star-Tribune*, September 12, 1992, A12.

75 **A recent attempt to** . . . Greater Yellowstone Coalition, Inc. v. Servheen, 665 F.3d 1015, 1026 (9th Cir. 2011).

76 **In this light, writes** . . . Michelle Marvier, Robert Lalasz, and Peter Kareiva. "Conservation in the Anthropocene: Beyond Solitude and Fragility," *Breakthrough* (Winter 2010), http://thebreakthrough.org/index.php/journal/past-issues/issue-2/conservation-in-the-anthropocene/.Marvier et al. Dr. Kareiva is the chief scientist and director of the Nature Conservancy, which relies upon funding from, inter alia, corporations involved in resource development. To be fair, he defends his position as pragmatic and necessary in a changing world (ibid.). For a cogent rebuttal, see Kieran Suckling, "Conservation for the Real World," *Breakthrough* (Winter 2010), http://thebreakthrough.org/index.php/journal/debates/conservation-in-the-anthropocene-a-breakthrough-debate/conservation-for-the-real-world/. Mr. Suckling is the founder and executive director and of the Center for Biological Diversity.

CHESAPEAKE & OHIO CANAL

78 **Canaling began here nearly** . . . See "Washington Patowmack Company," in Richard L. Stanton, *Potomac Journey: Fairfax Stone*

to Tidewater (Washington, D.C.: Smithsonian Institution Press, 1993), 43–83; and see, generally, Joe Achenbach, *The Grand Idea: George Washington's Potomac and the Race to the West* (New York: Simon and Schuster, 2004).

79 **Years later, however, a . . .** Mark Segraves, "Naked Ned Hunts for the Infinite along the Potomac," WTOP, November 11, 2011, http://wtop.com/41/2628604/Naked-Ned-hunts-for-the-infinite-along-the-Potomac. The account that follows is taken from this article.

80 **The C&O Canal, orders . . .** Harry Sinclair Drago, *Canal Days in America* (Seaton, Devon, U.K.: Bramhall, 1922), 45–72; see also George Washington Ward, *The Early Development of the Chesapeake and Ohio Canal Project* (Baltimore: Johns Hopkins University Press, 1899).

80 **In the 1950s, in . . .** T. Carter and M. Brach, "C&O Canal: Overview," Washington, D.C., History Matters, February 25, 2006, http://dchistorymatters.org/introduction.php?mod=9.

80 **Congress backed the idea . . .** "Associate Justice William O. Douglas," National Park Service, www.nps.gov/choh/historyculture/associatejusticewilliamodouglas.htm.

81 **Appointed to the high court . . .** Holmes, J. in State of New Jersey v. State of New York, 283 US 336 (Sup. Ct. 1931)

81 **Following the *Post* editorial . . .** William O. Douglas, letter to the editor, *Washington Post*, January 19, 1954, 14.

VERDE RIVER

84 **The Central Arizona . . .** Jennifer E. Zuniga, U.S. Bureau of Reclamation, "The Central Arizona Project 2," 2000, p. 50, www.usbr.gov/projects//ImageServer?imgName=Doc_1303158888395.pdf.

84 **That's why we are . . .** Jon Christenson, "Las Vegas Seeks Waterway Jackpot in Northern Nevada," *High Country News*, April 6, 1992, 10.

84 **Orme Dam would put . . .** 30th Annual Orme Dam Victory Days—Celebrating "The Dam That Never Was," Fort McDowell Yavapai Nation, www.ftmcdowell.org/communityevents/ormedam11/aboutormedam2011.html; Dr. Robert Witzeman to Matthew Landry, e-mail entitled "Orme Dam Salt-Verde River miles

impacted," August 27, 2013, and attached map, on file with author (dam and inundation).

85 **In 1976 President Carter** . . . For a full account of the president's hit-list war with Congress, see Marc Reisner, *Cadillac Desert: The American West and Its Disappearing Water* (New York: Viking, 1986), 317–43. The description that follows is taken principally from this source. The book is an excellent history of water resource development in the American West, perhaps the best of its kind.

86 **Out of the West** . . . Ibid., 326, 7.

88 **In November 2011, the** . . . 30th Annual Orme Dam Victory Days—Celebrating "The Dam That Never Was."

BLACKWATER RIVER

89 **Good forests in New England** . . . Jack Waugh, "Lumbering before Pinchot," 42 *American Heritage* 93 (1991).

90 **It dried and fires** . . . Ibid., 96.

90 **A timber company official** . . . Ibid.

SAINT JOHN RIVER

95 **wound up impounding** . . . See Zygmunt B. Plater, *The Snail Darter and the Dam: How Pork-Barrel Politics Endangered a Little Fish and Killed a River* (New Haven, Conn.: Yale University Press, 2013), 12–17, describing the onset of TVA hydroelectric projects in southern Appalachia.

96 **The Dickey-Lincoln project** . . . Leon Billings, president, Leon G. Billings LLC, interview by author, October 12, 2012. Mr. Billings, who had previously represented the American Public Power Association, served as Muskie's top assistant throughout the senator's career in Congress, and was directly involved in the initiatives described in this chapter, including the Dickey-Lincoln Dam, the Wild and Scenic Rivers Act, and the Clean Water Act.

96 **dams were seen** . . . Reisner, *Cadillac Desert*, 165–75.

97 **if the Dickey-Lincoln site was blocked** . . . Billings interview.

97 **The Corps at that time** . . . Reisner, *Cadillac Desert*; Oliver A. Houck, "Breaking the Golden Rule: Judicial Review of Federal

Water Project Planning," *Rutgers Law Review* 65, no. 17 (2012) (political popularity of Corps water projects).

97 **Then came another obstacle** . . . The act passed by overwhelming margins and was signed on New Year's Day, 1970, by President Nixon (The National Environmental Policy Act 42 USC § 4321 et seq.).

98 **Early litigation said otherwise** . . . See Envtl. Def. Fund, Inc. v. U.S. Army Corps of Eng'rs, 324 F. Supp. 878 (D.D.C. 1971) (Cross-Florida Barge Canal); Envtl. Def. Fund, Inc. v. U.S. Army Corps of Eng'rs, 325 F. Supp. 728 (E.D. Ark. 1971) (Gillham Dam project); Envtl. Def. Fund, Inc. v. Hoffman, 566 F.2d 1060 (8th Cir. 1977) (Cache River Project).

98 **The opposition included** . . . Rob Gardiner was the executive director of the Natural Resources Council of Maine and went on to a distinguished career in state government. A lawsuit was never filed, but its potential presented a serious threat to the Corps' justifications for the project that surfaced during the required environmental review. Tom Arnold, attorney, interview by author, Boston, Mass., February 9, 2010. Mr. Arnold was principally responsible for developing the legal issues and for a coalition called Friends of the St. John.

99 **Early in his governorship** . . . Billings interview.

100 **Those questions were never asked** . . . Senator Muskie in Senate Consideration of the Report of the Conference Comm. (Oct. 4, 1972), reprinted in *Senate Comm. on Public Works, 1 Legislative History of the Water Pollution Control Act Amendments of 1972, S. Rep. No. 1*, 93d Cong., 1st Sess. 164 (1973).

100 **Muskie's clean water bill** . . . The Clean Water Act, 33 United States Code § 1031 et seq. For its legislative history and a sense of the continuing controversy surrounding its requirements, see Oliver Houck, *The Clean Water Act TMDL Program*; Robert McClure, "Reforming the Clean Water Act—without Congress," Investigate West, June 21, 2012, www.invw.org/post/reforming-the-clean-water-1285.

101 **The first day was** . . . Address by James G. Watt, U.S. secretary of interior, to Conference of National Park Concessioners, March 9, 1981, p. 18, transcript on file with author.

101 **water project hit-list** . . . Carter's initiatives are described in Reis-

ner, *Cadillac Desert*, 317, 343; see also Nathaniel Reed, "G.O.P. Conservationism," editorial, *New York Times*, June 27, 1981, www. nytimes.com/1981/06/27/opinion/gop-conservationism.html.

101 **In 1984, sensing the** . . . www.csmonitor.com/1981/0929/092925. html/%28page%29/3 ("But Sen. George J. Mitchell [D] of Maine, a Dickey-Lincoln supporter who agreed to the deauthorization legislation, thinks the full project will someday be built"); www. sunjournal.com/news/maine/2013/02/24/dickey-lincoln-dam-fell-30-years-ago/1325548 ("But finally, in 1984, then-Sen. George Mitchell, the Maine Democrat later known as a champion of tougher environmental laws, said he could no longer 'in good conscience' support Lincoln School").

101 **It is said that** . . . Billings interview.

ATCHAFALAYA

109 **taking it on a western course to the Gulf of Mexico** . . . See John M. Barry, *Rising Tide: The Great Mississippi Flood of 1927 and How It Changed America* (New York: Simon and Schuster, 1997), 282–87. This flood inundated much of South Louisiana and spared New Orleans only after the levee below was dynamited to release the pressure, prompting major revisions of federal plans including creation of the Atchafalaya Floodway.

109 **undermined a man-made control structure** . . . Raphael G. Kazmann and David B. Johnson, *If the Old River Control Structure Fails?*, Bulletin 12, Louisiana Water Resources Research Institute, September 1980, Louisiana State University, Addendum B, 1–8. The Mississippi flood of 1973 opened the Morganza Floodway of the Atchafalaya for the first time.

115 **bought no-development easements instead** . . . See Corps of Engineers historian Martin Reuss's *Designing the Bayous: The Control of Water in the Atchafalaya Basin, 1800–1995* (College Station: Texas A&M University Press, 2004), 324–31.

115 **In the spring of 2010 . . . toward the Gulf of Mexico** . . . Associated Press, "Mississippi River Floodwaters Cover 100 Acres in Half an Hour in Morganza Floodway," May 14, 2011, www.nola. com/environment/index.ssf/2011/05/mississippi_river_floodwaters.html.

SHELL BANK BAYOU

116   **I get lost, but I mean that emotionally. I feel absolutely right** .
      . . Julia Sims, *Manchac Swamp: Louisiana's Undiscovered Wilderness* (Baton Rouge: Louisiana State University Press, 1996), 4. A photographed depiction of this now-unique environment, and by extension so much of this region at one time.

BUFFALO RIVER

128   **One dam in neighboring Missouri** . . . This is the Truman Dam on the Osage River. An environmental lawsuit against the project, which, among other things, inundated numerous caves of endangered bats, did not succeed (Envtl. Def. Fund, Inc. v. Froehlke, 477 F.2d 1033 [8th Cir. 1973]).

128   **engineer chiefs on the cover congratulating each other** . . . George Fisher, *U.S. Corps of Engineers Coloring Book,* undated, on file with author.

129   **setting aside lands from development of all kinds** . . . The Wilderness Act, 16 U.S.C. §§1131–1136 (2012), was first introduced in 1956 and enacted in 1964.

129   **untrammeled by man** . . . Ibid., 1131.

129   **the one use that altered them forever: dams** . . . The Wild and Scenic Rivers Act, 16 U.S.C. §§1271–1287 (2012).

HORN ISLAND

134   **a race of solo sailboats** . . . See Bernard Moitessier, *The Long Way* (Dobbs Ferry, N.Y.: Sheridan House, 1995) (a diary of his voyage); and Peter Nichols, *A Voyage for Madmen* (New York: HarperCollins, 2001), 197–98 (fuller account of the race). The description that follows is taken from both books.

135   **claimed to have shot more than three hundred of them** . . . Douglas Brinkley, *The Quiet World: Saving Alaska's Wilderness Kingdom* (New York: HarperCollins, 2011), 369, describing exploits of Alaska governor Jay Hammond.

136   **his wife from early years** . . . Agnes Anderson's memoir of her life

with Walter Anderson is a beautiful portrait, genius, violence, and all (see Agnes Grinstead Anderson, *Approaching the Magic Hour: Memories of Walter Anderson* [Jackson: University Press of Mississippi, 1989]). The descriptions and quotes are taken from this source.

137 **the government started bringing them in to protect and breed them** . . . U.S. Fish and Wildlife Service, "Red Wolf Recovery Program," *1st Quarter Report FY13*, October–December 2012, p. 2, www.fws.gov/redwolf/Images/20130110_RedWolf_QtrReport_ FY13-01.pdf.

137 **due to the likelihood of encounters with people** . . . Red Wolf Coalition, "Red Wolf Biology and Status," Red Wolf Coalition, http://redwolves.com/rwc/downloads/other/rw_biology_status. pdf.

HORTON RIVER

139 **In 1845, Sir John Franklin** . . . Information in this paragraph is found in Scott Cookman, *Ice Blink: The Tragic Fate of Sir John Franklin's Lost Polar Expedition* (New York: Wiley, 2000), 34–41; and Owen Beattie, *Frozen in Time* (London: Bloomsbury, 2004), 1–8.

139 **to discover which waters linked to the Pacific** . . . For a full account of these early explorations, see Bernard DeVoto, *The Course of Empire* (Kingsport, Tenn.: Kingsport Press, 1952).

140 **A protean body of water** . . . Ibid., 57.

140 **The end came for Sir John Franklin** . . . Cookman, *Ice Blink*,14–29, 30–35, 140–43.

141 **one on a search for him in 1850** . . . Sir Robert McClure, *The Discovery of a Northwest Passage* (Victoria, British Columbia: Touch-Wood Editions, 2013), 54.

142 **strongly impregnated . . . resembling lime-kilns** . . . Ibid.

142 **He had provisions** . . . Cookman, *Ice Blink*, 116–29, 140–43, 174–85; Beattie, *Frozen in Time*, 140–50. Speculation on the presence of lead and its possible effects on the health and sanity of the Franklin crew is taken from these sources, as is information on the subsequent Inuit siting.

143 **Some years later I read** . . . "Sputnik Sputters, Dies in Canada Woods," *Pittsburg, (N.Y.) Press-Republican*, January 25, 1978, 1.

143 **saving each of his men** . . . The Shackleton voyage, one of the most inspiring of exploration anywhere, is well told in Alfred Lansing's *Endurance: Shackleton's Incredible Voyage* (New York: McGraw-Hill, 1959).

143 **frenzy of search and rescue** . . . Martyn Beardsley, *Deadly Winter: The Life of Sir John Beardsley* (Annapolis, Md.: Naval Institute Press, 2002), 203–27.

144 **the entire herd** . . . Shirley Milligan and Walter Kupsh, eds., *Living Explorers of the Canadian Arctic* (Yellowknife, Northwest Territories: Outcrop, 1986), 191.

144 **They ran among the expedition's tents** . . . Ibid.

PEARL RIVER

146 **Edwin Edwards** . . . Governor Edwards courted scandal throughout his political career, documented in books and press accounts for three decades, beginning with Clyde C. Vidrine, *Just Takin' Orders: A Southern Governor's Watergate* (Baton Rouge, La.: self-published, 1977). After several criminal investigations of his activities, and an unsuccessful federal racketeering trial charging him with rigging state hospital licenses, he was finally convicted for rigging casino licenses instead. For all this and more, see Leo Honeycutt, *Edwin Edwards: Governor of Louisiana* (Baton Rouge, La.: Lisburn Press, 2009).

147 **As early as the 1880s** . . . See "U.S. Army Corps of Eng'rs, Pearl River Basin," undated, p. 97 (hereafter cited as "Pearl River Basin"). This history is summarized in a brief for the United States before the Supreme Court in 1990, State of Mississippi v. U.S. (1990). Government Briefs, Office of the Solicitor General, U.S. Dept. of Justice.

148 **reduced the living space** . . . U.S. Fish and Wildlife Service and Gulf States Marine Commission, "Gulf Sturgeon Recovery Plan," 1995, pp. 24, 25, describing a 90 percent loss of sturgeon habitat above the sills of the navigation project, from more than 320 to 48 miles on the mainstream Pearl alone, excluding tributaries.

148   **a flood of toxins** . . . Benjamin Alexander-Bloch, "Thousands of
        Pearl River Fish Die after Bogalusa Paper Mill Discharge," *New
        Orleans Times-Picayune,* August 15, 2011, Nola.com.

148   **The government captured six of them** . . . U.S. Fish and Wildlife
        Service, "Alabama Sturgeon Timeline," March 23, 2000, www.
        fws.gov/southeast/publications/ALsturgeontimeline3-23-00.pdf.

149   **In the late 1990s, pushed by Bogalusa again** . . . "Pearl River
        Basin."

150   **It turned out** . . . Hugh Penn, attorney, New Orleans, interview by
        author, August 9, 2012. Mr. Penn participated in lawsuits oppos-
        ing the project.

150   **chart for the trial** . . . Chart prepared by Hugh Penn and Michael
        Rolland from the Corps' Administrative Record, "Projected Ben-
        efits for the Pearl River Dredging Project: West Pearl River Com-
        modity Tonnages," on file with author.

150   **predicted staggering benefits** . . . Houck, "Breaking the Golden
        Rule," 22 and sources therein.

150   **the Pearl dredging was stopped** . . . Several lawsuits were filed
        against the project, one invalidating water quality approvals, "In
        the Matter of West Pearl River Navigation Project," 657 So. 2d
        640 (La. Ap. 1st Cir. 1995); another based on impacts to the stur-
        geon, Orleans Audubon Society v. Babbitt, Civ. Action No. CV
        00256-EEF, 1995, leading to a preliminary injunction against the
        project, which was subsequently abandoned (see Honey Island
        Swamp Tours v. Witherspoon, 1996 WL 56954 [E.D. La. 1996]).
        Yet another suit was filed compelling the federal government to
        designate critical (i.e., protected) habitat for the sturgeon, Sierra
        Club v. U.S. Fish and Wildlife Service (CA No. 98-3788 k-2 E.D.
        La.), which it then did, identifying five watersheds from Florida
        to Louisiana, one of which is the Pearl (see U.S. Fish and Wildlife
        Service and National Marine Fisheries Service, "Critical Habitat
        for Gulf Sturgeon," 50 C.F.R. 226.214). At times protecting the
        environment takes a village.

150   **where the local Klan killed** . . . Benjamin Alexander-Bloch, "The
        Klan Violently Reappears," *New Orleans Times-Picayune,* October
        15, 2008, nola.com. The account that follows is taken from this
        source.

GREEN RIVER

152 **We have an unknown distance yet to run** . . . John Wesley Powell,
     The Exploration of The Colorado River and Its Canyons (New York:
     Penguin, 1987), 247. Beyond this diary, perhaps the best account
     of Powell's expedition is that of Wallace Stegner, *Beyond the Hun-
     dredth Meridian: John Wesley Powell and the Second Opening of the
     West* (Rolling Meadows, Ill.: Riverside, 1954).

154 **Lugging a heavy telescope** . . . Stegner, *Beyond the Hundredth
     Meridian.* Major Powell had lost an arm at the battle of Shiloh
     while serving for the Union army in the Civil War.

157 **to advance the radical notion** . . . United States Geological Survey,
     "John Wesley Powell: Explorer, Geologist, Geographer," October
     15, 2012, www.usgs.gov/blogs/features/usgs_top_story/john-wes-
     ley-powell-explorer-geologist-geographer/.

157 **I wish to make it clear to you** . . . John Wesley Powell, Los Angeles
     International Irrigation Conference (1893), ibid.

GILA RIVER

158 **all the same river over time** . . . "Gila River," Geographic Names
     Information System, U.S. Geological Survey, Feb. 8, 1980, http://
     geonames.usgs.gov/apex/f?p=gnispq:3:::NO::P3_FID:42838;
     http://geonames.usgs.gov/pls/gnis.

158 **the Hohokam and Pima peoples** . . . "Gila National Forest,"
     U.S. Forest Service, Dec. 4, 2003 (Pima); and Jerry B. Howard,
     "Hohokam Legacy: Desert Canals," in Pueblo Grande Muse-
     um Profiles, http://waterhistory.org/histgories/hohokam2/
     (Hohokam).

158 **"God's First Temples** . . . " John Muir, "God's First Temples: How
     Shall We Preserve Our Forests?" *Sacramento Daily Union,* February
     5, 1876.

158 **Our way of managing nature** . . . Leopold was a first teacher of the
     interconnectedness of all life, captured in his iconic statement:
     "The last word in ignorance is the man who says of an animal or
     plant, 'What good is it?' If the land mechanism as a whole is good,
     then every part is good, whether we understand it or not. If the
     biota, in the course of aeons, has build something we like but do

not understand, then who but a fool would discard seemingly useless parts? To keep every cog and wheel is the first precaution of intelligent tinkering" (Aldo Leopold, "The Round River: From the Journals of Aldo Leopold," in *Sand County Almanac: And Sketches Here and There* [Oxford: Oxford University Press, 1949]).

158 **"Thinking Like a Mountain"** . . . Aldo Leopold, "Thinking Like a Mountain," in *Sand County Almanac*. The quotes that follow are taken from this text.

159 **Aldo Leopold made it happen** . . . John Murray, *The Gila Wilderness: A Hiking Guide* (Albuquerque: University of New Mexico Press, 1988).

159 **off-limits to roads and permits** . . . "History of the Gila Wilderness," U.S. Forest Service, www.fs.usda.gov/detail/gila/learning/history-culture/?cid=stelprdb5038907.

160 **"back country" areas** . . . Michael McCloskey and Jeffrey Sesautels, "A Primer on Wilderness Law and Policy," 13 *Environmental Law Reporter* 13 (Sept. 1983): 10278 et seq.

160 **three World War II German prisoners** . . . Harvey Miles, *The Island of Lost Maps: A True Story of Cartographic Crime* (New York: Random House, 2000), 154.

162 **The case tore the Supreme Court** . . . *United States v. New Mexico*, 438 U.S. 696 (1978). The majority opinion drew a vigorous dissent led by Justice Powell who, himself a fisherman, did not see the forests as the "lifeless" places envisioned by the Court, wrote: " In my view, the forests consist of the birds, animals and fish—the wildlife—that inhabit them, as well as the trees, flowers, shrubs, and grasses. I would therefore hold that the United States is entitled to so much water as is necessary to sustain the wildlife of the forests ." Id at 719. Justice Powell, meet Aldo Leopold.

162 **securing favorable conditions to water flows** . . . Organic Administration Act of June 4, 1897, 30 Stat. 34 (1897).

162 **Is education possibly a process** . . . Leopold, *Sand County Almanac*. For Leopold's passion for unspoiled rivers, see William Forbes, "Revisiting the 'River of the Mother of God': Leopold's Symbol of Global Wilderness," Center for Humans and Nature, www.humansandnature.org/revisiting-the--river-of-the-mother-of-god--article-28.php.

162 "The good life of any river" . . . Ibid.

162 "There is an hour" . . . Jorge Luis Borges, "El Fin," in *Ficciones* (Madrid: Bibiloteca Borges, 1999), 197.

BAYOU SAUVAGE

164 **official-looking map** . . . *Pontchartrain: New Town in Town*, prepared by New Orleans East, Inc., Wallace, McHarg, Roberts & Todd, Tippetts, Abbett, McCarthy, Stratton, and Gladstone Associates, undated, on file with author.

165 **to build a Houston version of New Orleans** . . . Todd Shallat, "Holding Louisiana," *Technology and Culture* 47, no. 1 (2006), www.historyoftechnology.org/eTC/v47no1/shallat.html#ref12.

165 **Merrill Lynch was caught holding the note** . . . Jane W. Apffel, "The Bayou Savage Urban Wildlife Refuge: A Definition of Land Use through Collaboration," unpublished paper, 1990, on file with author; author conversation with Patrick Noonan, March 1989. Mr. Noonan was president of the Nature Conservancy from 1973 to 1980 and founded the Conservation Fund in 1985. At a Christmas gathering in 1988, he met a former college classmate who complained about "a dog of a property" down in Louisiana for which he had the portfolio. Sensing opportunity, Noonan began negotiating a deal.

166 **yet another map** . . . Matt Scallan, "Nagin Will Propose New Site for Airport," *New Orleans Times-Picayune*, May 17, 2005.

166 **unstable marshes** . . . Subsidence rates for streets and residences in this area began to increase immediately after their construction (see J. O. Snowden et al., "Subsidence in Marshland Peat in the Greater New Orleans Area," in *Proceedings of the Third Coastal Marsh and Estuary Management Symposium* 1979), and continue to this day. Organic soils dry out and compact, roads crack open, and driveways separate from their garages—not ideal for arriving jetliners.

166 **sold the property** . . . Noonan conversation, 1989; Apffel, , "The Bayou Savage Urban Wildlife Refuge"; see also Coleman Warner, "Breaux Resolves Dispute over Control of Refuge," *New Orleans Times-Picayune*, October, 28, 1988.

DESCHUTES RIVER

172   **natives with highly unusual facial features** . . . Bernard DeVoto,
      Across the Wide Missouri (New York: Houghton Mifflin, 1947). The
      account of the Flatheads and the early Oregon settlers that follows
      is taken from this source.

172   **an 1855 treaty** . . . Robert J. Miller, "Indian Treaties as Sovereign Con-
      tracts," http://lawlib.lclark.edu/blog/native_america/?page_id=8.

173   **one of the most moving speeches** . . . There are at least two ver-
      sions of the Seattle speech, one more modern and the other from
      the notes of a newspaper reporter at the time. While the language
      differs, both exhibit a similar tone (see Jerry L. Clark, "Thus Spoke
      Chief Seattle: The Story of an Undocumented Speech," *Prologue
      Magazine*, 1985, www.archives.gov/publications/prologue/1985/
      spring/chief-seattle.html).

174   **which no longer exists** . . . U.S. Geological Survey, "Geo-
      graphic Names Information System: Feature Detail Report
      for Celilo Falls (historical)," http://geonames.usgs.gov/pls/
      gnispublic/f?p=132:3:7897726549718772::NO::P3_FID,P3_
      TITLE:1161648%2CCelilo%20Falls%20(historical). For a full
      account of the struggle between Native Americans and the dams,
      see Joseph C. Dupris, Kathleen S. Hill, and William H. Rodg-
      ers Jr., *The Si'lailo Way: Indians, Salmon, and Law on the Colum-
      bia River* (Durham, N.C.: Carolina Academic Press, 2006). The
      account of fishing practices and the subsequent dams is taken
      from this source.

174   **Warm Springs Indians had been promised** . . . The meaning and
      effect of the fishing rights accorded by these treaties has been the
      subject of constant litigation for a century (see Dupris, Hill, and
      Rodgers, *The Si'lailo Way*; and Mary Wood, "Restoring the Abun-
      dant Trust: Tribal Litigation in Pacific Northwest Salmon Recov-
      ery," 36 *Environmental Law Reporter*, 10163 [2006]). An uneasy
      truce has been reached acknowledging a Native American right to
      a subsistence baseline, and beyond that to mitigation measures to
      reduce the harm. A recent treaty case requires the State of Wash-
      ington to provide adequate fish passage under roads and through
      culverts: United States v. Washington, No. CV 70-9213, 2013 U.S.
      Dist. WL 1334391 (W.D. Wash. Mar. 29, 2013).

175   **the government now ferries** . . . The effects of these dams on endan-

gered salmon has also been in constant litigation, including the adequacy of barging them around the dams and of replacement fish hatcheries. See Trout Unlimited v. Lohn, 599 F.3d 946, 962 (9th Cir. 2009). and National Wildlife Federation v. National Marine Fisheries Service, 524 F.3d 917 (9th Cir. 2007). To date, these palliatives are the best the government has been willing to offer.

OLD RIVER

177 **blocked by a mile-long raft** . . . Charles R. Caillouet Jr., "A Limited History of the Atchafalaya Basin," www.basinbuddies.org/news/?page_id=611. After dynamiting the raft, Captain Shreve went on to pilot boats to New Orleans, including a steamer that broke a local monopoly and opened the Mississippi to steam-powered vessels (see Ari Kelman, *A River and Its City: The Nature of Landscape in New Orleans* [Berkeley: University of California Press, 2003], 49–58).

177 **began to swell** . . . Caillouet Jr., "A Limited History of the Atchafalaya Basin"; see also Kazman and Johnson, *If The Old River Control Structure Fails?*

177 **a dam across Old River** . . . Ibid.; John McPhee, "The Atchafalaya," in *The Control of Nature*, by McPhee (New York: Farrar, Straus and Giroux, 1990). Louisiana senator Bennett Johnston was so daunted by the proposal of the Atchafalaya capturing the Mississippi that he opened a hearing on the proposed new structure saying, "We are here to contemplate doomsday" (personal recollection of author).

178 **ivory-billed woodpecker** . . . The last documented sighting of the ivory-bill was by Dr. George M. Lowery of LSU, in 1935, on a tract just north of the Atchafalaya Swamp (see George H. Lowery Jr., *Louisiana Birds* [Baton Rouge: Louisiana State University Press, 1955], 415–19).

BAYOU SORREL

191 **first cash crop of the Atchafalaya** . . . For a description of life and commerce in the early Atchafalaya, see Malcolm L. Comeaux, "Atchafalaya Swamp Life: Settlement and Folk Occupations," *Geo-*

science and Man 2 (January 1972). Equally haunting is Timothy Gautreaux's recent novel on cypress logging at the turn of the last century, *The Clearing: A Novel* (New York: Vintage, 2003). For a photographic portrait, see C. C. Lockwood, *Atchafalaya: America's Largest River Basin Swamp* (Baton Rouge, La.: Beauregard Press, 1981).

192   **a $12 million** . . . Jack C. Isaacs and David Lavergne, "Louisiana Commercial Crawfish Harvesters Survey Report," Louisiana Department of Wildlife and Fisheries, 2010; the figure is an average between 1988 and 1995.

192   **easement with the landowners** . . . The negotiated easement is contained in U.S. Army Corps of Engineers, *Atchafalaya Basin Floodway System, Louisiana, Feasibility Study: Main Report and Final Environmental Impact Statement*, vol. 1 (1982), http://cdm16313.contentdm.oclc.org/cdm/ref/collection/p16313coll35/id/342. For more on the negotiations, which spanned a decade, see Martin Reuss, *Designing the Bayous: The Control of Water in the Atchafalaya Basin, 1800–1995* (College Station: Texas A&M University Press, 2004).

193   **not really navigating** . . . See Blanchard v Williams, Civ. Act. No. 92-0941 (W.D. La. 1992); see also Vicknair v. Louisiana Dept. of Wildlife and Fisheries, Civ. Nos. 6:11-0184, 11-406, 11-407, 11-834, 2013 U.S. Dist. WL 1180834, at *8 (W.D. La. Jan. 29, 2013).

193   **only gaming** . . . Tyler Bridges, *Bad Bet on the Bayou: The Rise of Gambling in Louisiana and the Fall of Governor Edwin Edwards* (New York: Farrar, Straus and Giroux, 2002), 60.

195   **to see Alcide** . . . Alcide Verret, like many Cajun men, was a superb cook and particularly proud of his mirlitons, which he called "molytones," saying he cooked them "nine different ways and they all delicious" (see Oliver A. Houck, "In Cajun Land, Molytones," *New York Times*, October 13, 1979, A-19).

GRANDE RONDE

198   **named by French trappers** . . . Mike Benbow, "Spectacular Fishing on Grande Ronde River," *Everett (Wash.) Herald,* September 25, 2011, www.heraldnet.com/article/20110925/SPORTS/709259913.

198   **heart of the Nez Perce nation** . . . See William R. Swagerty, "Chief Joseph and the Nez Perce Indians," Chief Washakie Foundation, www.windriverhistory.org/exhibits/chiefjoseph/chiefjoseph01. htm.

198   **more rattlers** . . . Grand Ronde in *Soggy Sneakers: A Paddler's Guide to Oregon Rivers* (Willamette, Ore: Willamette Kayak and Canoe Club, 1980).